Henry Harris Jessup, Charles Robinson, Woodbridge Riley

The Women of the Arabs

With a Chapter for Children

Henry Harris Jessup, Charles Robinson, Woodbridge Riley

The Women of the Arabs
With a Chapter for Children

ISBN/EAN: 9783744760720

Printed in Europe, USA, Canada, Australia, Japan

Cover: Foto ©ninafisch / pixelio.de

More available books at **www.hansebooks.com**

THE WOMEN

OF

THE ARABS.

WITH A CHAPTER FOR CHILDREN.

BY

REV. HENRY HARRIS JESSUP, D.D.,

Seventeen years American Missionary in Syria.

EDITED BY

REV. C. S. ROBINSON, D.D., & REV. ISAAC RILEY.

"The threshold weeps forty days when a girl is born."
—*Mt. Lebanon Proverb.*

LONDON:

SAMPSON LOW, MARSTON, LOW & SEARLE,

CROWN BUILDINGS, 188 FLEET STREET.

1874.

THIS BOOK

IS DEDICATED TO THE

CHRISTIAN WOMEN OF AMERICA.

PREFACE.

THE Orient is the birthplace of prophecy. Before the advent of our Lord, the very air of the East was resounding with the "unconscious prophecies of heathenism." Men were in expectation of great changes in the earth. When Mohammed arose, he not only claimed to be the deliverer of a message inspired of Allah, but to foretell the events of futurity. He declared that the approach of the latter day could be distinguished by unmistakable signs, among which were two of the most notable character.

Before the latter day, the *sun shall rise in the West*, and God will send forth a cold odoriferous wind blowing from *Syria Damascena*, which shall *sweep away* the souls of all the faithful, and *the Koran itself*. What the world of Islam takes in its literal sense, we may take in a deeper spiritual meaning. Is it not true, that far in the West, the gospel sun began to rise and shed its beams on Syria, many years ago, and that in our day that cold odoriferous wind of truth and life, fragrant with the love of Jesus and the love of man, is beginning to blow from Syria Damascena, over all the Eastern world! The church and the school, the printing press and the translated

Bible, the periodical and the ponderous volume, the testimony of living witnesses for the truth, and of martyrs who have died in its defence, all combine to sweep away the systems of error, whether styled Christian, Moslem or Pagan.

The remarkable uprising of christian women in Christian lands to a new interest in the welfare of woman in heathen and Mohammedan countries, is one of the great events of the present century. This book is meant to be a memorial of the early laborers in Syria, nearly all of whom have passed away. It is intended also as a record of the work done for women and girls of the Arab race; to show some of the great results which have been reached and to stimulate to new zeal and effort in their behalf.

In tracing the history of this work, it seemed necessary to describe the condition of woman in Syria when the missionaries first arrived, and to examine the different religious systems, which affect her position.

In preparing the chapter on the Pre-Islamic Arabs, I have found valuable materials in Chenery's Hariri, Sales and Rodwell's Koran, and Freytag's Arabic Proverbs.

For the facts about the Druze religion, I have consulted Col. Churchill's Works, Mount Lebanon, and several Arabic manuscripts in the mission library in Beirût.

Rev. S. Lyde's interesting book called the "Asian Mystery," has given me the principal items with regard to the Nusairîyeh religion. This confirms the statements of Suleiman Effendi, whose tract, revealing the secrets of the Nusairîyeh faith, was printed years ago at the Mission Press in Beirût, and translated by that ripe Arabic Scholar Prof. E. Salisbury of New Haven. The bloody Nusairîyeh never forgave Suleiman for revealing their mysteries; and having invited him to a feast in a village near Adana, 1871, brutally buried him alive in a dunghill!

For the historical statements of this volume, I am indebted to the files of the Missionary Herald, the Annual Reports of the Syria Mission, the archives of the mission in Beirût, the memoir of Mrs. Sarah L. Smith, and private letters from Mrs. Whiting, Mrs. De Forest, and various missionary and native friends.

Information on the general work of the Syrian Mission may be found in Dr. Anderson's "Missions to the Oriental churches," Rev. Isaac Bird's "Bible Work in Bible Lands," and the pamphlet sketches of Rev. T. Laurie and Rev. James S. Dennis.

The specimens of poetry from ancient Arabic poetesses, have been gathered from printed and manuscript volumes, and from the lips of the people.

Some accounts of child life in Syria and specimens of Oriental stories and nursery rhymes have been gathered into a "Children's Chapter." They have a value higher than that which is given by mere entertainment as they exhibit many phases of Arab home life. The illustrations of the volume consist of drawings from photographs by Bergheim of Jerusalem and Bonfils of Beirût.

The pages of Arabic were electrotyped in Beirût by Mr. Samuel Hallock, the skilful superintendent of the American Press.

I send out this record of the work carried on in Syria with deep gratitude for all that the Lord has done, and with an ardent desire that it may be the means of bringing this great field more vividly before the minds of Christian people, of wakening warmer devotion to the missionary cause, and so of hastening the time when every Arab woman shall enjoy the honor, and be worthy of the elevation which come with faith in Him who was first foretold as the seed of the woman.

HENRY HARRIS JESSUP.

BEIRUT, Syria, Nov. 28, 1872.

CONTENTS.

BEIRUT, SYRIA, *July*, 1873.

Owing to the impossibility of my attending personally to the editing of this volume, I requested my old friends, REV. C. S. ROBINSON, D.D., *and* REV. ISAAC RILEY, *of New York, to superintend the work, and would gratefully acknowledge their kind and disinterested aid, cheerfully proffered at no little sacrifice of time.*

H. H. JESSUP.

THE

WOMEN OF THE ARABS.

CHAPTER I.

STATE OF WOMEN AMONG THE ARABS OF THE JAHILIYEH, OR THE "TIMES OF THE IGNORANCE."

IN that eloquent Sura of the Koran, called Ettekwir, (lxxxi.) it is said, "When the *girl buried alive* shall be asked for what sin she was slain." The passage no doubt refers to the cruel practice which still in Mohammed's time lingered among the tribe of Temîm, and which was afterwards eradicated by the influence of Islam. The origin of this practice has been ascribed to the superstitious rite of sacrificing children, common in remote times to all the Semites, and observed by the Jews up to the age of the Captivity, as we learn from the denunciations of Jeremiah. But in later times daughters were buried alive as a matter of household economy, owing to the poverty of many of the tribes, and to their fear of dishonor, since women were often carried off by their enemies in forays, and made slaves and concubines to strangers.

So that at a wedding, the wish expressed in the gratulations to the newly-married pair was, "with concord and sons," or "with concord and permanence; with sons and no daughters." This same salutation is universal in Syria now. The chief wish expressed by women to a bride is, "may God give you an "arees," *i. e.* a bridegroom son.

In the Koran, Sura xiv, Moḥammed argues against the Arabs of Kinȧneh, who said that the angels were the daughters of God. "They (blasphemously) attribute daughters to God; yet they *wish them not for themselves.* When a female child is announced to one of them, his face grows dark, and he is as though he would choke."

The older Arab Proverbs show that the burying alive of female children was deemed praiseworthy.

"To send women before to the other world, is a benefit."
"The best son-in-law is the grave."

The Koran also says, that certain men when hearing of the birth of a daughter hide themselves "from the people because of the ill-tidings; shall he keep it with disgrace, or bury it in the dust." (Sura xvi.)

It is said that the only occasion on which Othman ever shed a tear, was when his little daughter, whom he was burying alive, wiped the dust of the grave-earth from his beard!

Before the Seventh Century this practice seems

to have been gradually abandoned, but was retained the longest in the tribe of Temîm. Naman, king of Hira, carried off among his prisoners in a foray, the daughter of Kais, chief of Temîm, who fell in love with one of her captors and refused to return to her tribe, whereupon her father swore to bury alive all his future female children, which he did, to the number of ten.

Subsequent to this, rich men would buy the lives of girls devoted to inhumation, and Sa Saah thus rescued many, in one case giving two milch camels to buy the life of a new-born girl, and he was styled "the Reviver of the Maidens buried alive."

The following Arabic Proverbs having reference to women and girls *will illustrate* the ancient Arab ideas with regard to their character and position, better than volumes of historic discourse :

"Obedience to women will have to be repented of."

"A man can bear anything but the mention of bis women."

"The heart of woman is given to folly."

"Leave not a girl nor a green pasture unguarded."

"What has a girl to do with the councils of a nation?"

"If you would marry a beauty, pay her dowry."

"Fear not to praise the man whose wives are true to him."

"Woman fattens on what she hears." (flattery)

"Women are the whips of Satan."

"If you would marry a girl, inquire about the traits of her mother."

"Trust neither a king, a horse, nor a woman. For the king is fastidious, the horse prone to run away, and the woman is perfidious."

"My father does the fighting, and my mother the talking about it."

"Our mother forbids us to err and runs into error."

"Alas for the people who are ruled by a woman!"

The position of woman among the Arabs before the times of Mohammed can be easily inferred from what has preceded. But there is another side to the picture. Although despised and abused, woman often asserted her dignity and maintained her rights, not only by physical force, but by intellectual superiority as well. The poetesses of the Arabs are numerous, and some of them hold a high rank. Their poetry was impromptu, impassioned, and chiefly of the elegiac and erotic type. The faculty of improvisation was cultivated even by the most barbarous tribes, and although such of their poetry as has been preserved is mostly a kind of rhymed prose, it often contains striking and beautiful thoughts. They called improvised poetry "the daughter of the hour."

The queen of Arabic poetesses is El Khunsa, who flourished in the days of Mohammed. Elegies on her two warrior brothers Sakhr and Mu'àwiyeh are among the gems of ancient Arabic poetry. She was not what would be called in modern times a refined or delicate lady, being regarded as proud and masculine in temper even by the Arabs of her own age. In the eighth year of the Hegira, her son Abbas brought a thousand warriors to join the forces of the Prophet. She came with him and recited her poetry to Mohammed. She lamented her brother for years. She sang of Sakhr:

"His goodness is known by his brotherly face,
Thrice blessed such sign of a heavenly grace:

You would think from his aspect of meekness and shame,
That his anger was stirred at the thought of his fame.
Oh rare virtue and beautiful, natural trait,
Which never will change by the change of estate!
When clad in his armor and prepared for the fray,
The army rejoiceth and winneth the day!"

Again, she lamented him as follows:

" Each glorious rising sun brings Sakhr to my mind,
I think anew of him when sets the orb of day;
And had I not beheld the grief and sorrow blind
Of many mourning ones o'er brothers snatched away,
I should have slain myself, from deep and dark despair."

The poet Nabighah erected for her a red leather tent at the fair of Okaz, in token of honor, and in the contest of poetry gave her the highest place above all but Maymûn, saying to her, " If I had not heard him, I would say that thou didst surpass every one in poetry. I confess that you surpass all women." To which she haughtily replied, " Not the less do I surpass all men."

The following are among the famous lines of El Khunsa, which gave her the title of princess of Arab poetesses. The translation I have made quite literal.

" Ah time has its wonders; its changes amaze;
It leaves us the tail while the head it slays;
It leaves us the low while the highest decays;
It leaves the obscure, the despised, and the slave,
But of honored and loved ones, the true and the brave,
It leaves us to mourn o'er the untimely grave.
The two new creations, the day and the night,
Though ceaselessly changing, are pure as the light:
But man changes to error, corruption and blight."

The most ancient Arab poetess, Zarîfeh, is supposed to have lived as long ago as the Second Century, in the time of the bursting of the famous dyke of Mareb, which devastated the land of Saba. Another poetess, Rakâsh, sister of the king of Hira, was given in marriage, by the king when intoxicated, to a man named Adî.

Alas, in these days the Moslem Arabs do not wait until blinded by wine, to give their daughters in marriage to strangers. I once overheard two Moslem young men conversing in a shop, one of whom was about to be married. His companion said to him, "have you heard anything about the looks of your betrothed?" "Not much," said he, "only I am assured that she is *white*."

In a book written by Mirai ibn Yusef el Hanbali, are the names of twenty Arab women who improvised poetry. Among them are Leila, Leila el Akhyalîyeh, Lubna, Zeinab, Afra, Hind, May, Jenûb, Hubaish, Zarifeh, Jemîleh, Remleh, Lotifeh, and others. Most of the verses ascribed to them are erotic poetry of an amatory character, full of the most extravagant expressions of devotion of which language is capable, and yet the greater part of it hardly bearing translation. It reminds one strikingly of Solomon's Song, full of passionate eloquence. And yet in the poetry of El Khunsa and others, which is of an elegiac character, there are passages full of sententious apothegms and proverbial wisdom.

CHAPTER II.

STATE OF WOMEN IN THE MOHAMMADAN WORLD.

OUR knowledge of the position of women among the Mohammedans is derived from the Koran, Moslem tradition, and Moslem practice.

I. In the first place, the Koran does not teach that women have no souls. Not only was Mohammed too deeply indebted to his rich wife Khadijah, to venture such an assertion, but he actually teaches in the Koran the immortality and moral responsibility of women. One of his wives having complained to him that God often praised the men, but not the women who had fled the country for the faith, he immediately produced the following revelation:

"I will not suffer the work of him among you who worketh to be lost, whether he be male or female." (Sura iii.)

In Sura iv. it is said:

"Whoso doeth good works, and is a true believer, whether male or female, shall be admitted into Paradise."

In Sura xxxiii:

"Truly, the Muslemen and the Muslimate, (fem.)
The believing men and the believing women,
The devout men and the devout women,

The men of truth and the women of truth,
The patient men and the patient women,
The humble men and the humble women,
The charitable men and the charitable women,
The fasting men and the fasting women,
The chaste men and the chaste women,
And the men and women who oft remember God;
For them hath God prepared
Forgiveness and a rich recompense."

II. Thus Mohammedans cannot and do not deny that women have souls, but their brutal treatment of women has naturally led to this view. The Caliph Omar said that "women are worthless creatures and soil men's reputations." In Sura iv. it is written:

"Men are superior to women, on account of the qualities
With which God has gifted the one above the other,
And on account of the outlay they make, from their substance
for them.
Virtuous women are obedient. . . . .
But chide those for whose refractoriness
Ye have cause to fear. . . . . . *and scourge them*."

The interpretation of this last injunction being left to the individual believer, it is carried out with terrible severity. The scourging and beating of wives is one of the worst features of Moslem domestic life. It is a degraded and degrading practice, and having the sanction of the Koran, will be indulged in without rebuke as long as Islamism as a system and a faith prevails in the world. Happily for the poor women, the husbands do not generally beat them so as to imperil their lives, in case their own relatives reside in the vicinity, lest the excruciating screams of the suffering should reach the ears of her parents and bring the husband into disgrace. But where there is no fear of interference or of discovery, the blows and kicks are applied in the most merciless and barbarous manner. Women are killed in this way, and no outsider knows the cause. One of my Moslem neighbors once beat one of his wives to death. I heard her screams day after day, and finally, one night, when all was still, I heard a dreadful shriek, and blow after blow falling upon her back and head. I could hear the brute cursing her as he beat her. The police would not interfere, and I could not enter the house. The next day there was a funeral from that house, and she was carried off and buried in the most hasty and unfeeling manner. Sometimes it happens that the woman is strong enough to defend herself, and conquers a peace; but ordinarily when you hear a scream in the Moslem quarter of the city and ask the reason, it will be said to you with an indifferent shrug of the shoulder, "that is only some man beating his wife."

That thirty-eighth verse of Sura iv. is one of the many proofs that the Koran is not the book of God, because it violates the law of love. "Husbands love your wives," is a precept of the Gospel and not of the Koran. Yet it is a sad fact that the nominal Christians of this dark land are not much better in this respect than their Moslem neighbors. The Greeks, Maronites and Papal Greeks beat their wives on the slightest provocation. In the more enlightened towns and cities this custom is "going out of fashion," though still often resorted to in fits of passion. Sometimes the male relatives of the wife retaliate in case a husband beats her. In the village of Schwire, in Lebanon, a man beat his wife in a brutal manner and she fled to the house of her brother. The brother watched his opportunity; waylaid the offending husband, and avenged his sister's injuries by giving him a severe flogging. In Eastern Turkey, a missionary in one of the towns noticed that not one woman attended church on Sunday. He expostulated with the Protestants, and urged them to persuade their wives to accompany them. The next Sunday the women were all present, as meek and quiet as could be wished. The missionary was delighted, and asked one of the men how they persuaded them to come? He replied, "We all beat our wives soundly until they consented to come!" This wife-beating custom has evidently been borrowed by the Christian sects from their Moslem rulers and oppressors, and nothing but a pure Christianity can induce them to abandon it.

III. Some have supposed that there will be no place in the Moslem Paradise for women, as their place will be taken by the seventy-two bright-eyed Houris or damsels of Paradise. Mohammed once said that when he took a view of Paradise he saw the majority of its inhabitants to be the poor, and when he looked down into hell, he saw the *greater part* of the wretches confined there to be *women!* Yet he positively promised his followers that the very meanest in Paradise will have eighty thousand servants, seventy-two wives of the Houris, *besides the wives he had in this world.* The promises of the Houris are almost exclusively to be found in Suras, written at a time when Mohammed had only a single wife of sixty years of age, and in all the ten years subsequent to the Hegira, women are only twice mentioned as the reward of the faithful. And this, while in four Suras, the proper wives of the faithful are spoken of as accompanying their husbands into the gardens of bliss.

> "They and their wives on that day
> Shall rest in shady groves." (Sura 36.)
> "Enter ye and your wives into Paradise delighted." (Sura 43.)
> "Gardens of Eden into which they shall enter
> Together with the just of their fathers, and their wives." (Sura 13.)

An old woman once desired Mohammed to intercede with God that she might be admitted to Paradise, and he told her that no old woman would enter that place. She burst into loud weeping, when he explained himself by saying that God would then make her young again.

I was once a fellow-passenger in the Damascus diligence, with a Mohammedan pilgrim going to Mecca by way of Beirût and Egypt, in company with his wife. I asked him whether his wife would have any place in Paradise when he received his quota of seventy-two Houris. "Yes," said he, looking towards his wife, whose veil prevented our seeing her, although she could see us, "if she obeys me in all respects, and is a faithful wife, and goes to Mecca, she will be made more beautiful than all the Houris of Paradise." Paradise is thus held up to the women as the reward of obedience to their husbands, and this is about the sum and substance of what the majority of Moslem women know about religion.

Women are never admitted to pray with men in public, being obliged to perform their devotions at home, or if they visit the Mosques, it must be at a time when the men are not there, for the Moslems are of opinion that the presence of women inspires a different kind of devotion from that which is desirable in a place set apart for the worship of God.

The Moslem idea of woman is vile and degraded. A Moslem absent from home never addresses a letter to his wife, but to his son or brother, or some male relative. It is considered a grievous insult to ask a Moslem about the health of his wife. If obliged to allude to a woman in conversation, you must use the word "ajellak Allah," "May God elevate you" above the contamination of this subject! You would be expected to use the same expression in referring to a donkey, a dog, a shoe, a swine or anything vile. It is somewhat like the Irish expression, "Saving your presence, sir," when alluding to an unpleasant subject.

A Greek christian (?) in Tripoli came to an American Missionary physician and said, "there is a woman, 'ajell shanak Allah' here who is ill. I beg your pardon for mentioning so vile a subject to your excellency." Said the doctor, "and who may it be?" "Ajellak, it is my wife!"

I remember once meeting the Mohammedan Mufti of Beirût in Dr. Van Dyck's study at the printing press. The Mufti's wife, (at least *one* of them,) was ill, and he wished medical advice, but could not insult the Doctor by alluding to a woman in his presence. So he commenced, after innumerable salutations, repeating good-morning, and may your day be happy, until he could decently proceed to business. "Your excellency must be aware that I have a sick man at my house. May God grant you health! Indeed, peace to your head. Inshullah, it is only a slight attack!" "He has pain in his back, headache, and he will not eat." "Has he any fever?" "A little." "I will come and see *her* this afternoon." "May God increase your good. Good morning, sir!"

The Mohammedan laws with regard to polygamy, inheritance and divorce, are a decided advance on the Pagan Arabs of "the Ignorance."

The Pagan Arabs allowed any number of wives. The Koran allows *only four* to any believer, the prophet himself having peculiar privileges in this respect. The modern practice of Mohammedans in taking a score or more of wives is directly contrary to the Koran. The Pagan Arabs suffered no woman to have any part of the husband's or father's inheritance, on the ground that none should inherit who could not go to war, and the widows were disposed of as a part of their husband's possessions. The

Koran says, (Sura iv.) "Women ought to have a part of what their parents leave." A male shall have twice as much as a female. But a man's parents, and also his brothers and sisters are to have equal shares, without reference to sex. "God commandeth you to give the male the portion of two females. If she be an only daughter, she shall have the half. Your wives shall have a fourth part of what ye leave, if ye have no issue."

Among the Pagan Arabs, divorce was a mere matter of caprice. The Koran says, (Sura ii.) "You may divorce your wives twice (and take them back again). But if the husband divorce her a third time, it is not lawful for him to take her again, until she shall have been actually married to another husband, and then divorced by him." I have known cases where the husband in a fit of passion has divorced his wife the third time, and, in order to get her back again, has *hired another man* to marry her and then divorce her. A rich Effendi had divorced his wife the third time, and wishing to remarry her, hired a poor man to marry her for a consideration of seven hundred piastres. He took the wife and the money, and the next day refused to give her up for less than five thousand piastres, which the Effendi was obliged to pay, as the woman had become the lawful and wedded wife of the poor man.

No Mohammedan ever walks with his wife in the street, and in Moslem cities, very few if any of men of other sects are willing to be seen in public in company with a woman. The women are closely veiled, and if a man and his wife have occasion to go anywhere together, he walks in advance and she walks a long distance behind him. Nofel Effendi, one of the most learned and intelligent Protestants in Syria, once gave me the explanation of this aversion to walking in public with women, in a more satisfactory manner than I have ever heard it before. Said he, "You Franks can walk with your wives in public, because their faces are unveiled, and it is *known that they are your wives*, but our women are so closely veiled that if I should walk with my wife in the street, no one would know whether I was walking with my own wife or another man's! You cannot expect a respectable man to put himself into such an embarrassing position!" No Moslem woman or girl would dare go into the street without a veil, for fear of personal chastisement from the husband and father, and the Greek, Maronite and other nominal Christian women in Syria shrink from exposing their faces, through fear of insult from the Mohammedans.

When European women, either residents or travellers, pass through the Moslem quarter of these cities of Syria and Palestine, with faces unveiled, they are made the theme of the most outrageous and insulting comments by the Moslem populace. Well is it for the feelings of the most of these worthy Christian women, that they do not understand the Arabic language. The Turkish governor of Tripoli was obliged to suppress the insulting epithets of the Moslems towards European ladies when they first began to reside there, by the infliction of the bastinado.

In 1857, the Rev. Mr. Lyons in Tripoli, hired Sheikh Owad, a Moslem bigot, to teach him the Arabic grammar. He was a conceited boor; well versed in Arabic grammar, but more ignorant of geography, arithmetic and good breeding than a child. One day Mrs. Lyons passed through the room where he was teaching Mr. L. and he turned his head away from her and spat towards her with a look of unutterable contempt. It was the last time he did it, and he has now become so civilized that he can say good morning to the wife of a missionary, and even consent to teach the sacred, pure and undefiled Arabic to a woman! I believe that he has not yet given his assent to the fact that the earth revolves on its axis, but he has learned that there are women in the world who know more than Sheikh Owad.

In ancient times Moslem women were occasionally taught to read the Koran, and among the wealthier and more aristocratic classes, married women are now sometimes taught to read, but the mass of the Moslem men are bitterly opposed to the instruction of women. When a man decides to have his wife taught to read, the usual plan is to hire a blind Mohammedan Sheikh, who knows the Koran by heart. He sits at one side of the room, and she at the other, some elderly woman, either her mother or her mother-in-law, being present. The blind Sheikhs have remarkable memories and sharp ears, and can detect the slightest error in pronunciation or rendering, so they are employed in the most of the Moslem-schools. The mass of the Mohammedans are nervously afraid of entrusting the knowledge of reading and writing to their wives and daughters, lest they abuse it by writing clandestine letters to improper persons. "Teach a *girl* to read and write!" said a Mohammedan Mufti in Tripoli to me, "Why, she will *write letters*, sir,—yes, *actually write letters!* the thing is not to be thought of for a moment." I replied, "Effendum, you put your foot on the women's necks and then blame them for not rising. Educate your girls and train them to intelligence and virtue, and then their pens will write only what ought to be written. Train the hand to hold a pen, without training the mind to direct it, and only mischief can result." "*Saheah, saheah,*" "very true, very true," said he, "But how can this be done?"

It has begun to be done in Syria. From the days of Mrs. Sarah L. Smith to the present time, Moslem girls have been taught to read and write and sew, and there are many now learning in the various American, British and Prussian schools. But it will be long before any true idea of the dignity of woman enters the debased minds of Arab Mohammedans. The simple fact is that there is no moral purity or elevation among the men, and how can it be expected among the women. The Moslem idea of woman is infinitely lower than the old Jewish idea. Woman in the time of Christ was highly honored. Believing women followed Christ throughout Galilee and Judea, and although enemies stood watching with hateful gaze on every side, not one word of insinuation was ever lisped against them. It is a most sadly impressive fact to one living in Syria at the present day, that the liberty and respect allowed to woman in the days of our Saviour would now be absolutely impossible. In purely Greek or Maronite or Armenian villages, the women enjoy far greater liberty than where there is a Moslem element in the population. And it is worthy of remark and grateful recognition, that although Christianity in the East has sunk almost to a level, in outward morality, with the Islamic and semi-Pagan sects, there is a striking difference between the lowest nominal Christian community and the highest Mohammedan, in the respect paid to woman. Ignorant and oppressed as the Greek and Maronite women may be, you feel on entering their houses, that the degrading yoke of Moslem brutality is not on their necks. Their husbands may be coarse, ignorant and brutal, beating their wives and despising their daughters, mourning at the birth of a daughter, and marrying her without her consent, and yet there are lower depths of coarseness and brutality, of cruelty and bestiality, which are only found among Mohammedans. I once suggested to a Tripoli Moslem, that he send his daughters to our Girls' School, then taught by Miss Sada Gregory, a native teacher trained in the family of Mrs. Whiting, and he looked at me with an expression of mingled pity and contempt, saying, "Educate a *girl!* You might as well attempt to educate *a cat!*"

Not two months since, I was conversing with several of the aristocratic Mohammedans of Beirût, who were in attendance at the commencement of the Beirût Protestant Medical College. The subject of the education of girls was introduced, and one of them said, "we are beginning to have our girls instructed in your Protestant schools, and would you believe it, I heard one of them read the other day, (probably his own daughter,) and she actually asked a question about the construction of a noun preceded by a preposition! I never heard the like of it. The things do distinguish and understand what they read, after all!" The others replied, "*Mashallah! Mashallah!*" "The will of God be done!"

Some ten years ago, an influential Moslem Sheikh in Beirût, who was a personal friend of Mr. Araman, the husband of Lulu, brought his daughter Wahïdy (only one) to the Seminary to be instructed, on condition that no man should ever see her face. As Mr. Araman himself was one of the teachers, and I was accustomed to make constant visits to the school, she was obliged to wear a light veil, which she drew adroitly over her face whenever the door was opened. This went on for months and years, until at length in recitation she would draw the veil aside. Then she used to listen to public addresses in the school without her veil, and finally, in June, 1867, she read a composition on the stage at the Public Examination, on, "The value of education to the women and girls of Syria," her father, Sheikh Said el Ghur, being present, with a number of his Moslem friends.

CHAPTER III.

THE DRUZE RELIGION AND DRUZE WOMEN.

THE great expounder and defender of the Druze religion is Hamzé, the "Universal Intelligence," the only Mediator between God and man, and the medium of the creation of all things. This Hamzé was a shrewd, able and unprincipled man. In his writings he not only defends the abominations of Hakem, but lays down the complete code of Druze doctrine and duty.

It is the belief of many, and said to be the orthodox view among the Druzes that their system as such is to last exactly 900 lunar years. The date of the Druze era is 408 Hegira, or 1020 A. D. The present year, 1872, corresponds to the year 1289 Anno Hegira, so that *in nineteen lunar years* the system will begin to come to an end according to its own reckoning, and after 1000 years it will cease to exist. Others have fixed this present year as the year of the great cataclysm, but the interpreters are so secret and reserved in their statements, that it is only by casual remarks that we can arrive at any idea of their real belief. Lying to infidels is such a meritorious act, that you cannot depend on one word they say of themselves or their doctrines.

Their secret books, which were found in the civil wars of 1841 and 1845, have been translated and published by De Lacy, and we have a number of them in the original Arabic manuscripts in the Mission Library in Beirût. From a chapter in one of these, entitled "Methak en Nissa," or the "Engagements of Women," I have translated the following passages, to show the religious position of women, as bearing upon my object in describing the condition of Syrian females.

"Believers are both male and female. By instruction women pass from ignorance to knowledge, and become angels like the Five Ministers who bear the Throne: *i. e.*, the Doctrine of the Unity. All male and female believers ought to be free from all impurity and disgrace and dishonor. Believing women should shun lying (to the brethren) and infidelity and concupiscence, and the appearance of evil, and show the excellency of their work above all Trinitarian women, avoiding all suspicion and taint which might bring ill upon their brethren, and avoiding giving attention to what is contrary to the Divine Unity.

"We have written this epistle to be read to all believing women who hold to the Unity of Hakem, who knows His Eternity and obey their husbands. But let no Dai or Mazûn read it to a woman until he is well assured of her faith and her religion, and she shall have made a written profession of her faith. He shall not read it to one woman alone, nor in a house where there is but one woman, even though he be worthy of all confidence, lest suspicion be awakened and the tongue of slander be loosed. Let there be assembled together at least three women, and let them sit behind a curtain or screen, so as not to be seen. Each woman must be accompanied by her husband, or her father, or brother or son, if he be a Unitarian. The Dai in reading must keep his eyes fixed on his book, neither turning towards the place where the women are, nor casting a glance towards it, nor listening to them. The woman, moreover, must not speak a word during the reading, and whether she is affected by a transport of joy, or moved by an impression of respect and fear, she must carefully abstain from showing her feelings either by smiles or tears. For the smiles, the tears, and the words of a woman may excite man's passions. Let her give her whole attention to the reading, receive it in her heart, and apply all the faculties of her mind to understand its meaning, in order clearly to conceive the true signification of what she is listening to. If she finds any passage obscure, let her ask the Dai, (the preacher,) and he shall answer, if he can, and if not, promise to ask those who are more learned, and when he has obtained the solution he must inform her, if she be deemed worthy.

"The highest duty of Unitarian women is to know our Moulah Hakem and the Kaim Hamzè. If they follow Him, let them know that He has released them entirely from the observance of the Seven Arbitrary Pillars of the Law (of Islam) which are (1) Prayer, (2) Fasting (3) Pilgrimage, (4) Asserting, There is no God but God and Mohammed is the Prophet of God, (5) Giving tithes, (6) War on infidels, (7) Submission to authority. But on the other hand, all believing women must perform the Seven Religious Duties : The First and greatest is Truth in your words : (i.e to the brethren and sisters) the Second is, To watch reciprocally over the safety of the brethren ; the Third is, to renounce wholly and entirely whatever religion you may have previously professed ; the Fourth is, To keep yourselves apart, clear and distinct from all who are in error ; the Fifth is, To recognize the existence of the Unity of our Lord in all ages, times and epochs ; the Sixth is, To be satisfied with His will and His works, whatever they may be ; The Seventh is, To abandon and resign yourselves to all His orders whether in prosperity or adversity. You must keep these Seven Commandments, and keep them strictly secret from all who are of a different religion. If the Druze women do all this and fulfil their duties, they are indeed among the good, and shall have their reward among the 159 Angels of the Presence and among the Prophets who were Apostles, and be saved from the snare of the accursed Iblîs (Diabolus). Praise then to our Lord Hakim, the praise of the thankful ! He is my hope and victory !"

What can you expect of the women, if the teachers are thus warped with hypocrisy and falsehood. They receive you politely. Dr. De Forest used to say, that there is not a boor in the Druze nation. But their very politeness confounds you. The old

An Arab Sheikh.

politely paid their salams, saying, "Naharkum Saieed," "May your day be blessed," "Allah yahtikum el afiyeh," "God give you health!"

When a Druze Sheikh wishes to marry, he asks consent of the father without having seen the daughter. If the father consents, he informs her, and if she consents, the suitor sends his affianced presents of clothes and jewelry, which remain in her hands as a pledge of his fidelity. She is pictured to him as the paragon of beauty and excellence, but he is never allowed to see her, speak to her, or write to her, should she know how to write. His mother or aunt may see her or bring reports, but he does not see her until the wedding contract is signed and the bride is brought to his house.

The following is the marriage ceremony of the Druzes. It is read by the Kadi or Sheikh, and in accordance to the Druze doctrine that they must outwardly conform to the religion of the governing power, it is a purely Mohammedan ordinance.

"Praise to God, the original Creator of all things; the Gracious in all His gifts and prohibitions; who has decreed and fixed the ordinance of marriage; may Allah pray for (bless) our Prophet Mohammed, and his four successors! Now after this, we say that marriage is one of the laws given by the prophets, and one of the statutes of the pious to guard against vice; a gift from the Lord of the earth and the heaven. Praise to Him who by it has brought the far ones near, and made the foreigner a relative and friend! We are assembled here to attend to a matter decreed and fated of Allah, and whose beginning, middle and end he has connected with the most happy and auspicious circumstances. This matter is the blessed covenant of marriage. Inshullah, may it be completed and perfected, and praise to Allah, the Great Completer! Amen!

In the name of God, the Merciful, the Compassionate. He is my portion and sufficiency. May Allah pray for his pure prophet!"

This is the marriage contract between the person named A. son of — of the village of — in the district of — in Lebanon, and his betrothed named B. the daughter of — of the village of — she being a maiden of full and marriageable age, with no legal obstacles to her marriage. (May Allah protect her veil, and have mercy on her relatives and friends!)

In view of the mercies of Allah and his prophet Mohammed, they pay fifty piastres ($2.00) of full and lawful number, weight and measure, of the Imperial mint of our Moulah the Sultan, (may the exalted and merciful One give him the victory!) and of new white silver. The agent of the husband is — and of the wife is—.

It is the absolute and bounden duty of the husband to provide clothing for the body of his wife and a crown for her head, and of the wife to give him his due honor and rights and do his work, and Allah will be with those who fear Him, and not suffer those who do well to lose their reward.

Signed Sheikh——————(seal)

Witnesses } seal
seal
seal

A whole week is given up to festivity before her arrival, and the retinue of the bride mounted on fine horses escort her amid the firing of musketry, the *zilagheet* shrieks of the women, and general rejoicing, to the bridegroom's house. Col. Churchill describes what follows: "The bride meantime, after having received the caresses and congratulations of her near relatives, is conducted to a chamber apart and placed on a divan, with a large tray of sweetmeats and confectionery before her, after which all the females withdraw and she is left alone, with a massive veil of muslin and gold thrown over her head and covering her face, breasts and shoulders down to the waist. What thoughts and sensations must crowd upon the maiden's mind in this solitude! not to be disturbed but by him who will shortly come to receive in that room his first impressions of her charms and attractions! Presently she hears footsteps at the door; it opens quietly; silently and unattended her lover approaches her, lifts the veil off her face, takes one glance, replaces it and withdraws."

He then returns to the grand reception-room, takes his seat at the head of the divan amid the throng of Sheikhs and other invited guests. He maintains an imperturbable silence, his mind being supposed to be absorbed by one engrossing object. It may be delight. It may be bitter disappointment. It is generally past midnight when the party breaks up and the family retires.

A plurality of wives is absolutely forbidden. If a Druze wishes to divorce his wife, he has merely to say, "You had better go back to your father," or she, the woman, wishes to leave her husband, she says, "I wish to go back to my father," and if her husband says, "Very well, go," the divorce in either case holds good, and the separation is irrevocable. Both parties are free to re-marry. Childlessness is a common cause of divorce.

The birth of a son is the occasion of great rejoicing and presents to the family. But the birth of a daughter is considered a misfortune, and of course not the slightest notice is taken of so inauspicious an event. This holds true among all the sects and peoples of Syria, and nothing but a Christian training and the inculcation of the pure principles of gospel morality can remove this deeply seated prejudice. The people say the reason of their dislike of daughters is that while a son builds up the house, and brings in a wife from without and *perpetuates the family name*, the daughter pulls down the house, loses her name, and is lost to the family.

The wealthier and more aristocratic Druze sitts or ladies are taught to read by the Fakih or teacher, but the masses of the women are in brutish ignorance. You enter a Druze house. The woman waits upon you and brings coffee, but you see only *one eye*, the rest of the head and face being closely veiled. In an aristocratic house, you would never be allowed to see the lady, and if she goes abroad, it is only at night, and with attendants on every side to keep off the profane gaze of strangers. If a physician is called to attend a sick Druze woman, he cannot see her face nor her tongue, unless she choose to thrust it through a hole in her veil. In many cases they suffer a woman to die sooner than have her face seen by a physician.

The Druzes marry but one wife at a time, and yet divorce is so common and so heartlessly practiced by the men, that the poor women live in constant fear of being driven from their homes.

In Abeih, we were startled one evening by the cry "Rouse ye men of self respect! Come and help us!" It was a dark, rainy night, and the earthen roof of a Druze house had fallen in, burying a young man, his wife and his mother, under the mass of earth, stones and timber. They all escaped death, but were seriously injured, the poor young wife suffering the most of all, having fallen with her left arm in a bed of burning coals, and having been compelled to lie there half an hour, so that when dug out, her hand was burned to a cinder! For several days the husband refused to send for a doctor, but at length his wife Hala was sent to the College Hospital (of the Prussian Knights of St. John) in Beirût where Dr. Post amputated the hand below the elbow.

One would naturally suppose that such a calamity, in which both so narrowly escaped death, would bind husband and wife together in the strongest bonds of affection and sympathy. But not so in this case. The poor young wife is now threatened with divorce, because she is no longer of any use to her husband, and her two little children are to be taken from her! She lies on her bed in the Hospital, the very picture of stoical resignation. Not a groan or complaint escapes her.

She said one day, "Oh how glad I am that this happened, for it has taken away all my sins, and I shall never have to suffer again in this world or the next!" This is the doctrine of the Druzes, and, cold and false as it is, she has made it her support and her stay.

Dr. Post and Mrs. Bliss have pointed her to the Lamb of God "who bore our sins in His own body on the tree," and she seems interested to hear and learn more.

Her younger sister is in the Beirût Seminary. May this poor sufferer find peace where alone it can be found, in trusting in the Lord Jesus Christ, whose blood cleanseth from all sin!

The cruelty of her husband, sanctioned as it is by the religious code of the Druzes, may be the means of opening her eyes to the falsity of that heartless Christless system, and lead her to the foot of the Cross!

Christians, who read these lines, pray for Hala of Abeih!

SITT ABLA.

More than twenty years ago in the little Druze village of Aitath, in Lebanon, about seven miles from Beirût, lived a family of Druze Sheikhs of the tribe of Telhûk. This tribe was divided into the great Sheikhs and the little Sheikhs, and among the latter was the Sheikh Khottar. The proximity of this village to Beirût, its elevated position, cool air, and fine fountain of water, made it a favorite summer retreat for the missionaries from the withering heats of the plain. Sheikh Khottar and his wife the Sitt, having both died, their orphan son Selim and daughter Abla, called the Sitt (or lady) Abla, were placed under the care of other members of the family of Telhûk. The missionaries opened a school for boys and Selim attended it. Dr. and Mrs. Van Dyck were living in Aitath at the time, and the young Druze maiden Abla, who was betrothed to a Druze Sheikh, became greatly attached to Mrs. Van Dyck, and came almost constantly to visit her. The light of a better faith and the truth of a pure gospel gradually dawned upon her mind, until her love for Mrs. Van Dyck grew into love for the Saviour of sinners. The Sheikh to whom she was betrothed was greatly enraged at her course in visiting a Christian lady, and meeting her one day when returning to her home, attacked her in the most brutal manner, and gave her a severe beating. She fled and took refuge in the house of Mrs. Van Dyck, who had taught her to read and given her a Bible. A short time after, several of her cousins seized her and scourged her most cruelly, and a violent persecution was excited against her and her brother Selim. She was in daily and hourly expectation of being killed by her male relatives, as it had never been heard of in the Druze nation that a young girl should dare to become a Christian, and Mr. Whiting, missionary in Abeih, sent over a courageous Protestant youth named Saleh, who took the Sitt Abla by night over the rough mountain road to Abeih in safety. But even here she was not safe. The Druzes of Lebanon at that time were at the height of their feudal power. Girls and women were killed among them without the least notice on the part of the mountain government. Abla was like a prisoner in the missionary's house, not venturing to go outside the door, and in order to be at peace, she went down with her brother to Beirût, where she has since resided. Selim united with the Church, but was afterwards suspended from communion for improper conduct, and joined himself to the Jesuits, so that Abla has had to endure a two-fold persecution from her Druze relatives and her Jesuit brother. On her removal to Beirût she was disinherited and deprived of her little portion of her father's estate, and her life has been a constant struggle with persecution, poverty and want. Yet amid all, she has stood firm as a rock, never swerving from the truth, or showing any disposition to go back to her old friends. At times she has suffered from extreme privation, and the missionaries and native Protestants would only hear of it through others who happened to meet her. Since uniting with the Church in 1849 she has lived a Christian life. In a recent conversation she said, "I count all things but loss for the excellency of the knowledge of Christ Jesus my Lord, *for whom I have suffered the loss of all things*. . . . and I still continue, by the grace of Him Exalted, and by the merits of Jesus

Christ my Saviour, awaiting a happy death, and everlasting rest."

KHOZMA.

Her Christian experience is like that of Khozma Ata. She is the only female member of the Protestant church in Syria from among the Druzes, except Sitt Abla. She was born in Beirût of the Druze family of Witwat, and when quite a child was taken by Dr. Beadle, then by Miss Tilden, living at one time in Aleppo, then in Jerusalem, and finally settled in the family of Dr. De Forest, where she continued until his departure for America in 1854. For several years she has been an invalid, and is not often able to leave her house, even to go to church. Two of her little girls are in the Female Seminary. In 1861 she taught a day school for girls in Beirût, and assisted Dr. De Forest in his work in the Beirût Seminary. I called upon her a few days since, and she handed me a roll of Arabic manuscript, which she said she had been translating from the English. It is a series of stories for children which she has prepared to be printed in our monthly journal for Syrian children. The name of the journal is "koukab es Subah," or "Morning Star." She has been confined to her bed a part of the summer, and when she gave me the manuscript, she apologized for the handwriting, on the ground that she had written the most of it sitting or lying on her bed. She has not forgotten the example and instructions of Dr. and Mrs. De Forest, and speaks of them with enthusiastic interest. Her husband failed in business some years ago, and she is in a constant struggle with want, but her old friends and loving sisters, Raheel and Lulu, who are among her nearest neighbors, are unremitting in their kind attentions to her.

What a difference between the faithful Christian nurture her little children are receiving at home, and the worse than no training received by the children of her Druze relatives at Ras Beirût, who are still under the shadow of their old superstitions. She never curses her children nor invokes the wrath of God upon them. She is never beaten and spit upon and tortured and threatened with death by her husband. It is worth much to have rescued a Khozma and an Abla from the degradation of Druze superstition! These two good women, with Adballah in Beirût, and Hassan, Hassein, Asaad and Ali, in Lebanon, are among the living witnesses to the preciousness of the love of Christ, who have come forth from the Druze community. They have been persecuted, and may be again, but they stand firm in Christ. Not a few Druze girls are gathered in our schools in Beirût, Lebanon, and the vicinity of Hermon, as well as in other schools in Damascus, Hasbeiya and elsewhere, and some of their young-men are receiving a Christian education.

CHAPTER IV.

NUSAIRIYEH.

TO the North of Mount Lebanon, and along the low range of mountains extending from Antioch to Tripoli, and from the Mediterranean on the West to Hums on the East, live a strange, wild, bloodthirsty race called the Nusairîyeh numbering about 200,000 souls, and now for the first time in their history coming within the range of Missionary effort.

The Druzes admit women to the Akkal or initiated class, but not so the Nusairîyeh. The great secret of the Sacrament is administered in a secluded place, the women being shut up in a house, or kept away from the mysteries. In these assemblies the Sheikh reads prayers, and then all join in cursing Abubekr, Omar, Othman, Sheikh et-Turkoman and the Christians and others. Then he gives a spoonful of wine, first to the Sheikhs present, and then to all the rest. They then eat fruit, offer other prayers, and the assembly breaks up. The rites of initiation are frightful in the extreme, attended by threats, imprecations and blasphemous oaths, declaring their lives forfeited if they expose the secrets of the order.

They use given signs and questions, by which they salute each other, and ascertain whether a stranger is one of them or not. In their books they employ the double interlacing triangle or seal of Solomon. They call each other brethren, and enjoin love and truthfulness, but *only to the brethren.* In this they are like the Druzes. So little do they regard all outside their own sect, that they *pray to God to take out of the hearts of all others than themselves, what little light of knowledge and certainty they may possess!* The effect of this secret, exclusive, and selfish system is shown in the conduct of the Nusairiyeh in robbing and murdering Moslems and Christians without compunction.

As it has been said, the Nusairiyeh women are entirely excluded from all participation in religious ceremonies and prayers, and from all religious teaching. The reason given is two-fold; the first being that women cannot be trusted to keep a secret, and the second because they are considered by the Nusairiyeh as something unclean. They believe that the soul of a wicked man may pass at death into a brute, or he may be punished for his sins in this life by being born in a woman's form in the next generation. And so, if a woman live in virtue and obedience, there is hope of her again being born into the world *as a man*, and becoming one of the illuminati and possessors of the secret. It is a long time for the poor things to wait, but it is a convenient reward for their husbands to hold out before them.

Yet the women are so religiously inclined by nature that they will have some object of worship, and while their husbands, fathers and sons are talking and praying about the celestial hierarchies, and the unfathomable mysteries, the wives, mothers and daughters will throng the "zeyarehs," or holy visiting shrines, on the hill tops, and among the groves of green trees, to propitiate the favor of the reputed saints of ancient days. These shrines are supposed to have miraculous powers, but Friday is the day when the prophets are more especially "at home," to receive visitors. On other days they may be "on a journey," or asleep. Whenever a Nuisaíyeh woman is in sorrow or trouble or fear, she goes to the zeyareh and cries in a piteous tone, "zeyareh, hear me!"

Their women do not veil themselves, and consequently there is more of freedom among them than among Moslems and Druzes, and in their great festivals, men and women all dance together.

When a young man sees a girl who pleases him, he bargains with her father, agreeing to pay from twenty dollars to two hundred, according to the dignity of her family; of which sum she receives but four dollars, unless her father should choose to give her a red bridal box and bedding for her outfit. She rides in great state to the bridegroom's house amid the firing of guns and shouts of the women, and on dismounting, the bridegroom gives her a present of from one to three dollars, called the "dismounting money."

Divorce needs only the will of the man, and polygamy is common. Lane says in speaking of Egypt, "The depraving effects of this freedom of divorce upon both sexes, may be easily imagined. There are many men in this country who, in the course of ten years, have married as many as twenty, thirty or more wives; and women, not far advanced in age, who have been wives to a dozen or more men successively."

The Nusairîyeh women smoke, swear, and use the most vile and unclean language, and even go beyond the men in these respects. Swearing and lying are universal not only among the Nusairîyeh, but among the most of the Syrian people. You never receive a direct reply from a Nusaîry. He will answer your question by asking another, in order, if possible, to ascertain your object in asking it and to conceal the true state of the case. Their Moslem and nominal Christian neighbors are not much better. They all lie, and swear, and deceive. Mr. Lyde illustrates the ignorance of the Greek clergy in Latakiah by the following incident. A ploughman who had learned something of the Bible, heard a Greek priest cursing the father of a little child. He said, "My father, is it right to curse?" "Oh," said he, "it was only from my lips." "But does not the psalmist say, Keep the door of my lips?" "That" replied the priest, "is only in the English Bible."

Walpole says of the Nusairîyeh women, "when young, they are handsome, often fair, with light hair and jet-black eyes; or the rarer beauty of fair eyes and coal-black hair or eyebrows."

When a fight takes place between the tribes, the women, like the women of the Druzes, enter into the spirit of it with demoniacal fury. During the battle they bring jars of water, shout, sing, and encourage the men, and at the close carry off the booty, such as pots, pans, chickens, quilts, wooden doors, trays, etc. In the Druze war of 1860, I saw the Druze women running with the men through Aitath, on their way to the scene of hostilities in the Metn. The Bedawin women likewise aid their husbands in the commissariat of their nomad warfare.

The Rev. Mr. Lyde was the first to undertake direct missionary labors among the Nusairiyeh, and his work has been carried on by the Reformed Presbyterian Mission in Latakiah. The Rev. J. Beattie sends me the following facts with regard to the work now going on among the women and girls.

The first convert under the labors of Mr. Lyde was Hammûd, of the village of Merj, a young man of fine mind and most lovely character, who gave promise of great usefulness. After he became a Christian, his mother, finding that no Nusaîry girl would marry a Christian, determined to secure a young girl and have her educated for Hammûd. So she paid four Turkish pounds for a little Nusaîry girl named Zahara or Venus, whose widowed mother had removed to her village. This payment was in accordance with Nusaîry customs, and constituted the girl's dowry. After the betrothal in 1863, Hammûd sent her to Latakiah, where she was taken into the family of the late Dr. Dodds for instruction and training. She gladly received the truth, and Hammûd labored earnestly for her enlightenment. Everything seemed bright and promising, until suddenly all their earthly hopes were dashed by the early death of Hammûd in December, 1864. He died in the triumphs of the Christian faith, and from that time she gave herself to the Lord. In August, 1865, she with several others was baptized and received into the communion of the Church. At her own request, she was baptized as Miriam.

In 1866 she was married to Yusef Jedid, and lived with him in several of the villages among the Nusairîyeh, where he was engaged in teaching. Her husband at length removed to Bahlulîyeh in 1870, and a wide door of usefulness was opened to them. Her little daughters Lulu and Helany were with her, and there was every prospect that she would be able to do much for Christ among her benighted sisters. But the same disease, consumption, which prostrated Hammûd, now laid her aside. It was probably brought on by a careless exposure of her health while lying down on the damp ground and falling asleep uncovered, as the natives of the mountain villages are in the habit of doing. The missionaries from Latakiah constantly visited her, and Dr. Metheny gave her the benefit of his medical skill, but all in vain. She loved to converse on heavenly things, and hear the Scriptures and prayer. But when the missionaries returned to the city, she was overwhelmed by the rebukes and merciless upbraidings of the fellaheen, who have no sympathy for the sick, the disabled and the dying. Her ears were filled with the sound of cursing and bitterness, and no wonder that she entreated the missionaries not to leave her. She told Mr. Beattie that she did not fear to die, for her trust was in Jesus Christ, but it was hard to be left among such coarse and unsympathizing people. At length she was brought into Latakiah, where she seemed to feel more at home. At times she passed through severe spiritual conflicts, and said she was struggling with the adversary, who had tried to make her blaspheme. At one time she was in great excitement, but when the 34th Psalm was read she became entirely composed and calm, and in turn began chanting the 23rd Psalm to the end. She sent for all of her friends and begged their forgiveness, commended her children to the care of Miss Crawford, and asked Mr. Beattie to pray with her again. Her bodily sufferings now increased, when suddenly she called out, "The Lord be glorified! To God give the glory!" Soon after, she gently fell "asleep in Jesus." Thus died the first woman, as far as we know, ever truly converted from among the Pagan Nusairîyeh. Her conversion opened the way for that work of moral, religious and intellectual elevation among the Nusaîry females which has since been carried on in Latakiah and vicinity.

The first Christian woman to undertake the direct task of educating and elevating the Nusairîyeh females was Miss Crawford. She commenced her work in 1869. The Mission had found that the Boarding School for boys was training a class of young men, who could not find, among the tens of thousands of families in their native mountains, a single girl fitted to be one's companion for life. The females were everywhere neglected, and Miss Crawford came to Syria just at the time of the greatest need. Under the care and direction of the Mission, she commenced a Boarding School for girls in Latakiah in the fall of 1869. At first, but few pupils could be persuaded to come. Only two attended during the first year. Their names were Sada and Naiuf, the sister of Zahara. The next year Sada left, and ten new ones entered the school: Marie, Howa, Naiseh, Shehla, Thaljeh, (snow,) Tumra, (fruit,) Ghazella, Husna, Bureib'han, and Harba. They were all from twelve to fourteen in age, and remained through the winter, but at the beginning of wheat harvest, their friends forced them to return to their homes for the summer. They made marked progress both in study and deportment, and before leaving for their homes passed a creditable examination both in their studies and in needlework. The fact was thus established to the astonishment of the citizens of Latakiah, that the Nusairiyeh girls were equal in intellect and skill in needlework to the brightest of the city girls. In the autumn of 1871 it was feared that the Pagan parents of the girls would prevent their return to the school, but, greatly to the gratification of the missionaries, all of the ten returned, bringing with them nine others; Hamameh, (dove,) Henîreh, Elmaza, (diamond,) Deebeh,(she-wolf,) Alexandra, Zeinab, Lulu, (pearl,) Howwa, (Eve,) and Naameh, (grace).

During the year the pupils brought new joy to the hearts of their teachers. Not only were their numbers greatly increased, but the older girls seemed all to be under the influence of deep religious impressions on their return to the school. Although they had spent the summer among the wild fellaheen and been compelled to listen to blasphemy, impurity and cursing on every side, they had been able by the aid of God's Spirit to discriminate between good and evil, and to contrast the lawless wickedness of the fellaheen with the holy precepts of the Bible. Finding themselves unable to meet the requirements of God's pure and holy law, they returned under serious distress of mind, asking what they should do to be saved? Such of them as could do so, had been in the habit of meeting together during the summer for prayer, and of repeating the ten commandments and other portions of Scripture with which they were familiar. They had been threatened and beaten by their friends on account of their religious views, but they remained unmoved. The child-like simple faith of some of them was remarkable. Marie was punished on one occasion by her father for attending the missionary service at B'hamra on the Sabbath. He forbade her to eat for a whole day, and she prayed that God would give her bread. Soon after, on her way to the village fountain, she found part of a merkûk, loaf of bread, by the wayside, which she picked up and ate most gratefully, regarding it as a direct answer to her prayer. Another Ghuzaleh, was brutally beaten because she would not swear and blaspheme, and all were threatened and insulted because they would not work on Sunday.

In November, 1871, seven of these girls, on their own application, were received into the membership of the Church. It was an interesting sight to see that group of Nusairîyeh heathen girls standing to receive the ordinance of Christian baptism. In the spring of 1872, another was added to the list. These little ones of Christ have all thus far shown themselves faithful. They were sent back to their homes in the summer, and several, if not the most, of them may be forbidden to return again to the school. Some may say, why allow them to go home? The policy of encouraging children to run away from their parents and connect themselves with foreign missionaries and missionary institutions, will lead the heathen to hate the very name of Christianity, and to charge it with being a foe to all social and family order, and on the broad ground of missionary usefulness, the girls can do far more good in their own homes than elsewhere.

CHAPTER V.

CHRONICLE OF WOMEN'S WORK FROM 1820 TO 1872.

IT must not be inferred from what has been said on a preceding page with regard to the favorable position occupied by the women of the nominal Christian sects of Syria as compared with the Mohammedan women, that the first missionaries found the Greek and Maronite women and girls who speak the Arabic language eager or even willing to receive instruction. Far from it. The effects of the Mohammedan domination of twelve hundred years have been to degrade and depress all the sects and nationalities who are subject to Islam. Not only were there not women and girls found to learn to read, but the great mass of the men of the Christian sects could neither read nor write. Many of the prominent Arab merchants in Beirût to-day can neither read nor write. I say Arab merchants, and yet very few of the Arabs of the Greek Church have more than a mere tinge of Arab blood in their veins. To call them Syrians, would be to confound them with the "Syrian" or "Jacobite" sect, who are found only in the vicinity of Hums, Hamath and Mardin. So with the Maronites. They are chiefly of a darker complexion than the Arab Greeks, and are supposed to have had their origin in Mesopotamia. Yet all these sects and races speak the common Arabic language, and hence it will be convenient to call them Arabs, although I am aware, that while many of the modern Syrians glory in the name "Oulad el Arab," many others regard it with dislike.

The Syrian Christianity, moreover, so often alluded to in the history of the Syrian Mission, is the lowest type of the religion of the Greek and Roman churches. Saint-worship and picture-worship are universal. An ignorant priesthood, and a superstitious people, no Bibles, and no readers to read them, no schools and no teachers capable of conducting them, prayers in unknown tongues, and a bitter feeling of party spirit in all the sects, universal belief in the efficacy of fasts and vows, pilgrimages and offerings to the shrines of reputed saints, churches without a preached gospel, and prayers performed as a duty without the worship of the heart, universal Mariolatry, a Sabbath desecrated by priests and people alike, God's name everywhere profaned by men, women and children, and truthfulness of lip almost absolutely unknown; the women and girls degraded and oppressed and left to the tender mercies of a corrupt clergy through the infamies of the confessional; all these practices and many others which space forbids us to mention, combined with the social bondage entailed upon woman by the gross code of Islam, rendered the women of the nominal Christian sects of Syria almost as hopeless subjects of missionary labor as were their less favored Druze and Moslem sisters.

In order to present the leading facts in the history of Mission Work for Syrian women, I propose to give a brief review of the salient points, in the order of time, as I have been able to glean them from the missionary documents within my reach.

The first Protestant missionary to Syria since the days of the Apostles, was the Rev. Levi Parsons, who reached Jerusalem January 16, 1821, and died in Alexandria February 10, 1822. In 1823, Rev. Pliny Fisk, and Dr. Jonas King reached Jerusalem to take his place, and on the 10th of July came to Beirût. Dr. King spent the summer in Deir el Kamr, and Mr. Fisk in a building now occupied by the Jesuit College in Aintûra.

On the 16th of November, 1823, Messrs. Goodell and Bird reached Beirût, and on the 6th of December, 1824, they wrote as follows: "Mr. King's Arabic instructor laughs heartily that the ladies of our company are served first at table. He said that if any person should come to his house and speak to his wife *first*, he should be offended. He said the English ladies have some understanding, the Arab women have none. It is the custom of this country that a woman must never be seen eating or walking, or in company with her husband. When she walks abroad, she must wrap herself in a large white sheet, and look like a ghost, and at home she must be treated more like a slave than a partner. Indeed, women are considered of so little consequence that

Arabic Lord's Prayer.

الصلوة الربّانيّة

ابانا الذي في السموات . ليتقدّس اسمك . ليأتِ ملكوتك .
لتكن مشيئتك كما في السماء كذلك على الارض . خبزنا كفافنا
أعطِنا اليوم . واغفر لنا ذنوبنا كما نغفر نحن ايضًا
للمذنبين الينا . ولا تدخلنا في تجربةٍ . لكن
نجّنا من الشرّير . لان لك الملك
والقوّة والمجد الى الابد .
آمين

know how to read and write. They are quite bad enough with what little they now know. Teach them to read and write, and *there would be no living with them!*'" That Tyrian priest of fifty years ago, was a fair sample of his black-frocked brethren throughout Syria from that time to this. There have been a few worthy exceptions, but the Syrian priesthood of all sects, taken as a class, are the avowed enemies of the education and elevation of their people. Some of the exceptions to this rule will be mentioned in the subsequent pages of this volume.

In 1826, there were three hundred children in the Mission schools in the vicinity of Beirût.

In 1827, there were 600 pupils in 13 schools, of whom *one hundred and twenty were girls!* In view of the political, social and religious condition of Syria at that time, that statement is more remarkable than almost any fact in the history of the Syrian Mission. It shows that Mrs. Bird and Mrs. Goodell must have labored to good purpose in persuading their benighted Syrian sisters to send their daughters to school, and to these two Christian women is due the credit of having commenced Woman's Work for Women in modern times in Syria. In that same year, the wives of Bishop Dionysius Carabet and Gregory Wortabet were received to the communion of the Church in Beirût, being the first spiritual fruits of Women's Work for Women in modern Syria.

During 1828 and 1829 the Missionaries temporarily withdrew to Malta. In 1833, Dr. Thomson and Dr. Dodge arrived in Beirût. The Mission now consisted of Messrs. Bird, Whiting, Eli Smith, Drs. Thomson and Dodge. In a letter written at that time by Messrs. Bird, Smith and Thomson, it is said, "Of the females, none can either read or write, or the exceptions are so very few as not to deserve consideration. Female education is not merely neglected, but discouraged and opposed." They also stated, that "the whole number of native children in the Mission Schools from the beginning had been 650; 500 before the interruption in 1828, and 150 since." "Female education as such is yet nearly untried."

During that year Mrs. Thomson and Mrs. Dodge commenced a school for girls in Beirût. Dr. Eli Smith speaks of this school as follows, in the Memoir of Mrs. S. L. Smith: "A few girls were previously found in some of the public schools supported by the Mission, and a few had lived in the Mission families. But these ladies wished to bring them more directly under missionary influence, and to confer upon them the benefit of a system of instruction adapted to females. A commencement was accordingly made, by giving lessons to such little girls as could be irregularly assembled for an hour or two a day at the Mission-house; such an informal beginning being not only all that the ladies had time to attempt, but being also considered desirable as less likely to excite jealousy and opposition. For the project was entered upon with much trembling and apprehension. Not merely indifference to female education had to be encountered, but strong prejudice against it existing in the public mind from time immemorial. The Oriental prejudice against innovations from any quarter, and especially from foreigners, threatened resistance. The seclusion of females within their own immediate circle of relationship originally Oriental, but strengthened by Mohammedan influence, stood in the way. And more than all, religious jealousy, looking upon the missionaries as dangerous heretics, and their influence as contamination, seemed to give unequivocal warning that the attempt might be fruitless. But the missionaries were not aware of the hold they had gained upon the public confidence. The event proved in this, as in many other missionary attempts, that strong faith is a better principle to act upon in the propagation of the gospel, than cautious calculation. Even down to the present time (1840) it is not known that a word of opposition has been uttered against the school which was then commenced.

"On the arrival of Mrs. S. L. Smith in Beirût in January, 1834, she found some six or eight girls assembled every afternoon in Mrs. Thomson's room at the Mission house, receiving instruction in sewing and reading. One was far enough advanced to aid in teaching, and the widow of Gregory Wortabet occasionally assisted. On the removal of Mrs. Thomson and Mrs. Dodge to Jerusalem, the entire charge of the school devolved upon Mrs. Smith, aided by Mrs. Wortabet. Especial attention was given to reading, sewing, knitting and good behavior. In November, 1835, Miss Rebecca Williams arrived in Beirût as an assistant to Mrs. Smith. The school then increased, and in the spring of 1836 an examination was held, at which the mothers of the children and some other female friends were present. The scholars together amounted to upwards of forty; the room was well-filled, "presenting a scene that would have delighted the heart of many a friend of missions. Classes were examined in reading, spelling, geography, first lessons in arithmetic, Scripture questions, the English language, and sacred music, and the whole was closed by a brief address from Mrs. Dodge. The mothers then came forward of their own accord, and in a gratifying manner expressed their thanks to the ladies for what they had done for their daughters." Of the pupils of this school, the greater part were Arabs of the Greek Church; two were Jewesses; and some were Druzes; and at times there were eight or ten Moslems.

A Sabbath School, with five teachers and thirty pupils, was established at the same time, the majority of the scholars being girls. A native female prayer-meeting was also commenced at this time, conducted by three missionary ladies and two native Protestant women. At times, as many as twenty were present, and this first female prayer-meeting in Syria in modern times, was attended with manifest tokens of the Divine blessing.

As has been already stated, the seclusion of

Oriental females renders it almost impossible for a male missionary to visit among them or hold religious meetings exclusively for women. This must be done, if at all, by the missionary's wife or by Christian women devoted especially to this work. It was true in 1834, and it is almost equally true in 1873. The Arabs have a proverb, "The tree is not cut down, but by a branch of itself;" *i. e.* the axe handle is of wood. So none can reach the women of Syria but women. The Church of Rome understands this, and is sending French, Italian and Spanish nuns in multitudes to work upon the girls and women of Syria, and the women of the Syria Mission, married and unmarried, have done a noble work in the past in the elevation and education of their Syrian sisters. And in this connection it should be observed, that a *sine qua non* of efficient usefulness among the women of Syria, is that the Christian women who labor for them should know the Arabic language. Ignorance of the language is regarded by the people as indicating a want of sympathy with them, and is an almost insuperable barrier to a true spiritual influence. The great work to be done for the women of the world in the future, is to be done in their own mother-tongue, and it would be well that all the Female Seminaries in foreign lands should be so thoroughly supplied with teachers, that those most familiar with the native language could be free to devote a portion of their time to labors among the native women in their homes.

In 1834 and 1835 Mrs. Dodge conducted a school

for Druze girls in Aaleih, in Lebanon. This School in Aaleih, a village about 2300 feet above the level of the sea, was once suddenly broken up. Not a girl appeared at the morning session. A rumor had spread through the village, that the English fleet had come up Mount Lebanon from Beirût, and was approaching Aaleih to carry off all the girls to England! The panic however subsided, and the girls returned to school. In 1836 Mrs. Hebard and Mrs. Dodge carried on the work which Mrs. Smith had so much loved, and which was only temporarily interrupted by her death.

In 1837, Mrs. Whiting and Miss Tilden had an interesting school of Mohammedan girls in Jerusalem, and Mrs. Whiting had several native girls in her own family.

In reply to certain inquiries contained in a note I addressed to Miss T. she writes: "I arrived in Beirût, June 16, 1835. Mr. and Mrs. Whiting in Jerusalem were desirous that I should take a small school that Mrs. Whiting had gathered, of Mohammedan girls. She had in her family two girls from Beirût, Salome, (Mrs. Prof. Wortabet,) and Hanne, (Mrs. Reichardt.) There were in school from 12 to 20 or more scholars, all Moslems. Only one Christian girl could be persuaded to attend. I think that the inducement they had to send their daughters was the instruction given in sewing and knitting, free of expense to them. Mrs. Whiting taught the same scholars on the Sabbath. The Scripture used in their instruction, both week days and on the Sabbath, was the Psalms. After a year and a half I went to Beirût and assisted in the girl's school, which was somewhat larger and more promising. Miss Williams had become Mrs. Hebard, and Miss Badger from Malta was teaching at the time. Mrs. Smith's boarding scholar Raheel, was with Mrs. Hebard. I suppose that female education in the family was commenced in Syria by Mr. Bird, who taught the girl that married Demetrius. (Miss T. probably meant to say Dr. Thomson, as Mariya, daughter of Yakob Agha, was first placed in his family by her father in 1834.) The girls taught in the different missionaries' families were Raheel, Salome, Hanne, Khozma, Lulu, Kefa, and Susan Haddad. Schools were taught in the mountains, and instruction given to the women, and meetings held with them as the ladies had strength and opportunity, at their different summer residences. The day scholars were taught in Arabic, and the boarding scholars in Arabic and English. I taught them Colburn's Arithmetic. I taught also written arithmetic, reading, etc., in the boys' school."

In 1841, war broke out between the Druzes and Maronites, and the nine schools of the Mission, including the Male Seminary of 31 pupils, the Girls' School of 25 pupils, and the Druze High School in Deir el Kamr, were broken up.

In 1842, the schools were resumed. In twelve schools were 279 pupils, of whom 52 were girls, and twelve young girls were living as boarders in mission families.

In 1843, there were thirteen schools with 438 pupils, and eleven young girls in mission families.

During the year 1844, 186 persons were publicly recognized as Protestants in Hasbeiya. Fifteen women attended a daily afternoon prayer-meeting, and expressed great surprise and delight at the thought that religion was a thing in which *women* had a share! A fiery persecution was commenced against the Protestants, who all fled to Abeih in Lebanon. On their return they were attacked and stoned in the streets, and Deacon Fuaz was severely wounded.

In 1845, Lebanon was again desolated with civil war, the schools were suspended, and the instruction of 182 girls and 424 boys interrupted for a time.

CHAPTER VI.

MRS. WHITING'S SCHOOL.

IN 1846, Mrs. Whiting commenced a girls' day-school in her family at Abeih, and in Beirût there were four schools for boys and girls together, and one school for girls alone. In 18 Mission schools there were 144 girls and 384 boys. This girls' school in Abeih in 1846 was taught by Salome (Mrs. Wortabet) and Hanne, (Mrs. Reichardt,) the two oldest girls in Mr. Whiting's family. It was impossible to begin the school before August 1st, as the houses of the village which had been burned in the war of the preceding year had not been rebuilt, and suitable accommodations could not readily be found. During the summer there were twelve pupils, and in the fall twenty-five, from the Druze, Maronite, Greek Catholic and Greek sects, and the greatest freedom was used in giving instruction in the Bible and the Assembly's and Watts' Catechisms. A portion of every day was spent in giving especial religious instruction, and on the Sabbath a part of the pupils were gathered into the Sabbath School. During the fall a room was erected on the Mission premises for the girls' school, at an expense of 100 dollars.

The following letter from Mrs. Whiting needs no Introduction. It bears a melancholy interest from

3*

the fact that the beloved writer died shortly afterwards, at Newark, N. J., May 18th, 1873.

"My first introduction to the women of Syria was by Mrs. Bird, mother of Rev. Wm. Bird and Mrs. Van Lennep. She was then in the midst of her little family of four children. I daily found her in her nursery, surrounded by native women who came to her in great numbers, often with their sick children. They were always received with the greatest kindness and ministered to. She might be seen giving a warm bath to a sick child, or waiting and watching the effect of other remedies. Mothers from the neighboring villages of Lebanon were allowed to bring their sick children and remain for days in her house until relief was obtained. She was soon known throughout Beirût and these villages as the friend of the suffering, and I have ever thought that by these Christian self-denying labors, she did much towards gaining the confidence of the people. And who shall say that while good Father Bird was in his study library among the 'Popes and Fathers,' preparing his controversial work 'The Thirteen Letters,' this dear sister, by her efforts, was not making a way to the hearts of these people for the reception of gospel truth, which has since been preached so successfully in the neighboring villages of Lebanon?

"In the autumn of 1834, Mr. Whiting was removed to the Jerusalem station. I found the women accessible and ready to visit me, and invite me to their houses, but unwilling to place their girls under my instruction. All my efforts for some time were fruitless. Under date of Aug. 22, I find this entry in Mr. Whiting's journal: "During the past week, three little Moslem girls have been placed under Mrs. Whiting's instruction for the purpose of learning to read and sew. They seem much pleased with their new employment, and their parents, who are respectable Moslems, express great satisfaction in the prospect of their learning. They say, in the Oriental style that the children are no longer theirs, but ours, and that they shall remain with us and learn everything we think proper to teach them. This event excited much talk in the city, particularly among the Moslem mothers. The number of scholars, chiefly Moslem girls, increased to twenty-five and thirty."

At a later date, Jan., 1836, "one of the girls in Mrs. Whiting's school, came with a complaint against a Jew who had been attempting to frighten her away from the school by telling her and her uncle (her guardian) that her teacher certainly had some evil design, and no doubt intended to select the finest of the girls, and send them away to the Pasha, and that it was even written so in the books which she was teaching the children to read. Whether the Jew has been set up by others to tell the people this absurd nonsense, I cannot say, but certainly it is a new thing for Jews to make any opposition, or to show any hostility to us. And this looks very much like the evil influence which has been attempted in another quarter."

"March 7. Yesterday Mrs. W. commenced a Sunday school for the pupils of her day school

They were much delighted. They began to learn the Sermon on the Mount."

"Sept. 7. Had a visit from two Sheikhs of the Mosque of David. One of them inquired particularly respecting Mrs. Whiting's school for Moslem girls, and wished to know what she taught them to read. I showed him the little spelling-book which we use, with which he was much pleased and begged me to lend it to him. I gave him one, with a copy of the Psalms, which he wished to compare with the Psalms of David as the Moslems have them. He invited me strongly to come and visit him, and to bring Mrs. Whiting to see his family."

The school continued with little interruption until October 3d, when Miss Tilden arrived and had the charge of the school for nearly two years. I left in feeble health, with Mr. Whiting, for the United States, where we spent more than one year. Miss Tilden during our absence was engaged in teaching in the boys' school in Beirût. On my return the Moslem school was not resumed, and soon after Mr. Whiting was again transferred to the Abeih station.

My work in the family school began in October, 1835, when Salome Carabet and Hanne Wortabet were placed by their parents in our family school. We afterwards added to the number Melita Carabet, and the two orphan girls Sada and Rufka Gregory. These two were brought to us in a very providential way. They were the children of Yakob Gregory, a respectable Armenian well known in Beirût.

He had two children, and when these were quite

young, he left his wife, and nothing was heard of him afterwards. The mother died soon after and left the children in the care of the American Mission and the Armenian Bishop. The old grandmother, who was in Aleppo, on hearing of her death, soon returned to Beirût to look after the children. She was allowed to visit them in the Bishop's family, where they were cared for, and one day, in a stealthy way, she took Sada into the city, placed her in the hands of a Jew, on board of a native boat bound for Jaffa. I suppose Sada was then about six years old. They set sail. The child cried bitterly on finding her grandmother was not on board as she had promised. There was on board the boat an Armenian, well acquainted with her father, who inquired of her the cause. On hearing her story he remonstrated with the Jew, who said she had been placed in his hands by her grandmother to be sent to Jerusalem. On their arriving at Jaffa, the affair was made known to Mr. Murad, the American Consul. He sent for the Jew, took the child from his hands, and dismissed him, and wrote to Mr. Whiting in Jerusalem an account of the affair, and was directed by him to send the child to us. Not long after, her grandmother came to Jerusalem bringing Rufka. She tried to interest the Armenian Convent in her behalf. Here I find an extract from Mr. Whiting's journal, which will give you all of interest on this point. "After being out much of the morning, I returned and found the grandmother of little Sada, who had brought her little sister Rufka to leave her with us. She had a quarrel with the convent, and fled for refuge to us. We cannot but be thankful that both these little orphans are at length quietly placed under our care and instruction."

The parents of three of the girls in our family, being Protestants, always gave their sanction to our mode of instructing and training them. Bishop Curabet likewise aided us in every way in his power, and ever seemed most grateful for what I was doing for his daughters. In his last sickness, when enfeebled by age, I often visited him. Once on going into his room, he was seated as usual on his Turkish rug. One of the family rose to offer me a chair, I said, "let me sit near you on your rug, that I may talk to you." With much emotion he replied, "*Inshullah tukodee jenb il Messiah fe melakoot is sema!*" "God grant that you may sit by the side of Christ in the kingdom of Heaven!"

We were from time to time encouraged by tokens of a work of God's Spirit in their hearts. Melita Curabet was the first to indulge a hope in Christ, and united with the Church in Abeih. Salome united in Beirût; Hanne in Hasbeiya, where her brother, Rev. John Wortabet, was pastor. Sada was received by Mr. Calhoun at Abeih, soon after Mr. Whiting's death, and Rufka in later years united with the United Presbyterian Church in Alexandria, Egypt. I have ever thought these girls were under great obligations to the American Churches and the American Mission, who for so many years supported and instructed them, and I have ever tried to impress upon them a sense of their obligation to impart to others of their countrywomen what they had received. I believe as early as 1836, they began assisting me in the Moslem school for girls in Jerusalem, in which they continued to assist Miss Tilden until the school was given up.

Soon after our removal to Abeih, October, 1844, we established a day-school for girls in the village on the Mission premises, of which Salome and Hanne had the entire charge under my superintendence. When the Station at Mosul was established, Salome was appointed by the Mission to assist Mrs. Williams in her work among the women, in which work she continued until her marriage with Rev. John Wortabet. Melita was afterwards appointed by the Mission to the Aleppo Station to assist Mrs. Eddy and Mrs. Ford in the work, and so they were employed at various stations in the work of teaching, until I left the Mission. I have kept up a continual correspondence with them, and have learned from others to my joy, that they were doing the work for which I had trained them."

The above deeply interesting letter from Mrs. Whiting is enough in itself to show what an amount of patient Christian labor was expended through a course of many years, in the education of the five young Syrian maidens who were entrusted in the providence of God to her care. I have been personally acquainted with four of them for seventeen years, and can testify, as can many others, of the good use they have made of their high opportunities.

The amount of good they have accomplished as teachers, in Abeih, Jerusalem, Deir el Komr, Hasbeiya, Tripoli, Aleppo, Mosul, Alexandria, Cairo, Melbourne, (Australia,) and in the Mission Female Seminary and the Prussian Deaconesses' Institute in Beirût, will never be known until all things are revealed. I have received letters from several of them, which I will give in their own language, as they are written in English. The first is from Salome, now the wife of the Rev. Prof. John Wortabet, M. D., of the Syrian Protestant College in Beirût.

"I do not consider my history worth recording, and it is only out of consideration of what is due to Mrs. Whiting for the labor she bestowed upon us, that I am induced to take up my pen to comply with your request. I was taken by Mrs. Whiting when only six years old, together with Hannie Wortabet, who was five years old, to be brought up in her family, she having no children of her own. Owing partly to the nature of the religious instruction we received, and partly to my own timid sensitive nature, I was, from time to time for many years, under deep spiritual terrors, without any saving result. When I was about sixteen, a revival of religion took place, under whose influence I was also brought. Mr. Calhoun was my spiritual adviser, and although my mind groped in darkness, and bordered on despair for many weeks, I hope I was then led to put my trust in Jesus, and if ever I am saved, my only hope now is, and ever shall be, in the merits of Jesus' blood and His promises."

The next letter is from Melita Carabet, daughter of the Armenian Bishop Dionysius Carabet, who became a Protestant in 1823. She writes as follows:

"Nothing could give me more pleasure than to comply with your request, and thereby recall some of the happy days and incidents of my childhood and youth, spent under the roof of my godly teachers, Mr. and Mrs. Whiting. I ought to remember them as far back as at the baptismal font, for I heard afterwards that they were both present on the occasion, which took place in Malta, where I was born. But as my memory does not carry me back so far, I must date my recollections from the time I was five years of age, when I came to live in their family. I can distinctly recollect the first texts of Scripture and verses of hymns that dear Mrs. Whiting taught my young lips to repeat, and my little prayer which I used to say at her knees on going to bed, I still repeat to this day, "Now I lay me," etc. One incident which happened about a year later, was so deeply impressed on my memory, and had such an effect upon me at the time, that I must mention it. It was this. Mrs. Whiting had given us girls (we were five in number, my sister Salome, and Hannie, Dr. Wortabet's sister, and Sada and Rufka Gregory) some raisins to pick over preparatory to making cake. I stole an opportunity after a while, to slip about a dozen of these raisins into my pocket. No one saw me do it, but from the moment I had done it, I began to feel very unhappy, and repented the deed. My companions went out to play, but I could not join in their sports. My heart was too heavy. I sat mourning over my sin, and could eat no supper, and had no rest until I had made a full confession to Mrs. Whiting at bed-time. She prayed and wept over me, and somehow I was comforted and went to my little bed much happier.

"I remember nothing more until a much later period, when I was about the age of twelve. About this time, there was a great awakening among the young girls in some of the Mission families. Mr. Calhoun's prayers and advice were very much solicited and sought, in guiding and praying with the young inquirers. One Sunday as I was reading the little tract "The Blacksmith's wife," (which I have kept to this day,) I felt a great weight and sense of sin. I trace my conversion to the reading of this tract. It was not long before I found peace. I have often since longed for those days and hours of sweet communion with my Saviour. I joined the Church a very short time after this, and at this early age was given charge of a Bible class in Abeih.

"Now I must pass over a few more years, when I went to Hasbeiya, to spend a little time with my sister Salome, now wife of Dr. John Wortabet, who was appointed pastor of the little Protestant Church there. I spent one year of my life here, during which time I took charge of a little day school for girls in my sister's house. Dr. Wortabet's sister Hannie had opened this school some years before I came. I do not remember the number of pupils, but there were five little Moslem princesses, grandchildren of the great Emir "Saad-ed-Deen," who was called some years later to Constantinople to be punished for having spoken disrespectfully of Queen Victoria. These little princesses were regular attendants at the school, and learned to read in the New Testament, and studied Watts' Catechism with the rest of the Christian children. I had also charge of a Bible class for women, who used to meet once a week in the Protestant Church. This was before the massacre of 1860. The rest of my life has been spent in teaching in Beirût. Since the massacres, I have been teaching the orphans in the Prussian School, where I at present reside. Indeed it has been my home ever since I undertook this work which I love dearly, and which I hope to continue so long as the Lord sees fit, and gives me strength to work for Him."

I am permitted to make the following extract from a letter written by Melita to Mrs. Whiting, in February, 1868. I give the exact language, as the letter is written in English:

PRUSSIAN INSTITUTION, BEIRUT,
February 23, 1868.

MY DEAR MRS. WHITING—

It is so cold this morning that I can with difficulty hold my pen. It has been a very cold and stormy month, and there seems no prospect of fair weather yet. The snow on the mountains is as low as the lowest hills, and I pity the poor creatures who must be suffering in consequence. J. enjoys the weather very much; indeed he seems so exhilarated and invigorated by it that one could almost wish it to last on his account, but I must say that I wish it was over, and the warm sunbeams shedding their genial rays again upon the cold frozen earth.

Trouble and grief are such a common complaint at present that you will not be surprised to hear me relate my share of them. I have indeed had my full share, and you would say so too had you seen how I was occupied during my holidays last summer, in taking care of my ill and suffering brother. And aside from my fatigue, for I was always on my feet until two or three hours after midnight, quite alone with him—merely to witness such indescribable suffering as he went through, was more than is generally allotted to human beings on earth. He had been unwell for some time previous, and had been advised by the Doctor to go up to the mountains, so Mr. Calhoun kindly offered him a place in the Seminary, where he could stop until his health was recruited, and in the meantime give a couple of English lessons during the day to the boys in the Seminary. He lodged with the Theological students in a little room above the school, but he had not been up there more than a week, when his whole body became suddenly covered with a burning eruption that was always spreading and increasing in size. He could neither lie nor sit in any possible position, and was racked with pains that seemed at times well nigh driving him mad. I trembled for his reason, and was so awed and terrified by the sight, that I was in danger of losing mine as well. No one would come near him, and Mrs. Calhoun had kindly asked me to come and spend the holidays with them, so it fell to my lot to nurse and take care of him. I used to go to him in the morning as soon as I got up, and sit (or stand) up with him until two or three o'clock at night, dressing his sores; running down only occasionally for my meals, and with my little lantern coming down in the dead of night, all alone, to lay my weary head and aching heart and limbs on my bed for a little rest. But not to sleep, for whenever I closed my eyes, I had that eternal picture and scene of suffering before me. I could find no one who was willing for love or for money to help me or relieve me for one night or day. The disease was so offensive as well as frightful, that no one could stop in the room. One of the Prussian "Sisters" who went up with me, kindly assisted me sometimes until she came down. In this state did J. find me on his return from England. His family was up in Aaleih, and he used to ride over occasionally to see P. and prescribe some new medicine for him, but his skill was baffled with this terrifying disease, and poor P. remained in this agonizing state of suffering for five whole months without leaving his bed. He was carried down on a litter to Beirût, where he has been since. He took a little room by himself, and gives lessons in English until something more prosperous turns up for him. Twenty years' experience seemed to be added to my life in those three months of anxiety I went through last summer; and what a picture of suffering and grief was I, after this, myself! No wonder if I feel entirely used up this winter, and feel it a great effort to live.

There is not the slightest prospect of my ever getting back my lost property from that man—as he has long since left the country, and is said to be a great scoundrel and a very dishonorable man. If he were not, he would never have risked the earnings of a poor orphan girl by asking for it on the eve of his bankruptcy. Had I my property I might perhaps have given up teaching for a while, and gone away for a little change and rest, but God has willed it otherwise, no doubt for some wise purpose, and to some wise end, although so difficult and incomprehensible at present. It is all doubtless for the trial of my faith and trust in Him. Let me then trust in Him! Yea, though He slay me, let me yet trust in Him! Has He ever yet failed me? Has He not proved Himself in all ages to be the Father and the God of the orphan and the widow? He must see that I need these troubles and sorrows, or He would not send them, for my Father's hand would never cause his child a needless tear. A bruised reed He will not break, but will temper the storm to the shorn lamb; I will then no longer be dejected and cast down, but look upward and trust in my Heavenly Father, feeling sure that He will make all right in the end.

My letter is so sad and melancholy that I cannot let it go without something more cheerful, so I will add a line to brighten and cheer it up a little. For life, with all the bitterness it contains, has also much that is agreeable and affords much enjoyment; for there is a wonderful elasticity in the human mind which enables it, when sanctified by divine grace, to bear up under present ills. So with all my griefs and ills, I have been able to enjoy myself too sometimes this winter. I have lately attended two Concerts, one here, given by the Prussian Sisters, for the benefit of the new Orphanage, "Talitha Kumi," at Jerusalem, lately erected by the Prussian Sisters there—and one given by the "Sisters of Charity," for the benefit of the orphans and poor of this town. Daood Pasha most generously gave up the large hall in his mansion for the occasion, as well as honoring it by his attendance. The Concert in our Institution was entirely musical, vocal and instrumental. All the Missionaries came. We had nearly three hundred tickets sold at five francs apiece, so that there was a nice little sum added to the Orphan's Fund at Jerusalem.

Ever your affectionate MELITA.

Saada Gregory was engaged in teaching at different times in Tripoli, Aleppo, Hasheiya and Egypt. Her school in Tripoli was eminently successful, and her labors in Alexandria were characterized by great energy and perseverance. She kept up a large school even when suffering from great bodily pain. She is now in the United States in enfeebled health.

AMERICAN MISSION HOUSE,
ALEXANDRIA, *November* 8, 1867.

MY DEAR MRS. WHITING,

I know you will be expecting a letter from me soon, partly in answer to yours sent by Mrs. Van Dyck, and especially because it is the day on which you expect all your children to remember you. I never do forget this day, but this time there are special reasons for my remembering it. Whenever the day has come around, I have felt more forcibly than at others, how utterly alone I have been, for since dear Mr. Whiting was taken away from us, it has seemed as though we were made doubly orphans, but this time it has not been so. I think I have been made to realize that I have a loving Father in heaven who loves and watches over and cares for me more than ever you or Mr. Whiting did. I do really feel now that God has given me friends, so this day has not been so sad a one to me as it usually is. Another source of thankfulness to-day is, that I have been raised up from a bed of pain and suffering from which neither I nor any of my friends thought I ever would rise. Weary days and nights of pain, when it was torture to move and almost impossible to lie still, and when it seemed at times that death would be only a relief, and yet here I am still living to praise Him for many, many mercies. Mr. Pinkerton waited on me day and night, often depriving himself of sleep and rest in order to do it, and when convalescence set in, and with the restlessness of a sick person, I used to fancy I would be more comfortable up stairs, he used to carry me up and down and gratify all my whims. For five weeks I was in bed, and many more confined to my room and the house. But the greatest reason for thankfulness is, that God has in His great mercy brought me to a knowledge of Himself, and of my own lost state as a guilty sinner. It was while lying those long weary days on the bed that I was made to see that for ten long years I had been deceiving myself. Instead of being a Christian and being prepared to die, I was still in the gall of bitterness and the bonds of iniquity, and if God had taken me away during that sickness, it would have been with a lie in my right hand. Now when I look back on those long years spent in sin and in self-deception, I wonder at God's loving kindness and patience in sparing me still to show forth in me His goodness and forbearance. Truly it is of His mercies that I was not consumed. How often I taught others and talked to them of the love of Christ, and yet I had not that love myself. How many times I sat down to His table with his children, and yet I had no portion nor lot in the matter. Sometimes when I think how near destruction I was, with literally but a step between me and death, eternal death, and yet God raised me up and brought me to Christ and made me love Him, and how ever since He has been watching over me giving me the measure of comfort and peace that I enjoy and giving me the desire to know and love Him more, I wonder at my own coldness, at the frequency with which I forget Him. How strong sin still is over me, how prone I am to wander away from Christ and to forget His love, to allow sin to come between me and Him, and yet He still follows me with His love, still He brings me back to Him, the good Shepherd. Oh! if I could live nearer Christ, if I could realize and rejoice in His love. Now when I think how near I may be to the eternal world, that at any moment a severe attack of pain may come on which will carry me off, it is good to know that my Saviour will be with me; that He is mine and I am His. It is not easy to look death calmly in the face and know that my days are numbered, yet can I not participate in the promise that He Himself will come and take me to be with Him where He is. I would like to be allowed to live longer and be permitted to bring souls to Christ, but I feel assured that He will do what is best, and that He will not call me away as long as He has any work for me to do here.

I have a feeling that this will be my last letter to you, and I now take the opportunity of thanking you for all you have done for me, for all the care you bestowed on me, the prayers you have offered for me, and the kind thoughtfulness you still manifest for my welfare. It would be a comfort to me if I could see and talk with you once more, but I fear that will never be in this world, but shall we not meet in our Saviour's presence, purified, justified and sanctified through His blood? With truest love and gratitude

I remain yours, SAADA.

CHAPTER VII.

DR. DE FOREST'S WORK IN BEIRUT.

IN 1847, Dr. and Mrs. De Forest commenced their work of female education, receiving two young women into their family. In 13 Mission schools there were 163 girls and 462 boys. During the year 1847, six schools were in operation in connection with the Beirût Station. One in the Mesaitebe with 32 pupils, of whom 10 were girls. This school was promising and 15 of the pupils could read in the Bible. Another was in the Ashrafiyeh, with 50 pupils, of whom 12 were girls. Nineteen in this school could read in the Bible. Another was on the Mission premises with seventy pupils. Another school, south of the Mission premises, had 60 pupils, of whom 15 were girls. In addition to these was the Female School with thirty girls, taught by Raheel.

In 1848, on the organization of the first Evangelical Church, nineteen members were received, of whom four were women. Dr. De Forest had seven native girls in his family, and there were fifty-five girls in other schools.

In 1849, Mrs. Thomson and Mrs. De Forest visited Hasbeiya to labor among the women, by whom they were received with great cordiality. The girls' school of that time was regularly maintained and well attended. Dr. De Forest had thirteen native girls boarders in his family in Beirût, and Mr. Whiting had five.

In the Annual Report of the Beirût Station for 1850, it is stated that "a more prayerful spirit prevails among the brethren and sisters. One pleasing evidence of this is the recent establishment of a weekly female prayer-meeting, which is attended by all the female members of the Church. Yet it is somewhat remarkable that in our little Church there is so small a proportion of females. Unhappily, only one of our native brethren is blessed with a pious wife. Some of them are surrounded with relatives and friends whose influence is such as to hinder rather than help them in their Christian course, and in the religious training of their children."

This difficulty still exists in all parts of the Protestant community, not only in Syria, but throughout the Turkish Empire, and probably throughout the missionary world. The young men of the Protestant Churches at the present time endeavor to avoid this source of trial and embarrassment by marrying only within the Protestant community, and the rapid growth of female education in these days gives promise that the time is near when the mothers in Syria will be in no respect behind the fathers in either virtue or intelligence. The Beirût Church now numbers 107 members, of whom 57 are men and 50 are women.

In 1851, Miss Anna L. Whittlesey arrived in Beirût as an assistant to Dr. and Mrs. De Forest, and died in a year less one day after her arrival, beloved and lamented by all. In July of that year five of the women in Hasbeiya united with the Church.

In 1852 and 1853 the Female Seminary in Beirût reached a high degree of prosperity, and the girls' schools in different parts of the land were well attended. Miss Cheney arrived from America to supply Miss Whittlesey's place.

In 1854, Dr. De Forest was obliged from failing health, to relinquish his work and return to the United States. A nobler man never lived. As a physician he was widely known and universally beloved, and as a teacher and preacher he exerted a lasting influence. The good wrought by that saintly man in Syria will never be fully known in this world. The lovely Christian families in Syria, whose mothers were trained by him and his wife, will be his monuments for generations to come. It is a common remark in Syria, that the great majority of all Dr. De Forest's pupils have turned out well.

I have not been able to find the official reports with regard to the Female Seminary of Dr. De Forest in Beirût for the years 1847, 1848, and 1849, but from the Reports made by Dr. De Forest himself for the years 1850, 1852 and 1853, I make the following extracts:

In 1850, the Doctor writes: "The Seminary now has seventeen pupils including two Khozma and Lulu, who act as teachers. The older class have continued to study the Sacred Scriptures as a daily lesson, and have nearly finished the Old Testament.

They have studied a brief Compend of History in Arabic, and have continued Arithmetic and English. Compositions have been required of them weekly in Arabic until last autumn, when they began to write alternately in English and Arabic. A brief course of Astronomy was commenced, illustrated by Mattison's maps, given by Fisher Howe, Esq., of Brooklyn, N. Y.

"Recently the pupils have been invited to spend every second Sabbath evening with the other members of the family in conversation respecting some missionary field which has been designated previously. The large missionary map is hung in the sitting-room, and all are asked in turn to give some fact respecting the field in question. Even the youngest, who have not yet learned to read with facility in their own language, furnish their mite of information.

"The instruction in this school has been given by Dr. and Mrs. De Forest, aided by Mrs. De Forest's parents and the two elder pupils who have rendered such efficient aid heretofore. The pupils of all the classes have made good progress in their various studies, and their deportment has been satisfactory. They are gaining mental discipline and intellectual furniture, and have acquired much evangelical knowledge. Deep seriousness has been observed on the part of some of the elder pupils at different times, and they give marked and earnest attention to the preached word.

"In our labors for the reconstruction of society

here, we feel more and more the absolute need of a sanctified and enlightened female influence; such an influence as is felt so extensively in America, and whose beneficent action is seen in the proper training of children, and in the expulsion of a thousand superstitions from the land. Christian schools seem the most evident means of securing such an end. Commerce and intercourse with foreigners, and many other causes are co-operating with missionary effort to enlighten the *men* of Beirût and its vicinity, but the women, far more isolated than in America, are scarcely affected by any of these causes, and they hinder materially the moral elevation of the other sex. Often the man who seems full of intelligence and enterprise and mental enlargement when abroad, is found when at home to be a mere superstitious child; the prophecy that his mother taught him being still the religion of his home, and the heathenish maxims and narrow prejudices into which he was early indoctrinated still ruling the house. The inquirer after truth is seduced back to error by the many snares of unsanctified and ignorant companionship, and the convert who did run well is hindered by the benighted stubbornness to which he is unequally yoked.

"While exerting this deleterious influence over their husbands and children, the females of the land have but little opportunity for personal improvement, and are not very promising subjects of missionary labor. His faith must be strong who can labor with hope for the conversion of women, with whom the customs of society prohibit freedom of intercourse, and who have not learning enough to read a book, or vocabulary enough to understand a sermon, or mental discipline enough to follow continuous discourse.

In the Report for 1852, Dr. De Forest writes: "At the date of our last Annual Report, Miss Whittlesey was in good health, was rapidly acquiring the Arabic, and was zealously pressing on in her chosen work, with well-trained intellect, steady purpose and lively hope. But God soon called her away, and she departed in "hope of eternal life which God that cannot lie promised before the world began." The Female Boarding School has suffered much from the loss of its Principal, but the same course of study has been pursued as before, though necessarily with less efficiency. One of the assistant pupils, (Lulu,) who has been relied upon for much of the teaching, and superintendence of the scholars, was married last autumn to the senior tutor of the Abeih Seminary. The number of pupils now in the school is fifteen. The communication of Biblical and religious knowledge has been a main object of this school. All the pupils, as a daily lesson, study the Assembly's Shorter Catechism, first in Arabic with proof-texts, and afterwards in English with Barker's Explanatory Questions and Scripture proofs, and they are taught a brief Historical Catechism of the Old and New Testaments. The first of proper school hours every day is occupied with the Scriptures by all the school. The Epistles to the Hebrews and the Romans formed the subject of these lessons until the autumn, when Mr. Calhoun's revised edition of thc "Companion to the Bible" was adopted as a text-book, and the Old Testament has been studied in connection with that work. The pupils all attend the service at the Mission Chapel, and have lessons appropriate to the Sabbath in the intervals of worship.

"The evening family worship is in Arabic, and is a familiar Bible Class. All the pupils are present, and not unfrequently some of their relatives and other strangers. In addition to this religious instruction, the several classes have studied the Arabic and English languages, some of them writing in both, geography and history, arithmetic mental and higher, astronomy, and some of the simple works on natural philosophy and physiology. Compositions have been required in Arabic and English. The lessons in drawing, commenced by Miss Whittlesey, have been continued under the instruction of Mrs. Smith, and plain and fancy needle-work have been taught as heretofore.

"To those who have watched the growth of intellect, and in some instances, we hope, the growth of grace in these few pupils, and in the other female boarding scholars in some of the mission families, who have seen the pleasing contrast afforded by Syrian females when adorned after the Apostolic recommendation by good works and a "meek and quiet spirit," with those who cover empty heads with pearls and enrobe untidy persons in costly array,—who have rejoiced to see one and another family altar set up, where both heads of the family and the hearts of both unite in acknowledging God, —this branch of our labors need offer no further arguments to justify its efficient prosecution.

"The library of the Seminary consists of 220 school books, and 148 volumes of miscellaneous books, chiefly for the young. The school has 6 large fine maps, and 50 of Mr. Bidwell's Missionary maps, and 16 of Mattison's astronomical maps. These maps were the gifts of Mrs. Dr. Burgess and of Fisher Howe, Esq. The school has a pair of globes, one Season's machine, one orrery, a pair of gasometers, a spirit-lamp and retort stand, a centre of gravity apparatus, a capillary attraction apparatus, a galvanic trough, a circular battery, an electro-magnet, a horse shoe magnet, a revolving magnet, a wire coil and hemispheric helices, and an electric shocking machine."

The report of the Female Seminary for 1853 is written in the handwriting of Mrs. De Forest, owing to the increasing infirmity of Dr. De Forest's health, and this report has a sad interest from its being the last one ever dictated by Dr. De Forest.

"A small day-school for girls has been taught by one of the pupils in Mrs. Whiting's family during the winter, and it is contemplated to continue the school hereafter in the Girl's School house on the Mission premises, under the instruction of a graduate of the Female Seminary. The demand for such instruction for girls is steadily increasing.

"The teaching force of the Seminary was increased last spring by the arrival of Miss Cheney, who entered at once upon the duties of her position, devoting a portion of her time to the acquisition of Arabic, and a part to the instruction of some classes in English. Still, on account of the repeated illnesses of Dr. De Forest, it was not deemed advisable to receive a new class last autumn. The only girls admitted during the year were one of Mrs. Whiting's pupils who was transferred to the Seminary for one year, one of the class who graduated two years since, and who desired to return for another year, and Sara, the daughter of Mr. Butrus Bistany. These three were received into existing classes, while it was not deemed' advisable under the circumstances to make up another class composed of new pupils.

"The course of instruction, Biblical and other, has been much the same as that hitherto pursued. Miss Cheney commenced "Watts on the Mind," with some of the older pupils, in English. All the pupils have had familiar lessons on Church History in Arabic, and some of them have begun an abridged work on Moral Philosophy. Much effort has been bestowed upon the cultivation of a taste for the reading of profitable books, and a number of the girls have read the whole of "D'Aubigné's History of the Reformation," and other history with Mrs. De Forest in the evening class, the atlas being always open before them. Mrs. Smith has given some instruction in the rudiments of drawing to a part of the pupils, and Mrs. Bird and Mrs. Calhoun have given lessons in vocal music, for which some of the pupils have considerable taste.

"After completing the 'Companion to the Bible' in Arabic, the whole school were engaged daily in a Harmony of the Gospels, and other Biblical and religious instruction has been continued as heretofore. We have ever kept in mind the necessity of not denationalizing these Arab children, and we believe that this desired result has been attained. The long vacation of six weeks in the spring, and the same in the autumn, the commencement of all instruction in Arabic, and the preponderance of Arabic study in the school, have contributed to this result. The older pupils have attained to a considerable knowledge of English, giving them access to books suitable for girls to read, and yet Arabic is the language of the school, and the pupils are Syrians still in dress and manners. The advantages of the school are more and more appreciated in the city, and the adjacent mountains. Many were exceedingly earnest in offering their daughters last autumn, both Protestant and other, and some when repulsed at the Seminary, besought the mission families to receive their children."

During the next year, the school was placed in the family of Mr. and Mrs. Wilson, under the charge of Miss Cheney. A class of eight graduated, and the pupils contributed to benevolent objects of the fruits of their industry, over 1200 piastres, or about fifty dollars.

In a report on Education, prepared by the Syria

Mission in 1855, it was stated, that "without entering into details in regard to the course of study pursued, we are happy to say that the results of Dr. De Forest's Seminary were very gratifying, and proved, if proof were needed, that there is the same capacity in the native female mind of the country that there is in the male, and that under proper instruction, and by the blessing of God, there will be brought forward a class of intelligent, pious and efficient female helpers in the great work of evangelizing this community."

The hope implied in the above sentence with regard to the raising up of " a class of intelligent, pious and efficient female helpers," has been abundantly realized. The list of Dr. De Forest's pupils is to a great extent the list of the leading female teachers and helpers in all the various departments of evangelic work in Syria.

Not having access to the records of the Seminary as they have been lost, I have obtained from several of the former pupils a list of the members of the various classes from 1848 to 1852. The whole number of pupils during that period was twenty-three. Of these two died in faith, giving good evidence of piety. Of the twenty-one who survive, twelve are members of the Evangelical Church, and nine are now or were recently engaged in *teaching*, although nearly twenty years have elapsed since they graduated. Twenty-one are at the head of families, esteemed and honored in the communities where they reside. The names of the whole class are as follows:

Ferha Jimmal, now Kowwar of Nazareth.
Sarra Haddad, now Myers of Beirût.
Sada Sabunjy, now Barakat of Beirût.
Sada Haleby, of Beirût.
Miriam Tabet, now Tabet of Beirût.
Khushfeh Mejdelany, now Musully of Beirût.
Khurma Mejdelany, now Ashy of Hasbeiya.
Mirta Tabet, now Suleeby of B-hamdûn.
Feifun Malûf, of Aramoon.
Katrin Roza, of Kefr Shima.
Mirta Suleeby, now Trabulsy of Beirût.
Sara Suleeby, of Beirût.
Esteer Nasif, now Aieed of Suk el Ghurb.
Hada Suleeby, now Shidoody of Beirût.
Helloon Lazûah, now Zuraiuk of Beirut.
Khushfeh Towîleh, now Mutr of Beirût.
Fetneh Suleeby, now Shibly of Suk el Ghurb.
Akabir Barakat, now Ghubrîn of Beirût.
Hamdeh Barakat, now Bû Rehan of Hasbeiya.
Eliza Hashem, now Khûri of Beirût.
Rufka Haddad, (deceased).
Sara Bistany, (deceased).
Durra Schemail, of Kefr Shima.

Two of the most successful of those engaged in teaching, are now connected with the British Syrian Schools. They are Sada Barakat and Sada el Haleby. The former has written me a letter in English in regard to her own history and religious experience, which

I take the liberty to transcribe here verbatim in her own language. She was one of the *least* religious of all the pupils in the school, when she was first received but the work of conviction and conversion was a thorough one, and she has been enabled by the grace of God to offer constant and most efficient testimony to the reality of Christian experience, in the responsible position she has been called upon to fill in the late Mrs. Thomson's institution.

SUK EL GHURB, MT. LEBANON,
September 3, 1872.

DEAR SIR—I am thankful to say, in reply to your inquiry, that I was not persecuted when I became a Protestant, like my other native sisters were when they became Protestants, because I was very young. I was about four years old when my father died, and a year after, my mother married a Protestant man. I came to live with my mother in her new home, with my two brothers. It was very hard to lose a dear loving father who loved his children so much as my mother tells me he did. But the Lord does everything right, because if the Lord had not taken my father away from us I should not have known the true religion. I lived in my step-father's house till I was twelve years old. I was then placed in Dr. De Forest's school, in the year 1848. I stayed there four years. I was not clever at my studies, and especially the English language was very difficult for me. Even until now I remember a lesson in English which was so hard for me that I was punished twice for it, and I could not learn it. Now it will make me laugh to think of these few words, which I could not translate into Arabic: "The hen is in the yard." My mind was more at play than at learning. I was very clever at housework, and at dressing dolls, and was always the leader in all games. From that you can see that I was not a very good girl at school. After the two first years I began to think how nice it would be to become a real Christian like my dear teacher Dr. De Forest. Then I used to pray, and read, especially the "Pilgrim's Progress," and my mind was so busy at it that I used sometimes to leave my lesson and go and sit alone in my room. Nobody knew what was the matter with me, but Dr. De Forest used to ask me why I did not go to school? I told him that I was very troubled, and he told me to pray to God very earnestly to give me a new heart. I did pray, but I did not have an answer then. Three or four times during my school time I began to wish to become a Christian. I prayed and was very troubled. I wept and would not play, and as I got no immediate answer, I left off reading and sometimes praying entirely. Everybody noticed that I did not much care to read, and especially a religious book. I felt that my heart had grown harder than before I had wished to become a Christian. The greatest trial was that I had no faith, and for that reason I used not to believe in prayer, but still I longed to become a real Christian. I left school in the year 1852, and went to live at home with my mother. I was taken ill, and when I was ill I was very much afraid of death, for I felt that God was very angry with me.

Till about two years after I left school, I had no religion at all. One evening a young man from Abeih came to our house. His name is Giurgius el Haddad, who is now Mr. Calhoun's cook. After a little while he began to talk about religion, and to read the book, "Little Henry and his Bearer." I felt very much ashamed that others who did not have the opportunity to learn about religion had religion, and I, who had learned so much, had none. That was the blessed evening on which I began to inquire earnestly about my salvation. I was three months praying and found no answer to my prayers. Christian friends tried to lead me to Christ, but I could not take hold of Him, till He Himself appeared to my soul in all His beauty and excellency. Before I found peace Dr. Eli Smith and Mr. Whiting wanted me to teach a day school for them. That was about three years after I left off learning. "Oh," thought I, "how can I teach others about Christ when I do not know Him myself?" However I began the school by opening and closing it with prayer, without any faith at all. So I began by reading from the first of Matthew, till I came to the 16th chapter. When I came to that chapter I read as usual, with blinded eyes; but when I came to the (13th) thirteen verse, and from there to the seventeenth, where it says, "Blessed art thou, Simon Barjona, for flesh and blood hath not revealed it unto thee, but my Father which is in heaven," I felt that this had been said to me, and were these words sounded from heaven I would not have felt happier. How true it is that no flesh could reveal unto me what God had revealed, because many Christian friends tried to make me believe, but I could not. I felt as if everything had become new and beautiful, because my Heavenly Father had made them all. I was sometimes with faith and sometimes doubting, and by these changes my faith was strengthened. After a short time, I asked Mr. Whiting to let me join the Church. He asked me if I saw any change in myself, and I said, "One thing I know, that I used to dislike Christian people, and now they are my best friends." After a short time I was permitted to join the Church. Then I left off teaching the day school, and was asked to teach in a Boarding school with Miss Cheney, in the same Seminary where I was brought up. We taught in that school only six months. Miss Cheney married, and I was engaged to be married. While I was engaged, I went to Mr. Bird's school for girls in Deir el Kamr, and taught there for more than a year. I was married by Mr. Bird in his own house to M. Yusef Barakat, and then we went to Hasbeiya. I stayed there seven months and then went to Beirût, and thence to Damascus with my husband, because he had to teach there. I had nothing to do there but to look after my house, my little boy, and my husband.

After some time, the massacre broke out in Damascus, (July 9, 1860,) so we came back as refugees to Beirût. Soon after my husband was taken ill and then died. In that same year 1860, dear Mrs. Bowen Thompson came to Beirut. She felt for the widows and orphans, being herself a widow. She asked me if I would come and teach a school for the widows and orphans, which I accepted thankfully. We opened the school with five children and seven women, and the work, by God's help has prospered, so that now, instead of one school, there are twenty-two schools. Until now I continue teaching in the Institution, and had I known that nearly all my life would be spent in teaching, I should have tried to gain more when I was a child. I can forget father and mother, but can never forget those who taught me, especially about religion. Although some of them are dead, yet still they live by their Christian example, which they have left behind. My whole life will be full of gratitude to those dear Christian friends, and I pray that God himself may reward them a hundred fold.

Yours respectfully,

SADA BARAKAT.

In the year 1851, the Missionary Sewing Society

of the Beirût Female Seminary heard of the interesting state of things in Aintab, and that the women there were anxious to learn to read. The missionaries in Aintab hired an old man to go around from house to house to teach the women to read in their homes, but the women were so eager to learn that the old man was unable to meet the demand. So children were employed to assist. The plan worked admirably, and in 1851, eighty women received instruction and became able to read God's Word. The Arab girls in Mrs. De Forest's school were called together, and it was proposed that they sew and embroider and send the proceeds of their work to pay the little girl teachers in Aintab. There were present, Ferha, (joy,) Sara, Saada Sabunjy, Miriam, Khushfeh, Khurma, Mirta, (Martha) Feifun, Katrina, Hada, Sada el Haleby, Esteer, Helloon, Fetny, Akabir, Hamdy, and Liza. The needles were briskly plied, and in due time, two hundred and fifty piastres were collected and forwarded to Aintab. Mrs. Schneider wrote back thanking the "dear Arab girls." The habits of benevolence thus acquired have continued with the most of these girls until now. The greater part of them are now church-members and the heads of families.

The following letter written by Mrs. De Forest in Feb. 1852, gives some account of Lulu Araman.

BEIRUT, SYRIA, *February*, 1852.

MY DEAR YOUNG FRIENDS IN THETFORD:

The quilt you sent came safely, and I thank you much for all the care and trouble you have taken to make and quilt it for me. I at first thought of keeping it for myself, but then it occurred to me that perhaps it might please you better and interest you more if I gave it to Lulu, one of my girls, who is to be married some time this year to Mr. Michaiel Araman, one of the teachers in the Abeih Seminary. You will thus have the pleasure of feeling that you have in one sense done something for the school, as she is an assistant pupil, or pupil teacher. She has been with me now for about eight years, and seems almost like my own daughter. Perhaps you will be interested in knowing something of her.

She was born in a pleasant valley, Wady Shehrûr, near Beirût, celebrated for its fine oranges, and indeed for almost all kind of fine fruits. She lost both her parents early in life. Her brothers (contrary to the usual custom here where girls are not much regarded or cared for) were very kind to her, and as she was a delicate child, they took great care of her, and often used to make vows to some saint in her behalf. At one time, when she was very ill, they vowed to Mar Giurgis (for they are members of the Greek Church, and St. George is one of the favorite saints of the Greeks, and indeed of all the Christian sects here, and they still show the spot where he is said to have killed the dragon) that if she recovered, she should carry to one of his shrines two wax candles as tall as herself and of a prescribed weight. While she was still feeble they provided the candles, and as she was too weak to walk, they carried her and the candles also, to the holy place and presented them.

When she was eight years old, they were persuaded by an acquaintance to place her in one of the Mission families. Here she was instructed in her own language, and especially in the Holy Scriptures. She was allowed, however, to keep her feasts and fasts, and to attend her own church, until she became convinced that these things would not save her and she wished to give them up. One feast day the lady with whom she lived gave her some sewing and told her to seat herself and do her task. She refused, saying it was a feast day, and it was unlawful work. A little while after she asked permission to go and visit her brother's family; but the lady told her, "No, if it is unlawful to work, it is unlawful to visit. I have no objection to your keeping your feast days, but if you do you must keep them as holy time." So she gave her a portion of Scripture to learn, and she was kept very quiet all day, as though it was the Sabbath, and without the day being made agreeable to her like the Sabbath by going to Church and Sabbath School. She did not at all like keeping a feast in this manner, which is very different from the manner in which such a day or even the Sabbath, is kept in this land, and was ever after ready to work when told to do so. When her brothers saw that she was beginning to give up their vain ceremonies, they became anxious to get her away, lest she should become a Protestant; and at one time, when she went home to attend the wedding of one of her relatives, they refused to allow her to return, and it was only through the good management of the native friend who was sent for her, and her own determination to come, that she was permitted to come back.

We hope that she became truly pious six years ago, in 1846, as her life evinces that she is striving to live according to the precepts of the gospel. She has never dared to go home again, although it has been a great trial for her to stay away, because she knew that she should be obliged to remain there, and to conform to the idolatrous rites of the Greek Church. She has assisted us in the School for nearly five years, besides teaching a day school at various times, before the Boarding School was commenced, and we shall feel very sorry to part with her. Still we hope that she will yet be useful to her countrywomen, and furnish them an example of a happy Christian home, of which there are so few at present in this country.

Our school has now nineteen pupils, most of whom are promising. Some we hope are true Christians. The girls opened their box the other day, and found that they had a little more than last year from their earnings. Some friends added a little, and they have now forty dollars. One half they send to China, and the other half give to the Church here.'

The hope expressed by Mrs. De Forest in 1852, with regard to the future usefulness of Lulu, has not been disappointed. Her family is a model Christian family, the home of piety and affection, the centre of a pure and hallowed influence. Her eldest daughter Katie, named from Mrs. De Forest, is now a teacher in the Beirût Female Seminary in which her father has been the principal instructor in the Bible and in the higher Arabic branches for ten years. For years this institution was carried on in Lulu's house, and she was the Matron while Rufka was the Preceptress, and its very existence is owing to the patient and faithful labors of those two Christian Syrian women. If any one who reads these lines should doubt the utility of labors for the girls and women of the Arab race, let him visit first the squalid, disorderly, cheerless and Christless homes of the mass of the Arab villagers of Syria, and then enter the cheerful, tidy, well ordered home of Mr. and Mrs. Araman, when the family are at morning prayers, listen to the voice of prayer and praise and the reading of God's word. Instead of the father sitting gloomily alone at his morning meal, and the mother and children waiting till their lord is through and then eating by themselves in the usual Arab way, he would see the whole family seated together in a Christian, homelike manner, the Divine blessing asked, and the meal conducted with propriety and decorum. After breakfast the father and Katie go to the Seminary to give their morning lessons, Henry (named for Dr. De Forest) sets out for the College, in which he is a Sophomore, and the younger children go to their various schools. Lulu's place at church is rarely vacant, and since that "relic of barbarism" the *curtain* which separated the men from the women has been removed from the building, the whole family, father, mother, and children sit together and join in the worship of God. Her brother and relatives from "Wady" are on the most affectionate terms with her, and her elder sister is in the domestic department of the Beirût Female Seminary.

This change is very largely due to the efforts of Mrs. De Forest, whose name with that of her sainted husband is embalmed in the memory of the Christian families of Syria, and will be held in everlasting remembrance. The *second generation* of Christian teachers is now growing up in Syria. Three of Mrs. De Forest's pupils have daughters now engaged in teaching. Khushfeh, Lulu, and Sada el Haleby; and Miriam Tabet has a daughter married to Mr. S. Hallock, of the American Press in Beirût.

FRUITS OF DR. DE FOREST'S GIRL'S SCHOOL.

In the autumn of 1852, there was a school of thirty girls in B'hamdûn, a village high up in Mt. Lebanon. Fifteen months before the teacher was the only female in the village who could read, and she had been taught by the native girls in Dr. De Forest's school. Quite a number of the girls of the village had there learned to read, and they all came to the school clean and neatly dressed. They committed to memory verses of Scripture, and it was surprising to see how correctly they recited them at the Sabbath School. At meeting they were quiet and attentive like the best behaved children in Christian lands. It would be difficult to sum up the results of that little school for girls twenty years ago in B'hamdûn. That village is full of gospel light. A Protestant church edifice is in process of erection, a native pastor, Rev. Sulleba Jerawan, preaches to the people, and the mass of the people have at least an intellectual acquaintance with the truth.

The picturesque village of B'hamdûn, where Dr. De Forest's school is established, is on the side of a lofty mountain. It is nearly 4000 feet above the level of the Mediterranean Sea. The village is compact as a little city, the streets narrow, rocky and crooked, the houses flat-roofed, and the floors of mud. One of the Protestants, the father of Miriam Tabet, has built a fine large house with glass windows and paved floors, which is one of the best houses in that part of Lebanon. The village is surrounded by vineyards, and the grapes are regarded as the finest in Mt. Lebanon. The people say that they never have to dig for the foundation of a house, but only to sweep off the dust with a broom. There is not a shade tree in the village. One day Dr. De Forest asked, "Why don't you plant a tree?" "We shall not live till it has grown," was the reply. "But your children will," said the Doctor. "Let them plant it then," was the satisfactory answer.

My first visit to B'hamdûn was made in February, 1856, a few days after my first arrival in Syria. On Sabbath morning I attended the Sabbath School with Mr. Benton, at that time a missionary of the A. B. C. F. M. One little girl named Katrina Subra, then nine years of age, repeated the Arabic Hymn "Kûmû wa Rettelû," "Awake and sing the song of Moses and the Lamb." She was a bright-eyed child of fair complexion and of unusual intelligence. At that time there was no children's hymn book in Arabic, and I asked Mr. B. to promise the children that when I had learned the Arabic, I would translate a collection of children's hymns into Arabic, which promise was fulfilled first in the printing of the "Douzan el Kethar," "The tuning of the Harp," in 1861. Katrina was the daughter of Elias Subra, one of the wealthiest men in the village, who had just then become a Protestant. She had been interested in the truth for some time, and though at the time only eight years old, was accustomed during the preceding summer to tell the Arab children that she was a Protestant, though they answered her with insults and cursing. At first she could not bear to be abused, and answered them in language more forcible than proper, but by the time of my visit she had become softened and subdued in her manner, and was never heard to speak an unkind word to any one. She undertook, even at that age, to teach the Greek servant girl in the family how to read. One day the old Greek Priest met her in the street and asked her why she did not go to confession as the other Greek children do. She replied that she could go to Christ and confess. The priest then said that her father and the rest of the Protestants go to the missionary and write out their sins on papers which he puts into rat holes in the wall! Katrina knew this to be a foolish falsehood and told the priest so. He then asked her how the Protestants confess. She replied that they confess as the Lord Jesus tells them to, quoting to him the language of Scripture, (Matt. 6: 6.) "But thou when thou prayest, enter into thy closet, and when thou hast shut the door, pray to thy Father which is in secret, and thy Father who seeth in secret shall reward thee openly." The priest was confounded by the ready truthful answer of the child, and turned away.

Three years later Katrina was a member of the Mission Female Seminary in Suk el Ghurb, a village three hours distant from Beirût, under the instruction of Miss Temple and Miss Johnson, and continued there until the Seminary was broken up by the massacres of May and June, 1860. I remember well the day when that procession of girls and teachers rode and walked down from Suk el Ghurb to Beirût. All Southern Lebanon was in a blaze. Twenty-five villages were burning. Druze and Maronite were in deadly strife. Baabda and Hadeth which we passed on our way to Beirût, were a smoking ruin. Armed bodies of Druzes passed and saluted us, but no one offered to insult one of the girls by word or gesture. Dr. and Mrs. Bliss gave us lunch at their home in the Suk as we came from Abeih, and then followed a few days later to Beirût. Miss Temple tried to re-open the school in Beirût, but the constant tide of refugees coming in from the mountains, and the daily rumors of an attack by Druzes and Moslems on Beirût, threw the city into a panic, and it was found impossible to carry on the work of instruction. The girls were sent to their parents where this was practicable, and the

Seminary as such ceased for a time to exist. Katrina, was married in 1864 to M. Ghurzûzy, a Protestant merchant of Beirût, who is now secular agent or Wakil of the Syrian Protestant College. In 1866, she united with the Evangelical Church in Beirût. She has had repeated attacks of illness, in which she has manifested the most entire submission to the Divine will, and a calm and sweet trust in her Lord and Saviour. Her home is a Christian home, and her children are being trained in "the nurture and admonition of the Lord."

A Syrian Woman.

CHAPTER VIII.

RE-OPENING OF THE SCHOOL IN BEIRUT.

IN 1856 Miss Cheney re-opened the Female Seminary with eight pupils, in Beirût, and in the 34 schools of the Mission there were 1068 pupils, of whom 266 were girls.

In 1857, there were 277 girls in the various schools.

In 1858, Miss Temple and Miss Johnson arrived from America, and the Female Seminary was opened in Suk el Ghurb in the family of Rev. Dr. Bliss, Miss Johnson and Miss Cheney having returned to the United States, Miss Mason came to aid Miss Temple in February, 1860. The girl's school in Beirut under the care of Rufka Gregory, had about 60 pupils. The civil war in Lebanon, followed by the massacres in Jezzin, Deir el Komr, Hasbeiya, Rasheiya and Damascus, beginning in May, and continuing until the middle of July, broke up all our schools and seminaries, and filled the land with sorrow and desolation.

Miss Temple and Miss Mason remained for a season in Beirût, studying the Arabic language, and in 1862 Miss Temple having returned to the U. S. A., Miss Mason opened a Boarding School for girls in Sidon.

5

It was decided that none but Protestant girls should be received into this school, that no English should be taught, and that the style of eating, sleeping and dress should be conformed as much as possible to the standard of native customs in the country villages, in order that the girls might the more readily return to their homes as teachers, without acquiring European tastes and habits. Miss Mason carried on this school until 1865, when she returned to the U. S. A., and it was decided if possible to carry it on with native instructors under the supervision of Mrs. Eddy.

In the winter of 1867 it was under the kind charge of Mrs. Watson of Shemlan and her adopted daughter, Miss Handumeh Watson, and is now conducted by two English young ladies, Miss Jacombs and Miss Stanton, who are supported by the London "Society for the Promotion of Female Education in the East." On the removal of the girls' Boarding School to Sidon, it was evident that the Female Seminary must be re-opened in Beirût. Owing to the depressed state of Missionary finances in America, arising from the civil war, it was deemed advisable to reorganize the Beirût Seminary on a new basis, with only native teachers. The Providence of God had prepared teachers admirably fitted for this work, who undertook it with cheerful hope and patient industry. It was decided to make a paying Boarding School of a higher order than any existing institution in Syria, and to resume instruction in the English language, giving lessons also in French and

Music to those who were willing to pay for these branches.

Mr. Michael Araman, for many years a teacher in the Abeih Seminary with Mr. Calhoun, and for some time a native preacher in Beirut. was appointed instructor in the Biblical History and the Higher Arabic branches; his wife Lulu, the Matron, and Miss Rufka Gregory, the Preceptress. Rufka was an orphan, as already stated, and was trained with her sister Sada in the family of Mr. and Mrs. Whiting for many years. As a teacher and a disciplinarian she had not an equal among the women of Syria, and under the joint management of this corps of teachers, aided by competent assistants in the various branches, the Seminary rose in public esteem, until it became one of the most attractive and prosperous institutions in Syria.

In March, 1862, Rufka's day school of seventy girls held a public examination in the Chapel. The girls were examined in Arabic reading, geography, grammar, catechism, arithmetic, Scripture lessons and English, with an exhibition of specimens of their needle work. In the fall it was commenced as a Boarding School, with two paying pupils and four charity pupils. The funds for commencing the boarding department were furnished by Mr. Alexander Van Rensselaer, Mrs. Henry Farnum, Col. Frazer, H. B. M. Commissioner to Syria, and others. The Seminary not being under the direction of the Mission as such, nor in connection with the American Board, was placed under the care of a local

Board of Managers, consisting of Dr. Thomson, Dr. Van Dyck, Consul J. A. Johnson, and Rev. H. H. Jessup. Dr. Thomson was indefatigable in his efforts to place it on a firm and permanent foundation, as a purely Native Protestant institution, and the fact that such a school could be carried on for a year without a single foreign instructor, was one of the most encouraging features in the history of the Syria Mission. It was the first purely native Female Seminary in Western Asia, and we hope it will not be the last.

It will continue to be the aim of the Mission, and of the present able faculty of the institution, to train up Native teachers qualified to carry on the work in the future.

At the same time in the fall of 1862, a school for Damascene girls was opened in an upper room of my house, under the care of one of Dr. De Forest's pupils, Sada el Haleby, who carried it on successfully with seventy girls until August, 1864, when, on my departure for the U. S. A. the school was taken up by the late Mrs. Bowen Thompson, whose Society has maintained it until this day.

In 1863, the number of paying boarders in the Seminary had increased to twenty, and in 1866 the pupils numbered eighty, and the income from native paying pupils was about fifteen hundred dollars in gold!

The Annual Examination was held in the latter part of June, in the Mission Chapel, and continued three days, thronged by a multitude of interested spectators. The Turkish official Arabic Journal of Beirut, the "Hadikat el Akhbar," published a lengthy report of the Examination, pronouncing it the most satisfactory examination of girls that ever took place in Syria. An English clergyman who was present refused to believe that they were Syrian girls, insisting that they must be English. The girls recited in Bible History, giving all the important dates from Adam to Christ, with an account of the rites, sacrifices and prophecies which refer to Christ, giving also the names of all the patriarchs, judges, kings and prophets in their order. Twenty-two different classes were examined, and many of the girls read original compositions.

On the Sabbath, July 1st, two of the assistant teachers, Asîn Haddad and Sara Sarkis (?) were received to the communion of the Beirût Church. They traced their religious awakening to the dying testimony of Sara Bistany, which is described in a subsequent chapter. Several of the younger pupils were much interested in the subject of religion at the time, and one little girl about seven years old said to her teacher, "I gave the Lord my heart, and He took it." Asîn died in Latakiah in 1869, triumphing in Christ. The women of the neighborhood came to the house of her brother to hear her joyous expressions of trust in Jesus, and her assurance that she should soon be with Him in glory. She was the second daughter of that young bride of fifteen years of age, who learned to read in 1825, in the school taught by her own husband, Tannus el Haddad.

In 1867, the health of Rufka having become seriously impaired, she removed to Egypt, where after a period of rest, she opened on her own account a school for girls in Cairo, which she maintained with her wonted energy, until her marriage with the Rev. Mr. Muir, a Scotch clergyman, whom she accompanied to Melbourne, Australia, in 1869. Since the death of her husband she has returned to her favorite employment of teaching, with marked success, among the British population of Melbourne.

While in Cairo, she passed through a deep and agonizing religious experience, which she described in the following letter to Mrs. Whiting, and the result of which was a new life in Christ.

CAIRO, EGYPT, *July* 9, 1868.

"I think I shall always remember my stay in Cairo with much pleasure, but the greatest advantage of this year is the opportunity I had of stopping to think of the interests of a never dying soul, of a neglected Saviour, an offended God. Yes, I have reflected, struggled, oh, how hard, and thanks to an ever merciful God, I trust I have been led by the Holy Spirit to see and feel my great sin, and casting myself at the feet of Jesus, stayed there with my sinful heart till a loving Saviour just came and took it up. Oh, how grieved was His tender heart when He saw how defiled it was with sin and wickedness, but He said, fear not, my blood will cleanse it and make it pure; then how He pleaded my case before His Father, setting forth His boundless love and infinite righteousness as a reason why He wished to be accepted. Yes, dear Mrs. Whiting, I hope I can now say, Thy God is my God, and the blessed Saviour you have loved so long is now very precious to me. The past winter has been a solemn time with me. Many hard struggles have I had, much fear that I might have forever grieved God's Holy Spirit, and for a long time it all seemed so dark, there seemed no hope for me who had been so long living away from the Saviour, but in great fear and despair I just rushed and cast myself at His feet, and asked Him to let me perish there if I must perish; there was nothing else for me to do, and I felt such happiness in just leaving myself in His care. How wonderful is His love! But what a life of constant prayer and watching is that of a Christian! in the first place to aim at close walking with God, leaving Him to order our steps for us, and trusting Him so to order our way as to best enable us to walk closely with Him. It has been a most comforting thought when I find it difficult to live right and feel my utter weakness, that Jesus is each day saying to His Father for me, "I pray not she should be taken out of the world, but that she should be *kept from the evil,*" and to live up to our privileges and to walk worthy of our high calling.

My precious teacher, I know you will rejoice and thank God with me for His great goodness to me in bringing me to the feet of Jesus. Oh, how precious He is to my poor soul! He is Heaven. How He blesses me every moment! His boundless love to *me* who am most unworthy of the least of His mercies. If ever any one had reason to boast of the loving kindness of the Lord, it surely must be myself. In His great mercy I have had the privilege of openly confessing my faith in Him, and publicly professing my determination to be the Lord's at the last communion in the Church here in May. I put it off till then hoping to do it in Beirût in the Church dear Mr. Whiting had preached in for so many years, and among the girls I had taught, and all the young friends there, but as that was not allowed me, I joined the Church here."

Her devoted friend and loving assistant teacher Luciyah, was deeply affected by what she learned from Rufka of her new spiritual life, and she too turned her thoughts to divine things, and soon after the arrival of Miss Everett and Miss Carruth in 1868, to take charge of the Seminary, she came out openly on the Lord's side, and in the midst of a fire of domestic persecution, publicly professed her faith in Jesus as her only Saviour.

Miss Carruth, after staying just long enough in the Seminary to win the hearts of teachers and pupils, was obliged to return to her native land, where she is still an efficient laborer in the New England Woman's Board of Missions.

The year following the departure of Rufka to Egypt was a critical time in the history of the Seminary. Lulu continued in charge of the domestic department, and Mr. Araman managed the business of the school, while Mrs. Salt (a sister of Melita and Salome) aided in several of the classes. But the institution owed its great success during that year, if not its very existence, to the untiring energy and efficient services of Mrs. Dr. Bliss and Mrs. Emilia Thomson, daughter of the Rev. Dr. Thomson. They each gave several hours every day to instruction in the English language, the Scriptures and music, and the high standard of excellence already attained in the Seminary was maintained if not surpassed.

Their perfect familiarity with the Arabic language gave them a great advantage in the management and instruction of the pupils, and their efforts on behalf of the Institution, in maintaining it in full and successful operation during the year previous to the arrival of Miss Everett and Miss Carruth, deserve grateful recognition.

In the winter of 1870 and 1871 Miss Sophia Loring, and Miss Ellen Jackson arrived from America as colleagues of Miss Everett, and under their efficient management aided by Mr. Araman, Luciyah and other native teachers, the Seminary is enjoying a high degree of prosperity.

In March, 1864, the Mission had issued an appeal for funds to erect a permanent home for this Seminary, and in 1866 the present commodious and substantial edifice was erected, a lasting monument of the liberality of Christian men and women in America and England.

Its cost was about eleven thousand dollars, and the raising of this sum was largely due to the liberality and personal services of Mr. Wm. A. Booth, of New York, who also kindly acted as treasurer of the building fund. The lumber used in its construction was brought from the state of Maine. The doors and windows were made under the direction of Dr. Hamlin of Constantinople, in Lowell, Mass., the tiles came from Marseilles, the stone from the sandstone quarries of Ras Beirût, the stone pavement partly from Italy and partly from Mt. Lebanon, and the eighty iron bedsteads from Birmingham, England. The cistern, which holds about 20,000 gallons, was built at the expense of a Massachusetts lady, and the portico by a lady of New York. The melodeon was given by ladies in Georgetown, D. C., and the organ is the gift of a benevolent lady in Newport, R. I.

Time would fail me to recount the generous offerings of Christian men and women who have aided in the support of this school during the ten years of its history. Receiving no pecuniary aid from the American Board, the entire responsibility of its support fell upon a few members of the Syria Mission. Travellers who passed through the Holy Land, sometimes assumed the support of charity pupils, or interested their Sabbath Schools in raising scholarships, on their return home, and a few noble friends in the United States have sent on their gifts from time to time unsolicited, to defray the general expenses of the Institution. Its support has been to some of us a work of *faith*, as well as a labor of love. Not unfrequently has the end of the month come upon us, without one piastre in the treasury for paying the teachers' salaries or buying bread for the children, when suddenly, in some unknown and unexpected way, funds would be received, sufficient for all our wants. About two years since the funds were entirely exhausted. More than a hundred dollars would be owing to the teachers and servants on the following day. The accounts were examined, and all possible means of relief proposed, but without avail. At length one of the members of the Executive Committee asked leave to look over the accounts. He did so, and said he could not find any mention of a sum of about thirty Napoleons, which he was sure he had paid into the treasury several months before, as a donation from Mr. Booth of New York, whose son had died in Beirût. The money had *not* been paid into the school treasury. The vouchers were all produced, and there was left no resort but prayer. There was earnest supplication that night that the Lord would relieve us from our embarrassment, and provide for the necessities of the school. The next morning the good brother, above mentioned, recalled to mind his having given that money to Dr. Van Dyck in the Mission Library for the School. Dr. Van Dyck was consulted, and at once replied, "Certainly I received the money. It is securely locked up in the safe where it has been for months awaiting orders." The safe was opened, and the money found to be almost to a piastre the amount needed for obligations of the School.

Since the transfer of the Syria Mission to the board of Missions of the Presbyterian Church, the pecuniary status of the Seminary has been somewhat modified. The Women's Boards of Missions of New-York and Philadelphia have assumed the responsibility of raising scholarships for its support among the Auxiliary Societies and Sabbath Schools; the salaries of the teachers are provided for by individuals and churches, and several of the old friends of the school retain their interest in it, while the danger of a deficit is guarded against, by the guarantees of the good Christian women who are doing so grand and noble a work in this age for the world's evangelization. The annual cost of supporting a pupil now is about sixty dollars gold. The number of paying pupils is increasing, and the prospect for the future is encouraging.

In the year 1864, a letter was received from certain Christian women in America, addressed to the girls of the School, and some of the older girls prepared a reply in Arabic, a translation of which was sent to America. It was as follows:

"From the girls of the Beirût School in Syria, to the sisters beloved in the Lord Jesus, in a land very far away. We have been honored in reading the lines which reached us from you, O sisters, distant in body but near in spirit, and we have given glory to God the Creator of all, who has caused in your hearts true love to us, and spiritual sympathies which have prompted you, dear sisters in the Lord, to write to us. Yes, it is the Lord Jesus who has brought about between us and between you (Arabic idiom) a spiritual intercourse, without the intercourse of bodily presence. For we have never in our lives seen you, nor your country, nor have we spoken to you face to face, and so you likewise have not seen us. Had neither of us the Word of God, the Holy and Only Book which is from one Father and a God unchangeable, to tell us that we have one nature, and have all fallen into one transgression, and are saved in one way, which is the Lord Jesus, we could not, as we now can, call you in one union, our sisters. The Lord Jesus calls those who love Him His brethren, and since He is the only bond and link, are we not His sister, and thus sisters to each other? Truly, O dear sisters, we are thirsting to see you, and we all unite in offering prayers and praises to God, through His Son Immanuel, the possessor of the glorious Name, praying that we may see you; but we cannot in this world, for we are in the East, and you are in the West, far, very far. But, O dear

A Jew with the Phylactery.

friends, as we hope for the resurrection from the dead, so after our period in this world is ended, we shall meet by the blessing of God in those bright courts which are illumined by the light of the Saviour, which need not sun nor moon to give them light,—that holy place which is filled with throngs of angels who never cease to offer glory to God. There we may meet and unite with all the saved in praising the Saviour. There we may meet our friends who have passed on before us "as waiting they watch us approaching the shore," as we sing in the hymn. There around the throne of the glorious Saviour, there in the heavenly Jerusalem, our songs will not be mingled with tears and grief, for the Lord Jesus Himself will wipe away all tears from our eyes. There will not enter sin nor its likeness into our hearts sanctified by the Holy Spirit. There this body which shall rise incorruptible, will not return to the state in which it was in this world. In those courts we shall be happy always, and the reason is that we shall always be with the Great Shepherd, as it is said in the Book of Revelation, 'He shall shepherd them and lead them to fountains of living waters and wipe all tears from their eyes.' Our sisters, were it not for the Holy Bible which the Lord has given to His people, we should have no comfort to console us with regard to our friends whom we have lost by means of death. We beg you to help us by offering prayers to the living and true God that He will make us faithful even unto death, —that He will bless us while on the sea of this life, until we reach the shore of peace without fear or trouble, that we may be ready to stand before the seat of the Lord Jesus the Judge of all, clothed in the robes of His perfect righteousness, which he wove for us on the Cross, and is now ready to give to those who ask Him. Let us then all ask of God that this our only treasure may be placed where no thief can break in and steal, and no moth shall corrupt. And may the Lord preserve you!

We love to sing this hymn,

> 'Holy Bible, Book Divine,
> Precious treasure, thou art mine!'

and we entreat you that when you sing it, you will let it be a remembrancer from us to you."

In March, 1865, a little girl was brought to the school under somewhat peculiar circumstances. Years ago, in the days of Mr. Whiting, a Maronite monk named Nejm, became enlightened, left the monastery and was married to a Maronite woman named Zarifeh, by Mr. Whiting. For years the poor man passed through the fires of persecution and trial. Even his wife, in her ignorance, though not openly opposing him, trembled with fear every time he read the Scriptures aloud. At the time mentioned above, their little daughter Resha was about five years of age. The Papal Maronite Bishop of Beirût made a visit to Nejm's village, Baabda, to dispense indulgences, in accordance with the Pope's Encyclical letter. Nejm was called upon to pay his portion of the sum assessed upon the people, but having been a Protestant fifteen years, he refused to pay it. At the instigation of the priests, his wife was then taken from him, and his little Resha, his only child, was carried off by one of the priests to Beirût, and thrust inside the gates of the convent of the French Sisters of Charity. The poor father came to me, well-nigh broken-hearted, pleading for assistance. I laid the case before His Excellency Daûd Pasha, Governor of Lebanon, who was then in Beirût, and drew up a petition to the Pasha of Beirût also, on the subject. Nejm went about weeping and wringing his hands, and my feelings became deeply enlisted in his behalf. Three weeks afterwards, after a series of petitions and visits to the Pasha of Beirût, the girl Resha was removed from the convent and taken by Nejm's enemies to a house near Nahr Beirût, about two miles distant, and just over the border line of the Mountain Pashalic. I then addressed another letter to Daûd Pasha, and he promptly ordered her to be restored to her father. The manner in which Nejm, the father, finally secured the child was not a little amusing. He had been searching for his child for several weeks, waiting and watching, until his patience was about exhausted, when he heard that Resha was again in the hands of the priests in Baabda. The mother followed the child, and the priests threatened to kill her, if she informed her husband where the girl was secreted. Daûd Pasha was then at his winter palace in Baabda, and Nejm took my letter to him. While awaiting a reply at the door, some one informed him that his daughter was at the fountain. Without waiting further for official aid, he ran to the fountain, took up his daughter, put her on his back, and ran for Beirût, a distance of about four miles, where he brought her to my house, and placed her in my room, with loud ejaculations of thanks to God. "Neshkar Allah; El mejd lismoo." Thanks to God! Glory to His name! The mother soon followed, and the girl was sent as a day scholar to the Seminary. They are now living in Baabda. The mother, Zarify, united with the Evangelical Church of Beirût, July 21, 1872, giving the best evidence of a true spiritual experience. The little girl is anxious to teach, and it was proposed to employ her as an assistant in the girls' school in Baabda, but the tyrannical oppressions of the priesthood upon the family who had offered their house for the school, and the refusal of the Pasha of Lebanon to grȧnt protection to the persecuted, have obliged the brethren there to postpone their request for a school for the present.

Alas for the poor women of Syria! Even when they seek to obtain the consolations of the Gospel by learning to read the Word of life, they are surrounded by priests and Sheikhs who watch their chance to destroy the "Bread of Life!" In March, 1865, a Maronite woman called at the Press to buy a book of poems, to teach her boy to read. "Why not buy a Testament?" asked the bookseller. "I did buy an Engeel Mushekkel," (a voweled Testament.) "Be careful of it then," said Khalil, "for the edition is exhausted, and you cannot get another for months." "It is too late to be careful now, for the book *has been burned.*" "Burned? by whom?" "By the Jesuits, who gathered a large pile and burned them." God grant that as Tyndale's English New Testament, first printed in 1527 was only spread the more widely for the attempts of the Papal Bishop of London to burn it, so the Arabic Bible may receive a new impulse from the similarly inspired efforts of the Bishop's successors!

CHAPTER IX.

LUCIYA SHEKKUR.

THE work done for Christ and for Syrian girls in the families of Missionaries in Syria, may well compare with that done in the established institutions of learning. Mrs. Whiting was not alone in the work of training native Arab girls in her own home. The same work had been done by other Missionaries before her, and has been carried on with no little success by Mrs. Bird, Mrs. Calhoun and others, up to the present time.

It is an interesting sight to see the Thursday afternoon Women's meeting in the house of Mrs. Calhoun in Abeih, and to know that a large part of that company of bright, intelligent and tidily dressed young native women, who listen so intently to the Bible lesson, and join so heartily in singing the sweet songs of Zion, were trained up either in her own family, or under her own especial influence. By means of her own example in the training of her children, she has taught the women of Abeih, and through them multitudes of women in other villages, the true Christian modes of family government and discipline, and introduced to their notice and practice many of those little conveniences and habits in the training of children, whose influence will be felt for many generations.

When Mr. and Mrs. Bird removed to Deir el Komr in 1855, they not only opened a large school for the education of girls, with Sada Haleby, one of Dr. De Forest's pupils, as teacher, but received into their own family three young girls, named Luciya, Sikkar and Zihry, all of whom entered upon spheres of usefulness. Zihry became a teacher, in Deir el Komr, and has continued to teach until the present time. She was at one time connected with the Beirût Female Seminary, and is now teaching in the Institution of Mrs. Shrimpton, under the auspices of the British Syrian Schools.

Luciya taught in Deir el Komr until the school was overwhelmed in the fires and blood of the Massacre year, 1860.

In 1862 she taught in the Sidon School, and afterwards married the Rev. Sulleba Jerwan, the first native pastor in Hums. In that great city, and amid the growing interest of the young Protestant community, she found a wide and attractive field of labor. She was a young woman of great gentleness and delicacy of nature, and of strong religious feeling, and entered upon the work of laboring among the women and girls of Hums, with exemplary zeal and discretion. She became greatly beloved, and her Godly example and gentle spirit will never be forgotten.

But at length her labors were abruptly cut short. Consumption, a disease little known in Syria, but which afterwards cut down her brother and only sister Sikkar, fastened upon her, and she was obliged, in great suffering, to leave the raw and windy climate of Hums, for the milder air of Beirût. Her two brothers being in the employ of Miss Whately in Cairo, she went, on their invitation, to Egypt, where after a painful illness, she fell asleep in Jesus. Amid all her sufferings, she maintained that same gentle and lovely temper of mind, which made her so greatly beloved by all who knew her.

She has rested from her labors, and her works do follow her. Not long after her sister Sikkar, who had also been trained in Mrs. Bird's family, died in her native village Ain Zehalteh.

Her last end also, was peace, and although no concourse of Druze Sheikhs came barefoot over the snow to her funeral, as they did on the death of the Sitt Selma, in the same village, no doubt a concourse of higher and holier beings attended her spirit to glory.

When Luciya was in Beirût before her departure to Egypt, I used to see her frequently, and I shall never forget the calm composure with which she spoke of her anticipated release from the pains and sufferings of life. Christ was her portion, and she lived in communion with him, certain that ere long she should depart and be with him forever.

The poor Moslem women in the houses adjoining her room used to come in, and with half-veiled faces look upon her calm and patient face with wonder. Would that they too might find her Saviour precious to them, in their hours of sickness, suffering and death!

Truly, there is no religion but that of Jesus Christ, that can soften the pillow of suffering, and take away the sting and dread of death.

One of the most serious difficulties in the way of the higher female education in Syria, is the early age at which girls are married. One young girl attended the Beirût Seminary for two years, from eight to ten, and the teachers were becoming interested in her progress, when suddenly her parents took her out of the school, and gave her to a man in marriage. After the festivities of the marriage week were over at her husband's house, she went home to visit her mother, *taking her dolls with her* to amuse herself!

The Arabic journal "the Jenneh" of Beirût, contained a letter in June, 1872, from its Damascus correspondent, praising the fecundity of Syria, and stating that a young woman who was married at nine and a half, became a grandmother at twenty! Such instances are not uncommon in Damascus and Hums, where the chief and almost the only concern of parents is to marry off their daughters as early as nature will allow, without education, experience or any other qualification for the responsible duties of married life. When the above mentioned letter from Damascus was published, Dr. Van Dyck took occasion to write an article in the "Neshra," the Missionary Weekly, of which he is the editor, exposing the folly and criminality of such early marriages, and demonstrating their disastrous effects on society at large.

Since the establishment of schools and seminaries of a high grade for girls, this tendency is being decidedly checked in the vicinity of Beirût, and girls are not given up as incorrigibly old, even if they reach the age of seventeen.

Dr. Meshakah of Damascus, who has long been distinguished for his learned and eloquent works on the Papacy, is a venerable white-bearded patriarch and his wife looks as if she were his daughter. I once asked him how old she was when married, and he said *eleven.* I asked him why he married her so young? He said that in his day, young girls received no training at home, and young men who wished properly trained wives, had to marry them young, so as to educate them to suit themselves!

Education is rapidly obviating that necessity, and young men are more than willing that girls to whom they are betrothed, should complete their education, lest they be eclipsed by others who remain longer at school. I once called on a wealthy native merchant in Beirût, who remarked that "the Europeans have a thing in their country which we have not. They call it ed-oo-cashion, and I am anxious to have it introduced into Syria." This "ed-oo-cashion" is already settling many a question in Syria which nothing else could settle, and the natives are also learning that something more than mere book-knowledge is needed, to elevate and refine the family. One of the most direct results of female education thus far in Syria has been the abolition from certain classes of society of some of those superstitious fears which harass and torment the ignorant masses.

CHAPTER X.

RAHEEL.

NO sketch of Woman's Work for Syrian women would be complete which did not give some account of the life and labors of that pioneer in work for Syrian women, Mrs. Sarah L. H. Smith, wife of Dr. Eli Smith. She reached Beirût, January 28, 1834, full of high and holy resolves to devote her life to the benefit of her Syrian sisters. From the first to the very last of her life in Syria, this was the one great object of her toils and prayers. As soon as April 2, she writes, "Our school continues to prosper, and I love the children exceedingly. Do pray that God will bless this incipient step to enlighten the women of this country. You cannot conceive of their deplorable ignorance. I feel it more and more every day. Their energies are expended in outward adorning of plaiting the hair and gold and pearls and costly array, literally so. I close with one request, *that you will pray for a revival of religion in Beirût.*" Again she writes, June 30, 1834, "I feel somewhat thoughtful, this afternoon, in consequence of having heard of the ready consent of the friends of a little girl, that I should take her as I proposed, and educate her. I am anxious to do it, and yet my experience and observation in reference to such a course,

الحروف الهجائية

ا ب ت ث ج ح خ د ذ ر ز س

ش ص ض ط ظ ع غ ف ق

ك ل م ن ه و لا ي

Arabic Alphabet.

and my knowledge of the sinful heart of a child, lead me to think I am undertaking a great thing. I feel, too, that my example and my instruction will control her eternal destiny." This girl was Raheel Ata. Again, August 16: " It is a great favor that so many of the men and boys can read. Alas, our poor sisters! the curse rests emphatically upon them. Among the Druze princesses, some, perhaps the majority, furnish an exception and can read. Their sect is favorable to learning. Not so with the Maronites. I have one scholar from these last, but when I have asked the others who have been here if they wished to read, they have replied most absolutely in the negative, saying that it was for boys, and not for them. I have heard several women acknowledge that they knew no more than the donkeys."

August 23. A Maronite priest compelled two little girls to leave her school, but the Greek priest sent " his own daughter, a pretty, rosy-cheeked girl" to be taught by Mrs. Smith. On the 22d of September, 1834, she wrote from B'hamdûn, a village five hours from Beirût, on Lebanon, "Could the females of Syria be educated and regenerated, the whole face of the country would change; even, as I said to an Arab a few days since, to the appearance of the houses and the roads. One of our little girls, whom I taught before going to the mountains, came to see me a day or two since, and talked incessantly about her love for the school, and the errors of the people here, saying that they 'cared not for Jesus Christ, but only for the Virgin Mary.'"

October 8. She says, "A servant woman of Mrs. Whiting, who has now lived long enough with her to love her and appreciate her principles, about a year and a half since remarked to some of the Arabs, that the people with whom she lived did 'not lie, nor steal, nor quarrel, nor do any such things; but poor creatures,' said she, 'they have no religion.'"

On the 22d of October, she wrote again, "Yesterday I went up to Mr. Bird's to consult about the plan of a *school-house now commenced for females.* I can hardly believe that such a project is actually in progress, and I hail it as the dawn of a happy change in Syria. Two hundred dollars have been subscribed by friends in this vicinity, and I told Mr. B. that if necessary he might expend fifty more upon the building, as our Sabbath School in Norwich had pledged one hundred a year for female education in Syria."

The principal contributor to this fund was Mrs. Alexander Tod, formerly Miss Gliddon, daughter of the U. S. Consul in Alexandria.

The building stood near where the present Church in Beirût stands, and was removed, and the stones used in the extension of the old Chapel. In the year 1866 Mr. Tod revisited Beirût and contributed £100 towards the erection of the new Female Seminary, saying that as Mrs. Tod aided in the first Female Seminary building in Beirût, he wished to aid in the second. The school-house was a plain structure, and was afterwards used as a boy's school, and the artist who photographed the portraits printed in this volume received his education there under the instruction of the late Shahîn Sarkis, husband of Azizy.

In the latter part of October, 1834, Mrs. Smith writes, "Yesterday I commenced the female school with four scholars, which were increased to ten to-day, and the number will probably continue to augment as before from week to week. As I walked home about sunset this evening, I thought, 'Can it be that I am a schoolmistress, and the only one in all Syria?' and I tripped along with a quick step amid Egyptians, Turks and Arabs, Moslems and Jews, to my quiet and pleasant home."

November 9. "I sometimes indulge the thought that God has sent me to the females of Syria—to the little girls, of whom I have a favorite school—for their good."

January 5, 1835. "On Friday I distributed rewards to twenty-three little girls belonging to my school, which, as they are all poor, consisted of clothing. Our Sabbath School also increases. Eighteen were present last Sabbath."

On the 11th of January Dr. Thomson wrote, "Mrs. Smith's female school prospers wonderfully, but it is the altar of her own health; and I fear that in the flame that goeth up toward heaven from off that altar, she will soon ascend as did Manoah's angel. We can hardly spare her; she is our only hope for a female school in Beirût at present."

The state of society in Syria at that time is well

pictured in the following language, used by Mrs. Smith in a letter dated February 12, 1835: "Excepting the three or four native converts, we know not one pious religious teacher, one judicious parent, one family circle regulated by the fear of God; no, *not even one!*"

"I wish I had strength to do more, but my school and my studies draw upon my energies continually." Even at that early day Moslem girls came to be taught by Mrs. Smith. She writes June 2, "A few days since, one of my little Moslem scholars, whose father was once an extensive merchant here, came and invited me to make a call upon her mother. I took Raheel and accompanied her to their house which is in our neighborhood. I found it a charming spot and very neatly kept. Hospitality is regarded here as a religious act, I think, and a reputation for it is greatly prized."

In July she wrote of what has not ceased to be a trial to all missionaries in Beirût for the past forty years, the necessity of removing to the mountains during the hot summer months. The climate of the plain is debilitating to foreigners, and missionary families are obliged to spend three months of the hot season in the Lebanon villages. "My school interests me more and more every day, and I do not love to think of suspending it even for a few weeks during the hot season. Day before yesterday a wealthy Jewish lady came with her two daughters to the school, and begged me to take the youngest as a scholar."

July 19. "At our Sabbath School to-day were *twenty-eight* scholars, twenty-one girls and seven boys."

July 31. "To-day I closed my school for the month of August by the distribution of rewards to *thirty little girls.* The American and English Consuls and a few Arab friends were present, and expressed much pleasure at the sight of so many young natives in their clean dress. A few of the more educated scholars read a little in the New Testament."

August 8. "On Saturday I closed my school for the month of August. It was increasing every day in numbers and I would gladly have continued it. Last Sabbath we had at the Sabbath School forty-six scholars, a *fourth of whom were Moslems.*"

September 29. "Yesterday I commenced my school again with twenty scholars; which, for the first day, was a good number. Mrs. Whiting has ten little Moslem girls in Jerusalem, and the promise of more."

December 14. "On Saturday, our native female prayer-meeting consisted of twenty, besides two children. Fourteen were Arabs, more than were ever present before. We met in the girls' school room, where we intend in future to assemble. We sung part of a psalm, as we have begun to teach music in our school. We find the children quite as capable of forming musical sounds as those in our own country; but alas, *we have no psalms or hymns adapted to their capacities.* The Arabic cannot be simplified like the English, without doing violence to Arab taste; at least such is the opinion now. What changes may be wrought in the language, we cannot tell. Of this obstacle in the instruction of the young here, you have not perhaps thought. It is a painful thought to us, that *children's literature*, if I may so term it, is *incompatible with the genius of this language:* of course, infant school lessons must be bereft of many of their attractions."

It may be interesting to know whether present missionary experience differs from that of Mrs. Smith and her husband in 1835, with regard to children's literature in the Arabic language.

In 1858, Mr. Ford prepared, with the aid of Mr. Bistany, (the husband of "Raheel," Mrs. Smith's adopted child,) a series of children's Scripture Tracts in simple and yet perfectly correct Arabic, so that the youngest child can understand them. In 1862, we printed the first Children's Hymn-book, partly at the expense of the girls in Rufka's school. We have now in Arabic about eighty children's hymns, and a large number of tracts and story books designed for children. We also publish an Illustrated Children's Monthly, called the "Koukab es Subah," "The Morning Star," and the children read it with the greatest eagerness.

The Koran, which is the standard of classic Arabic, cannot be changed, and hence can never be a book for children. It cannot be a family book, or a women's book. It cannot attract the minds of the young, with that charm which hangs around the exquisitely simple and beautiful narratives of the Old and New Testament. It is a gem of Arabic poetry, but like a gem, crystalline and unchanging. It has taken a mighty hold upon the Eastern world, because of its Oriental style and its eloquent assertion of the Divine Unity. It is reverenced, but not loved, and will stand where it is while the world moves on. Every reform in government, toleration and material improvement in the Turkish Empire, Persia and Egypt, is made in spite of the Koran and contrary to its spirit. The printing of the Koran is unlawful, but it is being printed. All pictures of living objects are unlawful, but the Sultan is photographed, Abd el Kader is photographed, the "Sheikh ul Islam" is photographed. European shoes are unlawful because sewed with a swine's bristle, but Moslem Muftis strut about the streets in French gaiters, and the women of their harems tottle about in the most absurd of Parisian high-heeled slippers.

The Arabic Bible translated by Drs. Eli Smith and Cornelius Van Dyck, is voweled with the grammatical accuracy and beauty of the Koran with the aid of a learned Mohammedan Mufti, and yet has all the elegant simplicity of the original and is intelligible to every Arab, old and young, who is capable of reading at all. The stories of Joseph, Moses, and David, of Esther, Daniel and Jonah are as well adapted to the comprehension of children in the Arabic as in the English.

Not a few of the hymns in the Children's Hymn book are original, written by M. Ibrahim Sarkis, husband of Miriam of Aleppo, and M. Asaad Shidoody, husband of Hada. This Hymn book was published in 1862, with Plates presented by Dr. Robinson's Sabbath School of the First Presbyterian Church, Brooklyn.

This digression seemed necessary, in order to show the great progress that has been made since 1836, in preparing a religious literature. It is no longer true as in Mrs. Smith's day, "that we have no psalms or hymns adapted to the capacities of children. Nor is it longer true that "*children's literature is incompatible with the genius of the Arabic language.*"

In a letter addressed to the young women in the "Female Academy at Norwich," February, 1836, Mrs. Smith gives a vivid description of the "average woman" of Syria in her time, and the description holds true of nine-tenths of the women at the present day. There are now native Christian homes, not the least attractive of which is the home of her own little protegé Raheel, but the great mass continue as they were forty years ago. She says, "My dear friends, will you send your thoughts to this, which is not a heathen, but an unevangelized country. I will not invite you to look at our little female school of twenty or thirty, because these form but a drop among the thousands and thousands of youth throughout Syria; although I might draw a contrast even from this not a little in your favor. But we will speak of the young Syrian females at large, moving in one unbroken line to the land of darkness and sorrow. Among them you will find many a fine form and beautiful face; but alas! the perfect workmanship of their Creator is rendered tame and insipid, for want of that mental and moral culture which gives a peculiar charm to the human countenance. It is impossible for me to bring the females of this country before you in so vivid a manner that you can form a correct idea of them. But select from among your acquaintances a lady who is excessively weak, vain and trifling; who has no relish for any intellectual or moral improvement; whose conversation is altogether confined to dress, parties, balls, admiration, marriage; whose temper and faults have never been corrected by their parents, but who is following, unchecked, all the propensities of a fallen, corrupt nature. Perhaps you will not be able to find any such, though I have occasionally met with them in America. If you succeed, however, in bringing a person of this character to your mind, then place the thousands of girls, and the women, too, of this land, once the land of patriarchs, prophets and apostles, in her class." "These weak-minded Syrian females are not attentive to personal cleanliness; neither have they a neat and tasteful style of dress. Their apparel is precisely such as the Apostle recommended that Christian females should avoid; while the ornament of a meek and quiet spirit is thrown wholly out of the account. They have no books, and no means of moral or intellectual improvement. It is considered a disgrace for a female to know how to read and write, and a serious obstacle to her marriage, which is the principal object of the parent's heart. This abhorrence of learning in females, exists most strongly in the higher classes. Nearly every pupil in our school is very indigent. Of God's word they understand nothing, for a girl is taken to church perhaps but once a year, where nothing is seen among the women but talking and trifling; of course she attaches no solemnity to the worship of God. No sweet domestic circle of father, brother, mother and sister, all capable of promoting mutual cheerfulness and improvement, greets her in her own house. I do not mean to imply that there exists no family affection among them, for this tie is often very strong; but it has no foundation in respect, and is not employed to promote elevation of character. The men sit and smoke their pipes in one apartment, while in another the women cluster upon the floor, and with loud and vociferous voices gossip with their neighbors. The very language of the females is of a lower order than that of the men, which renders it almost impossible for them to comprehend spiritual and abstract subjects, when first presented to their minds. I know not how often, when I have attempted to converse with them, they have acknowledged that they did not understand me, or have interrupted me by alluding to some mode or article of dress, or something quite as foolish." "Thus you see, my young friends, how unhappy is the condition of the females of Syria, and how many laborers are wanted to cultivate this wide field. On the great day of final account, the young females of Syria, of India, of every inhabited portion of the globe, who are upon the stage of life with you, will rise up, either to call you blessed, or to enhance your condemnation." "God is furnishing American females their high privileges, with the intention of calling them forth into the wide fields of ignorance and error, which the world exhibits. I look over my country and think of the hundreds and thousands of young ladies, intelligent, amiable and capable, who are assembled in schools and academies there; and then turn my eye to Jerusalem, Hebron, Nazareth, Sychar, Damascus, Tyre, Sidon, Jaffa, and to the numerous villages of Mount Lebanon, and think, 'Why this inequality of condition and privileges? Why can there not be stationed at every one of those morally desolate places, at least one missionary family, and one single female as a teacher? Does not Jesus Christ, the Good Shepherd, require it of His youthful friends in America, that from love to Him, gratitude for their own distinguished mercies, compassion for perishing souls, and the expectation of perfect rest and happiness in heaven, they should spread themselves over the wide world, and feed the sheep and the lambs scattered without a shepherd upon the mountains?' Yes, He requires it, and angels will yet behold it; but shall we not see it in our day?"

Great changes have come over Syria since the above words were written. Not less than twelve high schools for girls have been established since then in Syria and Palestine, and not far from forty common schools, exclusively for girls, under the auspices of the different Missionary Societies.

In February, 1836, Mrs. Smith also undertook the work of *systematic visiting among the mothers of her pupils.* She says, "Perhaps it will be a very long time before we shall see any fruit. Indeed those who enter into our labors may gather it in our stead; yet I am anxious that we should persevere until we die, though no apparent effect be produced."

In April, 1836, she wrote, "My mind is much upon a female boarding school; and if I can get the promise of ten girls, we shall, God willing, remove the press from our house, and commence one in the fall."

In May she commenced a new term of her day school with twenty-six scholars. She says, "The wife of a persecuted Druze is very anxious to learn to read, and she comes to our house every day to get instruction from Raheel." She also says, "We feel the want of books exceedingly. The little girl whom I took more than a year since, and who advances steadily in intelligence and knowledge, has no book but the Bible to read, not one." Then again, "Should our press get into successful operation, I despair in doing anything in the way of infant schools, because the Arabic language cannot be simplified, at least under existing prejudices. If every hymn and little story must be dressed up in the august habiliments of the Koran, what child of three and six years old will be wiser and better for them! How complete is the dominion of the Great Adversary over this people! All the links of the chain must be separated, one by one. And what a long, I had almost said, tedious process! But I forget that to each one will be assigned a few only of these links. We are doing a little, perhaps, in this work; if faithful, we shall rest in heaven, and others will come and take our places and our work."

On the eleventh of June, Mrs. Smith's health had become so impaired from the dampness of the floor and walls of her school building, that her physician advised a sea voyage for her. After suffering shipwreck on the coast of Asia Minor, and enduring great hardships, she reached Smyrna, where she died on the 30th of September, in the triumphs of the Gospel. Her Memoir is a book worthy of being read by every Christian woman engaged in the Master's service.

In a letter written from Smyrna, July 28, she says, "I had set my heart much upon taking Raheel with me. Parents, however, in Syria, have an especial aversion to parting with their children for foreign countries. One of my last acts therefore was to make a formal committal of her into the hands of my kind friend Miss Williams. I had become so strongly attached to the little girl, and felt myself so much rewarded for all my efforts with her, that the circumstances of this separation were perhaps more trying than any associated with our departure."

Mrs. Smith had from the first a desire to take a little Arab girl to be brought up in her family, and at length selected Raheel, one of the most promising scholars in her school, when about eight years of age, and with the consent of her parents adopted her. In her care, attentions and affections, she took almost the rank of a daughter. She was trained to habits of industry, truth and studiousness, and although Mrs. S. had been but nine months in the country when she adopted her, she commenced praying with her in Arabic from the very first.

Dr. Eli Smith says, "In a word, the expectations Mrs. Smith had formed in taking her, were fully answered; and she was often heard to say, that she had every day been amply repaid for the pains bestowed upon her. It will not be wondered at, that her affections became entwined very closely around so promising a pupil, and that the attachment assumed much of the character of parental kindness. Mrs. Smith's sharpest trial, perhaps, at her departure from Beirüt, arose from leaving her behind."

After the departure of Mrs. Smith, her fellow-laborer, Miss Williams, afterwards Mrs. Hebard, took charge of Raheel, who remained with her five years. She then lived successively with Mrs. Laneau and Mrs. Beadle, and lastly with Dr. and Mrs. De Forest.

When in the family of Dr. De Forest, she became engaged to be married to Mr. Butrus Bistany, a learned native of the Protestant Church, who was employed by the Mission as a teacher. Her mother and friends were opposed to the engagement, as they wished to marry her to a man of their own selection. On Carnival evening, February 20, in the year 1843, her mother invited her to come and spend the feast with the family. She hesitated, but finally consented to go with Dr. De Forest and call upon her family friends and return before night. After sitting several hours, the Doctor arose to go and she prepared to follow him. Her mother protested, saying that they would not allow her to return to her home with the missionary. Finding that the mother and brother-in-law were preparing to resist her departure by violence, Dr. De Forest retired, sending a native friend to stay in the house until his return. He repaired to the Pasha and laid the case before him. The Pasha declared her free to choose her own home, as she was legally of age, and sent a janizary with Dr. De Forest to examine the case and insure her liberty of action. On entering the house, the janizary called for Raheel and asked her whether she wished to go home or stay with her mother? She replied, "I wish to go home to Mrs. De Forest." The janizary then wrote down her request, and told her to go. She arose to go, but could not find her shoes. There was some delay, when her brother-in-law seized her arm and attempted to drag her to an inner room. The Pasha's officer seized the other arm and the poor girl was in danger of having her shoulders dislocated. At length the officer prevailed and she escaped. Her mother and the women who had assembled from the neighborhood, then set up a terrific shriek, like a funeral wail, "She's lost! she's dead! wo is me!" It was all pre-arranged. The brother-in-law had been around to the square to a rendezvous of soldiers, and told them that an attempt would be made to abduct his sister by force, and if they heard a shriek from the women, to hasten to his house. The rabble of soldiers wanted no better pastime than such a melée among the infidels, and promised to come. When they heard the noise they started on a run. Raheel, having suspected something of the kind, induced Dr. De Forest to take another road, and as they turned the corner to enter the mission premises, they saw the rabble running in hot haste towards her mother's house, only to find that the bird had flown.

In the following summer she was married to Mr. Bistany, who was for eight years assistant of Dr. Eli Smith in the work of Bible translation, and for twenty years Dragoman of the American Consulate. He is now Principal of a private Boarding School for boys, called the "Medriset el Wutanîyet" or "Native School," which has about 150 pupils of all sects. He and his son Selim Effendi are the editors and proprietors also of three Arabic journals; the *Jenan*, a Monthly Literary Magazine, illustrated by wood-cuts made by a native artist, and having a circulation of about 1500; the *Jenneh*, a semi-weekly newspaper published Tuesday and Friday; and the *Jeneineh*, published Monday, Wednesday, Thursday and Saturday. There is not a more industrious man in Syria than Mr. Bistany, and he is doing a great work in the enlightenment of his countrymen.

Raheel's home is one of affection, decorum, and Christian refinement, and she has fulfilled the highest hopes and prayers of her devoted foster mother, in discharging the duties of mother, neighbor, church member, and friend. May every missionary woman be rewarded in seeing such fruits of her labors!

In January, 1866, Sarah, one of Raheel's daughters, named after Mrs. Sarah L. Smith, was attacked by typhoid pneumonia. From the first she was deeply impressed on the subject of religion, and in deep concern about her soul. She sent for me, and I found her in a very hopeful state of mind. Day after day I called and conversed and prayed with her, and her views of her need of Christ were most clear and comforting, and she wished her testimony to His love to be known among all her young companions. Her friends from the school gathered at her request to see her, and she urged them to come to Christ, and several who have since united with the Church traced their first awakening to her words on her death-bed.

One day Sarah said to me, "How thankful I am for this sickness! It has been the voice of God to my soul! I have given myself to Jesus forever? I have been a great sinner, and I have been thinking about my sins, and my need of a Saviour, and I am resolved to live for Him hereafter." On her father's coming into the room, she said in English, "Papa, I am so happy that the Lord sent this sickness upon me. You cannot tell how I thank him for it."

After a season spent in prayer, I urged her, on leaving, to cast herself entirely on the Saviour of sinners, before another hour should pass. The next day as I entered the room, she said, "I am at peace now. I *did* cast myself on Jesus and He received me. I know His blood has washed my sins away." She had expressed some fear that she might not be able to live a consistent Christian life should she recover, "but," said she, "I could trust in Christ to sustain me." After a few words of counsel and prayer, and reading a portion of Scripture, she exclaimed, "It is all one now, whether I die or live. I am ready to go or stay. The Lord knows best."

At the last interview between her and her father, she expressed her determination to make the Bible henceforth her study and guide, and requested him to read the 14th chapter of John, which seemed to give her great comfort. Soon after that she ceased to recognize her friends, and on Monday night, January 5, she gently fell asleep. I was summoned to the house at 2 A.M. by a young man who said, "She is much worse, hasten." On reaching the house I met Rufka, teacher of the Seminary, who exclaimed, "She is gone, she is gone." Entering the mukod room, I found all the family assembled. There were no shrieks and screams and loud wailings, as is the universal custom in this land. All were seated, and the father, Abû Selim, was reading that chapter which Sarah had asked him to read. I then led the family in prayer, and all were much comforted. She had lived a blameless life, beloved by all who knew her, and had been a faithful and exemplary daughter and sister, but her only trust at the last was in her Saviour. She saw in her past life only sin, and hoped for salvation in the blood of Christ alone.

The funeral was attended by a great concourse of people of all sects, and the Protestant chapel was crowded.

CHAPTER XI.

HUMS.

THE city of Hums, the ancient Emessa, is situated about one mile east of the river Orontes, and about half way between Aleppo and Damascus. It is in the midst of a vast and fertile plain, extending to Palmyra on the east, and to the Orontes on the west. With the exception of a few mud-built villages along the east and near the city, there is no settled population between Hums and Palmyra. The wild roving Bedawin sweep the vast plains in every direction, and only a few years ago, the great gates of Hums were frequently closed at midday to prevent the incursion of these rough robbers of the desert. On the west of the city are beautiful gardens and orchards of cherry, walnut, apricot, plum, apple, peach, olive, pomegranate, fig and pear trees, and rich vineyards cover the fields on the south. It is a clean and compact town of about 25,000 inhabitants, of whom 700 are Greek Christians, 300 Jacobites, and the rest Mohammedans. The houses are built of sun-dried bricks and black basaltic rock, and the streets are beautifully paved with small square blocks of the same rock, giving it a neat and clean appearance. There are few windows on the street;

the houses are one story high, with diminutive doors, not more than four feet high; and the low dull walls stretching along the streets, give the city a dismal and monotonous appearance. The reason of building the doors so *low*, is to prevent the quartering of Turkish government horsemen on their families, as well as to prevent the Bedawin Arabs from plundering them. On the southwest corner of the city stands an ancient castle in ruins, built on an artificial mound of earth of colossal size, which was once faced with square blocks of black trap rock, but this facing has been all stripped off to build the modern city.

The people are simple and country-like in dress and manners, and the most of them have a cow-yard within the courts of their houses, thus combining the pastoral with the citizen life. The majority of the Greeks are silk-weavers and shoemakers, weaving girdles, scarfs and robes for different parts of Syria and Egypt, and supplying the Bedawin and the Nusairy villagers with coarse red-leather boots and shoes.

Hums early became the seat of a Christian Church, and in the reign of Diocletian, its bishop, Silvanus, suffered martyrdom. In 636 A. D., it was captured by the Saracens, (or "Sherakîyeen," "Easterns," as the Arab Moslems were called,) and although occupied for a time by the Crusaders, it has continued a Moslem city, under Mohammedan rule. The Greek population have been oppressed and ground to the very dust by their Moslem neighbors and rulers, and their women have been driven for protection into a seclusion and degradation similar to that of the Moslem hareems.

The Rev. D. M. Wilson, a missionary of the A. B. C. F. M., took up his residence in Hums in October, 1855, and remained until obliged to leave by the civil war which raged in the country in 1860. Mr. and Mrs. Aiken went to Hums in April, 1856, but Mrs. Aiken died June 20, after having given promise of rare usefulness among the women of Syria.

After Mr. Wilson left Hums, a faithful native helper, Sulleba Jerwan, was sent to preach in Hums. His wife, Luciya Shekkoor, had been trained in the family of Rev. W. Bird in Deir el Komr, and was a devoted and excellent laborer on behalf of the women of Hums. In October, 1862, one of the more enlightened men among the Greeks was taken ill, and sent for Pastor Sulleba to come and make him a religious visit. He went, and found quite a company of relatives and friends present. The sick man asked him to read from the Word of God, and among the passages selected, was that containing the Ten Commandments. While he was reading the *Second* Commandment, the *wife* of the sick man exclaimed, "Is that the Word of God? If it is, read it again." He did so, when she arose and tore down a wooden painted picture of a saint, which had been hung at the head of the bed, declaring that henceforth there should be no idol worship in that house. Then taking a knife, she scraped the paint from the picture, and took it to the kitchen to serve as the cover to a saucepan! This was done with the approbation of all present. The case was the more remarkable, as it was one of the first cases in Syria in which a woman has taken such a decided stand against picture-worship and saint-worship, in advance of the rest of the family.

In the year 1863, before the ordination of Pastor Sulleba, there being no Protestant properly qualified to perform the marriage ceremony in Hums, I went to that city to marry two of the Protestant young men. It was the first time a Protestant marriage had ever taken place in Hums, and great interest was felt in the ceremony. It is the custom among the other sects to *pronounce* the bride and groom husband and wife, neither giving an opportunity to spectators to object, nor asking the girl if she is willing to marry the man. The girl is oftentimes not consulted, but simply told she is to marry such a man. If it pleases her, well and good. If not, there is no remedy. The Greek Church gives no liberty in this respect, although the priest takes it for granted that the friends have satisfied both bride and groom with regard to the desirableness of the match. If they are not satisfied, the form of the ceremony gives neither of them the right of refusal.

The two young men, Ibrahim and Yunis, called upon me soon after my arrival, to make arrangements for the marriage. I read them the form of the marriage ceremony and they expressed their approval, but said it would be necessary to give the brides very careful instructions as to how and when to answer, lest they say yes when they should say *no*, and *no* when they wished to say *yes!* I asked them to accompany me to the houses of the girls, that I might give them the necessary directions. They at once protested that this would not be allowed. They had never called at the brides' houses when the girls were present, and it would be a grievous breach of decorum for them to go even with me. So certain of the male relatives of the girls were sent for to accompany me, and I went to their houses. On entering the house of the first one, it was only after long and elaborate argument and diplomatic management, that we could induce the bride to come in from the other room and meet me. At length she came, with her face partially veiled, and attended by several married women, her relatives.

They soon began to ply me with questions. "Do you have the communion before the ceremony?" "No." "Do you use the "Ikleel," or crown, in the service?" "No, we sometimes use the ring." Said one, "I hear that you ask the girl if she is willing to take this man to be her husband." "Certainly we do." "Well, if that rule had been followed in my day, I know of *one* woman who would have said *no;* but they do not give us Greek women the chance."

I then explained to them that the bride must stand beside the bridegroom, and when I asked her if she knew of any lawful reason why she should *not* marry this man, Ibrahîm, she should say *No*,—and when I asked her if she took him to be her lawful

Women Grinding at a Mill.

and wedded husband, she must answer *Yes*. Some of the women were under great apprehension that she might answer No in the wrong place; so I repeated it over and over again until the girl was sure she should not make a mistake. The woman above alluded to now said, "I would have said No in the *right* place, if I had been allowed to do it!" I then went to the house of the other bride and gave her similar instructions. The surprise of the women who came in from the neighborhood, that the girl should have the right to say yes or no, was most amusing and suggestive. That one thing seemed to give them new ideas of the dignity and honor of woman under the Gospel. Marriage in the East is so generally a matter of bargain and sale, or of parental convenience and profit, or of absolute compulsion, that young women have little idea of exercising their own taste or judgment in the choice of a husband.

This was new doctrine for the city of Heliogabalus, and, as was to be expected, the news soon spread through the town that the next evening a marriage ceremony was to be performed by the Protestant minister, in which the bride was to have the privilege of refusing the man if she wished. And, what was even more outrageous to Hums ideas of propriety, it was rumored that the brides were to walk home from the Church *in company with their husbands!* This was too much, and certain of the young Hums-ites, who feared the effect of conferring such unheard-of rights and privileges on women, leagued together to mob the brides and grooms if such a course were attempted. We heard of the threat and made ample preparations to protect Protestant women's rights.

The evening came, and with it such a crowd of men, women and children, as had never assembled in that house before. The houses of Hums are built around a square area into which all the rooms open, and the open space or court of the mission-house was very large. Before the brides arrived, the entire court, the church and the schoolroom, were packed with a noisy and almost riotous throng. Men, women and children were laughing and talking, shouting and screaming to one another, and discussing the extraordinary innovation on Hums customs about to be enacted. Soon the brides arrived, accompanied by a veiled and sheeted crowd of women, all carrying candles and singing as they entered the house. We took them into the study of the native preacher Sulleba, and after a reasonable delay, we forced a way for them through the crowd into the large square room, then used as a church. My brother and myself finally succeeded in placing them in a proper position in front of the pulpit, and then we waited until Asaad and Michaiel and Yusef and Nasif had enforced a tolerable stillness. It should be said that silence and good order are almost unknown in the Oriental churches. Men are walking about and talking, and even laughing, while the priests are "performing" the service, and they are much impressed by the quiet and decorum of Protestant worship.

The two brides were closely veiled so that I could not distinguish the one from the other. Ibrahim was slender and tall, at least six feet three, and Yunis was short and corpulent. So likewise, one of the brides was very tall, and the other even shorter than Yunis. As we could not see the brides' faces, we arranged them according to symmetry and apparent propriety, placing the tall bride by the tall groom, and the two short ones together. After the introductory prayer, I proceeded to deliver a somewhat full and practical address on the nature of marriage, and the duties and relations of husband and wife, as is our custom in Syria, not only for the instruction of the newly married pair, but for the good of the community. No Methodist exhorter ever evoked more hearty responses, than did this address, from the Hums populace. "That is true." "That is news in *this* city." "Praise to God." *Mashullah!* A woman exclaimed on hearing of the duties of husband to wife, "Praise to God, women are something after all!" I then turned to the two pairs, and commenced asking Ibrahim the usual question, "Do you" etc., etc.,) when a woman screamed out, "Stop, stop, Khowadji, you have got the wrong bride by that man. He is to marry the short girl!" Then followed an explosion of laughter, and during the confusion we adjusted the matter satisfactorily. A Moslem Effendi who was present remarked after listening to the service throughout, "that is the most sensible way of getting married that I ever heard of."

After the ceremony, we sent the newly married pairs to the study to await the dispersion of the multitude, before going into the street. But human curiosity was too great. None would leave until they saw the extraordinary sight of a bride and groom walking home together. So we prepared our lanterns and huge canes, and taking several of the native brethren, my brother and myself walked home first with Ibrahim and wife, and then with Yunis and his wife. We walked on either side of them, and the riotous rabble, seeing that they could not reach the bride and groom, without first demolishing two tall Khowadjis with heavy canes, contented themselves with coarse jokes and contemptuous laughter.

This was nine years ago, and on a recent visit to Hums, the two brides and their husbands met me at the door of the church on Sunday, to show me their children. Since that time numerous Protestant weddings have taken place in Hums, and a new order of things is beginning to dawn upon that people.

The present native pastor, the Rev. Yusef Bedr, was installed in June, 1872. His wife Leila, is a graduate of the Beirût Female Seminary, and has been for several years a teacher. Her father died in January, 1871, in the hospital of the Beirût College, and her widowed mother, Im Mishrik, has gone to labor in Hums as a Bible Woman. When her father was dying, I went to see him. Noticing his emaciated appearance, I said, "Are you very ill, Abû Mishrik?" "No my friend, *I* am not ill. My body is ill, and wasting away but *I* am well. I am happy. I cannot describe my joy. I have no desire to return to health again. If you would fill my hands with bags of gold, and send me back to Abeih in perfect health, to meet my family again, I would not accept the offer, in the place of what I *know* is before me. I am going to see Christ! I see Him now. I know He has borne my sins, and I have nothing now to fear. It would comfort me to see some of my friends again, and especially Mr. Calhoun, whom I love; but what are my friends compared with Christ, whom I am going so soon to see?" After prayer, I bade him good bye, and a few hours after, he passed peacefully away.

The teacher of the Girls' School in Hums, is Belinda, also a former pupil of the Beirût Seminary. Her brother-in-law, Ishoc, is the faithful colporteur, who has labored so earnestly for many years in the work of the Gospel in Syria. His grandfather was a highway robber, who was arrested by the Pasha, after having committed more than twenty murders. When led out to the gallows, the Pasha offered him office as district governor, if he would turn Moslem. The old murderer refused, saying that he had not much religion, but he would not give up the Greek Church! So he was hung, and the Greeks regarded him as a martyr to the faith! Ishoc's father was as bad as the grandfather, and trained Ishoc to the society of dancing girls and strolling minstrels. When Ishoc became a Protestant, the father took down his sword to cut off his head, but his mother interceded and saved his life. Afterwards his father one day asked him if it was possible that a murderer, son of a murderer, could be saved. He read the gospel to him, prayed with him, and at length the wicked father was melted to contrition and tears. He died a true Christian, and the widowed mother is now living with Ishoc in Beirût. Belinda has a good school, and the wealthiest families of the Greeks have placed their daughters under her care.

CHAPTER XII.

MIRIAM THE ALEPPINE.

THE city of Aleppo was occupied as a Station of the Syria Mission for many years, until finally in 1855 it was left to the Turkish-speaking missionaries of the Central Turkey Mission. It is one of the most difficult fields of labor in Turkey, but has not been unfruitful of genuine instances of saving faith in Christ. Among them is the case of Miriam Nahass, (or Mary Coppersmith,) now Miriam Sarkees of Beirût.

From a letter published in the Youth's Dayspring at the time, I have gathered the following facts:

In 1853 and 1854 the Missionaries in Aleppo, Messrs. Ford and Eddy, opened a small private school for girls, the teacher of which was Miriam Nahass. When the Missionaries first came to Aleppo, her father professed to be a Protestant, and on this account suffered not a little persecution from the Greek Catholic priests. At times he was on the point of starvation, as the people were forbidden to buy of him or sell to him. One day he brought his little daughter Miriam to the missionaries, and asked them to take her and instruct her in all that is good, which they gladly undertook, and her gentle pleasant ways soon won their love.

Her mother was a superstitious woman, who hated the missionaries, and could not bear to have her daughter stay with them. She used for a long time to come almost daily to their house and bitterly complain against them and against her husband for robbing her of her daughter. She would rave at times in the wildest passion, and sometimes she would weep as if broken-hearted; not because she loved her child so much, but because she did not like to have her neighbors say to her, "Ah! You have let your child become a Protestant!"

It may well be supposed that this was very annoying to the missionary who had her in special charge, and so it was; but he found some profit in it. He was just then learning to speak the language, and this woman by her daily talk, taught him a kind of Arabic, and a use of it, not to be obtained from grammars and dictionaries. He traced much of his ready command of the language to having been compelled to listen so often to the wearisome harangues of Miriam's mother. Sometimes the father would be overcome by the mother's entreaties and would take away the girl, but after awhile he would bring her back again, to the great joy of those who feared they had lost her altogether. This state of things continued two or three years, while Miriam's mind was daily improving and her character unfolding, and hopes were often entertained that the Spirit of God was carrying on a work of grace in her soul.

One day her father came to the missionary, and

asked him to loan him several thousand piastres (a thousand piastres is $40,) with which he might set up business. This was of course refused, when he went away greatly enraged. He soon returned and took away his daughter, saying that Protestantism did not pay what it cost. It had cost him the loss of property and reputation; it had cost him the peace of his household and the presence of his little girl, and it did not bring in to him in return even the loan of a few piastres, and he would try it no longer. Prayer continued to be offered without ceasing for Miriam, thus taken back to an irreligious home; and though the missionaries heard of her return and her father's return to the corrupt Greek Catholic Church, and of the exultation of the mother over the attainment of her wishes, yet they did not cease to hope that God would one day bring her back and make her a lamb of His fold.

An Arab young woman, Melita, trained in the family of Mrs. Whiting in Beirût, was sent to Aleppo about this time to open a girls' school there. The Greek Catholic priests then thought to establish a similar school of their own sect to prevent their children from attending that of the Protestants. They secured Miriam as their teacher. As she went from her home to the school and back again, she used sometimes to run into the missionary's house by stealth, and assure him that her heart was still with him, and her faith unchanged. The school continued a few weeks, but the priests having failed to pay anything towards its support, her father would let her teach no more. Perhaps two years passed thus, with but little being seen of Miriam, but she was not forgotten at the throne of grace.

The teacher from Beirût having returned to her home, it was proposed to Miriam's father that she should teach in the Protestant school. Quite unexpectedly he consented, with the understanding that she was to spend every evening at home. At first, little was said to her on the subject of religion; soon she sought religious conversation herself, and brought questions and different passages of Scripture to be explained. After about a month, having previously conversed with the missionary about her duty, when her father came for her at night, she told him that she did not want to go home with him, but to stay where she was. She ought to obey God rather than her parents. They had made her act the part of a hypocrite long enough; to pretend to be a Catholic when she was a Protestant at heart, and they knew that she was. Her father promised that everything should be according to her wishes, and then she returned with him.

Two or three days passed away and nothing was seen or heard of Miriam. A servant was then sent to her father's house to inquire if she was sick, and he was rudely thrust away from the door. The missionary felt constrained to interfere, that Miriam might at least have the opportunity of declaring openly her preference. According to the laws of the Turkish government, the father had no right to keep her at her age, against her will, and it was neces sary that she have an opportunity to choose with whom she wished to live. The matter was represented to the American Consul, who requested the father to appear before him with his daughter. When the officer came to his house, he found that the father had locked the door and gone away with the key. From an upper window, however, Miriam saw him and told him that she was shut up there a prisoner, not knowing what might be done with her, and she begged for assistance. She had prepared a little note for the missionary, telling of her attachment to Christ's cause, and closing with the last two verses of the eighth chapter of Romans, " For I am persuaded, that neither death nor life, nor angels, nor principalities, nor powers, nor things present nor things to come, nor height nor depth, nor any other creature, shall be able to separate us from the love of God which is in Christ Jesus our Lord." The janizary proposed to her to try if she could not get out upon the roof of the next house; and descend through it to the street, which she successfully accomplished, and was soon joyfully on her way to a place of protection in the Consulate.

Miriam, after staying three days at the Consul's house, returned to that of the missionary. Her parents tried every means to induce her to return. They promised and threatened and wept, but though greatly moved at times in her feelings, she remained firm to her purpose. They tried to induce her to go home for a single night only, but she knew them too well to trust herself in their hands. Her mother had artfully arranged to meet her at the house of a friend; but her brother came, a little before the time, to warn her that a plan was laid to meet her at this house with a company of priests who were all ready to marry her forcibly to a man whom she knew nothing about, as is often done in this country. Miriam thus gave up father and mother, brothers and sisters, for the sake of Christ and his gospel.

In the year 1855 Mr. Ford removed to Beirût, and Miriam accompanied him. She made a public profession of her faith in Christ in 1856, and was married in 1858 to Mr. Ibrahim Sarkees, foreman and principal proof reader of the American Mission Press. Her father has since removed to Beirût, and all of the family have become entirely reconciled to her being a Protestant. Her brother Habibis is a frequent attendant on Divine service, and regards himself as a Protestant.

Miriam is now deeply interested in Christian work, and the weekly meetings of the Native Women's Missionary Society are held at her house. The Protestant women agree either to attend this Sewing Society, or pay a piastre a week in case of their absence.

I close this chapter with the mention of Werdeh, [Rose,] daughter of the celebrated Arabic poet Nasif el Yazijy, who aided Dr. Eli Smith in the translation of the Bible into Arabic. She is now a member of the Evangelical Church in Beirût. She herself has written several poems of rare merit; one an elegy upon the death of Dr. Smith; another expressing grate-

Werdeh's Arabic Poem, Lamenting the Death of Farah Bistany.

قالت ترثي سارة بنت المعلم بطرس البستاني

يا بين ويحك هل ابقيت في البشرِ　　عينًا بلا دمعةٍ حرَّى ولا كدرِ

وهل تركتَ بذي الدنيا لنا كبدًا　　سليمةً وفؤادًا غيرَ منفطرِ

قطفتَ زهرةَ بستانٍ ستنبت في　　روضِ الجنانِ نظيرَ الانجمِ الزُّهرِ

ويحي على غصنِ بانٍ مالَ منكسرًا　　وايُّ قلبٍ عليهِ غير منكسرِ

يا من مضت وهي عني غير غائبةٍ　　وشخصها لم يفُتْ سمعي ولا بصري

تبكي على فقدكِ الأترابُ دمعَ دمٍ　　اغنت ثراكِ بهِ عن مدمعِ المطرِ

قد كنتِ بينَ بناتِ العصرِ جوهرةً　　عظيمةَ الشانِ تزري بافضلَ الدررِ

اينَ اللغاتُ واين العلمُ وا اسفا　　لم يتركِ البينُ من عينٍ ولا أثرِ

يا ويحَ قلبِ أبٍ يبكي ووالدةٍ　　حزينةٍ تستعيضُ النوم بالسهرِ

ان كنتِ سرتِ عن الابصار نازحةً　　فان شخصكِ في الاكبادِ لم يسرِ

لبستِ ثوبَ بياضٍ في النعيم كما　　ألبستِ كلَّ حزينٍ أسودَ الحبرِ

يا قبرُ اكرِم فتاةً فيكَ قد نزلت　　كريمةً من ذواتِ الطهرِ والخفرِ

سارت بغير وداعٍ سارةٌ عجلًا　　فهل سلامٌ لها ياتي من السفرِ

يا نومةً ما لها من يقظةٍ ابدًا　　وغيبةً ما لها في الدهرِ من حضرِ

ان لم تعُدْ نحوَنا يومًا فنحنُ غدًا　　نسعى اليها ولو كنّا على حذرِ

ful thanks to Dr. Van Dyck for attending her sick brother. Only this can be introduced here, a poem lamenting the death of Sarah Huntington Bistany, daughter of Raheel, who died in January, 1866. Sarah's father and her own father, Sheikh Nasif, had been for years on the most intimate terms, and the daughters were like sisters. The account of Sarah's death will be found in another part of this volume.

Oh sad separation! Have you left among mortals,
An eye without tears, hot and burning with sorrow?
Have you left on this earth a heart without anguish,
Or a soul unharrowed with grief and emotion?
Thou hast plucked off a flower from our beautiful garden,
Which shall shine like the stars in the gardens celestial.
Wo is me! I have lost a fair branch of the willow
Broken ruthlessly off. And what heart is *not* broken?
    Thou hast gone, but from me thou wilt never be absent.
    Thy person will live to my sight and my hearing.
Tears of blood will be shed by fair maids thy companions,
Thy grave will be watered by tears thickly falling.
Thou wert the fair jewel of Syrian maidens,
Far purer and fairer than pearls of the ocean.
Where now is thy knowledge of language and science?
This sad separation has left to us nothing.
    Ah, wo to the heart of fond father and mother,
    No sleep,—naught but anguish and watching in sorrow
    Thou art clad in white robes in the gardens of glory,
    We are clad in the black robe of sorrow and mourning.
Oh grave, yield thy honors to our pure lovely maiden,
Who now to thy gloomy abode is descending!
    Our Sarah departed, with no word of farewell,
    Will she ever return with a fond word of greeting?
Oh deep sleep of death, that knows no awaking!
Oh absence that knows no thought of returning!
    If she never comes back to us here in our sorrow,
    We shall go to her soon. 'Twill be but to-morrow!

CHAPTER XIII.

MODERN SYRIAN VIEWS WITH REGARD TO FEMALE EDUCATION.

IN the year 1847, a Literary Society was formed in Beirût, through the influence of Drs. Thomson, Eli Smith, Van Dyck, De Forest and Mr. Whiting, which continued in operation for about six years, and numbered among its members the leading men of all the various native communities. Important papers were read on various scientific and social subjects. The missionaries had been laboring for years to create an enlightened public sentiment on the subject of female education, contending against social prejudices, profound ignorance, ecclesiastical tyranny and selfish opposition, and at length the fruit of their labors began to appear. In the following articles may be seen something of the views of the better class of Syrians. The first was read before the Beirût Literary Society, Dec. 14, 1849, by Mr. Butrus Bistany, who, as stated above, married Raheel, and is now the head of a flourishing Academy in Beirût, and editor of three Arabic journals. I have translated only the salient points of this long and able paper :—

We have already spoken of woman in barbarous lands. The Syrian women, although better off in some respects than the women of barbarous nations, are still in the deepest need of education and elevation, since they stand in a position midway between the barbarous and the civilized. How few of the hundreds of thousands of women in Syria know how to read! How few are the schools ever established here for teaching women! Any one who denies the degradation and ignorance of Syrian women, would deny the existence of the noonday sun. Do not men shun even an allusion to women, and if obliged to speak of them, do they not accompany the remark with "a jellak Allah," as if they were speaking of a brute beast, or some filthy object? Are they not treated among us very much as among the barbarians? To what do they pay the most attention? Is it not to ornament and dress, and refining about styles of tatooing with the "henna" and "kohl?" What do they know about the training of children, domestic economy and neatness of person, and the care of the sick? How many abominable superstitions do they follow, although forbidden by their own religions? Are not the journals and diaries of travellers full of descriptions of the state of our women? Does not every one, familiar with the state of society and the family among us, know all these things, and mourn over them, and demand a reform? Would that I might awaken among the women the desire to learn, that thus they might be worthy of higher honor and esteem!

"Woman should be instructed in *religion*. This is one of her highest rights and privileges and her bounden duty.

"She should be taught in her own vernacular tongue, so as to be able to express herself correctly, and use pure language. Woman should learn to *write.*

"She should be taught to *read.* How is it possible for woman to remember all her duties, religious and secular, through mere oral instruction? But a written book, is a teacher always with her, and in every place and circumstance. It addresses her without a voice, rebukes her without fear or shame, answers without sullenness and complaint. She consults it when she wishes, without anxiety and embarrassment, and banishes it if not faithful or satisfactory, or even burns it without crime!

"Why forbid woman the use of the only means she can have of sending her views and feelings where the voice cannot reach? *Now* when a woman wishes to write a letter, she must go, closely veiled to the street, and hire a professional scribe to write for her, a letter which she cannot read, and which may utterly misrepresent her!

"Woman should also have instruction in the *training of children.* The right training of children is not a natural instinct. It is an art, and a lost art among us. It must be learned from the experience and observation of those who have lived before us; and where do we now find the woman who knows how to give proper care to the bodies and souls of her children?"

Mr. Bistany then speaks of the importance of teaching woman domestic economy, sewing, cooking, and the care of the sick, as well as geography, arithmetic, and history, giving as reasons for the foregoing remarks, that the education of woman will benefit herself, her husband, her children and her country.

" How can she be an intelligent wife, a kind companion, a wise counsellor, a faithful spouse, aiding her husband, lightening his sufferings, training his children, and caring for his home, without education? Without education, her taste is corrupt. She will seek only outward ornament, and dress, and painting, as if unsatisfied with her Creator's work; becoming a mere doll to be gazed at, or a trap to catch the men. She will believe in countless superstitions, such as the Evil Eye, the howling of dogs, the crying of foxes, etc., which are too well known to need mention here. He who would examine this subject, should consult that huge unwritten book, that famous volume called " Ketab en Nissa," the " Book of the Women," a work which has no existence among civilized women ; or ask the old wives who have read it, and taught it in their schools of superstition.

" Let him who would know the evils of neglecting to educate woman, look at the ignorant, untaught woman in her language and dress, her conduct at home and abroad; her notions, thoughts, and caprices on religion and the world ; her morals, inclinations and tastes ; her house, her husband, her children and acquaintances, when she rejoices or mourns, when sick or well; and he will agree with us that an uneducated woman is a great evil in the world, not to say the greatest evil possible to be imagined.

"In the reformation of a nation, then, the first step in the ladder is the education of the women from their childhood. And those who neglect the women and girls, and expect the elevation of the people by the mere training of men and boys, are like one walking with one foot on the earth, and the other in the clouds! They fail in accomplishing their purpose and are barely able, by the utmost energy, to repair that which woman has corrupted and destroyed. They build a wall, and woman tears down a castle. They elevate boys one degree, and women depress them many degrees.

"Perhaps I have now said enough on a subject never before written upon by any of our ancestors of the sons of the Arabs. My object has been to prove the importance of the education of woman, based on the maxim, that, 'she who rocks the cradle with her right hand, moves the world with her arm.'"

The next article I have translated from Mr. Bistany's Semi-monthly Magazine, called the "Jenan," for July, 1870. It was written by an Arab *woman* of Aleppo, the Sitt Mariana Merrash. She writes with great power and eloquence in the Arabic; and her brother, Francis Effendi, is one of the most powerful writers of modern Syria. The paper of the Sitt Mariana is long, and the introduction is most ornate and flowery. She writes on the condition of woman among the Arabs, and refutes an ancient Arab slander against women that they are cowardly and avaricious, because they will not fight, and carefully hoard the household stores. She then proceeds:—

"Wo to us Syrian women, if we do not know enough to distinguish and seek after those qualities which will elevate and refine our minds, and give breadth to our thoughts, and enable us to take a proper position in society! We ought to attract sensible persons to us by the charm of our cultivation and refinement, not by the mere phantom of beauty and personal ornament. Into what gulfs of stupidity have we plunged! Do we not know that the reign of beauty is short, and not enough of itself to be worthy of regard? And even supposing that it were enough of itself, in the public estimation, to make us attractive and desirable, do we not know assuredly that after beauty has faded, we should fall at once into a panic of anxiety and grief, since none would then look at us save with the eye of contempt and ridicule, to say nothing of the vain attempts at producing artificial beauty which certain foolish women make, as if they were deaf to the insults and abuse heaped upon them? Shall we settle down in indolence, and never once think of what is our highest advantage and our chiefest good? Shall we forever run after gay attire and ornament? Let us arise and run the race of mental culture and literary adornment, and not listen for a moment to those who insult us by denying the appropriateness of learning to women, and the capacity of women for learning!

"Were we not made of the same clay as men? Even if we are of weaker texture, we have the same susceptibility which they have to receive impressions from what is taught to us. If it is good, we receive good as readily as they; and if evil, then evil. Of what use is a crown of gold on the brow of ignorance, and what loveliness is there in a jewelled star on the neck of coarseness and brutality, or in a diamond necklace over a heart of stupidity and ignorance? The great poet Mutanebbi has given us an apothegm of great power on this very subject. He says:

'Fukr el jehûl bela okl ila adab,
Fukr el hamar bela ras ila resen,'

'A senseless fool's need of instruction is like a headless donkey's need of a halter.'

"Let us then gird ourselves with wisdom and understanding, and robe ourselves with true politeness and meekness, and be crowned with the flowers of the 'jenan' (gardens) of knowledge (a pun on the name of the magazine) now opened to us. Let us pluck the fruits of wisdom, lifting up our heads in gratulation and true pride, and remain no longer in that cowardice and avarice which were imputed to the women of the Arabs before us!"

The next article I shall translate, is a paper on the Training of Children in the East, by an Arab woman of Alexandria, Egypt, the Sitt Wustina Mesirra, wife of Selim Effendi el Hamawy. It was printed in the "Jenan" for Jan., 1871. After a long and eloquent poetical introduction, this lady says:—

"Let us put off the robes of sloth and inertness, and put on the dress of zeal and earnestness. We belong to the nineteeth century, which exceeds all the ages of mankind in light and knowledge. Why shall we not show to men the need of giving us the highest education, that we may at the least contribute to *their* happiness and advantage, and rightly train our children and babes, not to say that we may pluck the fruits of science, and the best knowledge for ourselves? Let them say to us, you are weak and lacking in knowledge. I reply, by perseverance and patience, we shall attain our object.

"Inasmuch as every one who reaches mature years, must pass by the road of childhood and youth, everything pertaining to the period of childhood becomes interesting and important, and I beg permission to say a word on the training of children.

"When it pleased God to give us our first child, I determined to train it according to the old approved modes which I had learned from my family relatives and fellow-countrywomen. So I took the baby boy soon after his birth, and put him in a narrow cradle provided with a tin tube running down through a perforation in the little bed, binding and tying him down, and wrapping and girding him about from his shoulders to his heels, so that he was stiff and unmovable, excepting his head, which rolled and wriggled about from right to left, with the rocking of the cradle, this rocking being deemed necessary for the purpose of inducing sleep and silence in the child. My lord and husband protested against this treatment, proving to me the evil effects of this wrapping and rocking, by many and weighty reasons, and even said that it would injure the little ones for life, even if they survived the outrageous abuse they were subjected to. I was astonished, and said, how can this be? We were all trained and treated in this manner, and yet lived and grew up in the best possible style. All our countrymen have been brought up in this way, and none of them that I know of have ever been injured in the way you suggest. He gave it up, and allowed me to go on in the old way, until something happened which suddenly checked the babe in his progress in health and happiness. He began to throw up his milk after nursing, and to grow ill, giving signs of brain disease, and then my lord said, you must now give up these customs and take my counsel. So, on the spur of the moment, I accepted his advice and gave up the cradle. I unrolled the bindings and wrappings and gave up myself to putting things in due order. I clothed my child with garments adapted to his age and circumstances, and to the time and place, and regulated the times of his eating and play by day, and kept him awake as much as might be, so that he and his parents could sleep at night. I soon saw a wonderful change in his health and vigor, though I experienced no little trouble from my efforts to wean him from the rocking of the cradle to which he was accustomed. My favorable experience in this matter, led me to use my influence to induce the daughters of my race, and my own family relatives, to give up practices which are alike profitless, laborious and injurious to health. My husband also aided me in getting books on the training of children, and I studied the true system of training, learning much of what is profitable to the mothers and fathers of my country in preserving the health of their children in mind and body. The binding and wrapping of babes in the cradle prevents their free and natural movements, and the natural growth of the body, and injures their health."

The next paper is from the pen of Khalil Effendi, editor of the Turkish official journal of Beirût. It appeared in the columns of the "Hadikat el Akhbar" of January, 1867. It represents the leading views of a large class of the more enlightened Syrians with regard to education, and by way of preface to the Effendi's remarks, I will make a brief historical statement.

The Arab race were in ancient times celebrated for their schools of learning, and although the arts and sciences taught in the great University under the Khalifs of Baghdad, were chiefly drawn from Greece, yet in poetry, logic and law the old Arab writers long held a proud preëminence. But since the foundation of the present Ottoman Empire, the Arabs have been under a foreign yoke, subject to every form of oppression and wrong, and for generations hardly a poet worth the name has appeared excepting Sheikh Nasif el Yazin. Schools have been discouraged, and learning, which migrated with the Arabs into Spain, has never returned to its Eastern home. There are in every Moslem town and city common schools, for every Moslem boy must be taught to read the Koran; but with the exception of the Egyptian school of the Jamea el Azhar in Cairo, there had not been up to 1867 for years even a high school under native auspices, in the Arabic-speaking world. But what the Turks have discouraged and the Arab Moslems have failed to do, is now being done among the nominal Christian sects, and chiefly by foreign educators. During the past thirty years a great work in educating the Arab race in Syria has been done by the American Missionaries. Their Seminary in Abeih, on Mount Lebanon, has trained multitudes of young men, who are now scattered all over Syria and the East, and are making their influence felt. Other schools have sprung up, and the result is, that the young men and women of Syria are now talking about the "Asur el Jedid," or "New Age of Syria," by which they mean an age of education and light and advancement. The Arabic journal, above referred to, is owned by the Turkish government, or rather subsidized by it, and its editor is a talented young Greek of considerable poetic ability. It is not often that he ventures to speak out boldly on such a theme as education, but the pressure from the people upon the Governor-General was so great at the time, that he gave permission to the editor to utter his mind. I translate what he wrote, quite literally.

بِسْمِ ٱللَّهِ ٱلرَّحْمَٰنِ ٱلرَّحِيمِ

١ ٱلْحَمْدُ لِلَّهِ رَبِّ ٱلْعَالَمِينَ ٢ ٱلرَّحْمَٰنِ ٱلرَّحِيمِ ٣ مَالِكِ يَوْمِ
ٱلدِّينِ ٤ إِيَّاكَ نَعْبُدُ وَإِيَّاكَ نَسْتَعِينُ ٥ إِهْدِنَا ٱلصِّرَاطَ ٱلْمُسْتَقِيمَ
٦ صِرَاطَ ٱلَّذِينَ أَنْعَمْتَ عَلَيْهِمْ ٧ غَيْرِ ٱلْمَغْضُوبِ عَلَيْهِمْ وَلَا ٱلضَّالِّينَ

The same Anglicized by Rodwell

1 Bismillahi' rahmani' rraheem
2 El-hamdoo lillahi rabi' lalameen
3 Arrahmani' raheem
4 Maliki yowmi-d-deen
5 Eyaka naboodoo waéyaka nestáeen
6 Ihdina' ssirat almostakeem
7 Sirat alezeena anamta aleihim, gheiri-'lmoghdoobi aleihim
wala' daleen. Ameen,

Burton's rhyming translation of same

1 In the Name of Allah, the Merciful the Compassionate!
2 Praise be to Allah who the three worlds made,
3 The Merciful the Compassionate.
4 The King of the day of Fate.
5 Thee alone do we worship and of thee alone do we ask aid
6 Guide us to the path that is straight—
7 The path of those to whom thy love is great,
Not those on whom is hate,
Nor they that deviate. Amen.

"There can be no doubt that the strength of every people and the source of their happiness, rest upon the diffusion of knowledge among them. Science has been in every age the foundation of wealth and national progress, and since science and the arts are the forerunners of popular civilization. and the good of the masses and their elevation in the scale of intellectual and physical growth, therefore primary education is the necessary preparation for all scientific progress. And in view of this, the providence of our most exalted government has been turned to the accomplishment of what has been done successfully in other lands, in the multiplication of schools and colleges. And none can be ignorant of the great progress of science and education, under His August Imperial Excellency the Sultan, in Syria, where schools and printing presses have multiplied, especially in the city of Beirût and its vicinity. For in Beirût and Mount Lebanon, there are nearly two thousand male pupils, large and small, in Boarding Schools, learning the Arabic branches and foreign languages, and especially the French language, which is more widely spread than any other. The most noted of these schools are the French Lazarist School at Ain Tura in Lebanon, the American Seminary in Abeih, the Jesuit School at Ghuzir, and the Greek School at Suk el Ghurb, the most of the pupils being from the cities of Syria. Then there are in Beirût the Greek School, the school of the Greek Catholic Patriarch, the Native National College of Mr. Butrus el Bistany, and there are also nearly a thousand *girls* in the French Lazarist School, the Prussian Protestant Deaconesses, the American Female Seminary and Mrs. Thompson's British Syrian School, and other female schools. And here we must mention that all of these schools, (excepting the Druze Seminary,) are in the hands of *Christians*, and the Mohammedans of Beirût have not a single school other than a common school, although in Damascus and Tripoli they have High Schools which are most successful, and many of their children in Beirût, are learning in Christian schools, a fact which we take as a proof of their anxiety to attain useful knowledge, although they have not as yet done aught to found schools of their own. And though the placing of their children in Christian schools is a proof of the love and fellowship between these two sects in this glorious Imperial Age, we cannot but say that it would be far more befitting to the honor and dignity of the Mussulmen to open schools for their own children as the other sects are doing. And lately the Imperial Governor of Syria has been urging them to this step, and they are now planning the opening of such a school, which will be a means of great benefit and glory to Islam."

The editor then states that the great want of Syria is a school where a high *practical* education can be given, and says:—

"We now publish the glad tidings to the sons of Syria that such a College has just been opened in Syria, in the city of Beirût, by the liberality of good men in America and England, and called the "Syria Protestant College." It is to accommodate eventually one thousand pupils, will have a large library and scientific apparatus, including a telescope for viewing the stars, besides cabinets of Natural History, Botany, Geology and Mineralogy. It will teach all Science and Art, Law and Medicine, and we doubt not will meet the great want of our native land."

Five years have passed since the above was written. Since that time the number of pupils in the various schools in Beirût has trebled, and new educational edifices of stately proportions are being built or are already finished, in every part of the city. It may be safely said that the finest structures in Beirût are those built for educational purposes. The Latins have the Sisters of Charity building of immense proportions, the Jesuit establishment, the Maronite schools, and the French Sisters of Nazareth Seminary, which is to be one of the most commanding edifices of the East. The Greeks have their large High School, and the Papal-Greeks, or Greek-Catholics their lofty College. The Moslems have built with funds drawn from the treasury of the municipality, a magnificent building for their Reshidiyeh, while the Protestants have the imposing edifices occupied by the American Female Seminary, the British Syrian Schools, the Prussian Deaconesses Institute, and most extensive and impressive of all, the new edifices of the Syrian Protestant College at Ras Beirût.

As another illustration of public sentiment in Syria with regard to evangelical work, I will translate another paragraph from this official newspaper:

"We have been writing of the progress of the Press in Syria, and of Arabic literature in Europe, but we have another fact to mention which will no doubt fill the sons of our country with astonishment. You know well the efforts which were put forth some time since in the printing of the Old and New Testaments in various editions in the Arabic language, in the Press of the American Mission in Beirût. This work is under the direction of the distinguished scholar Dr. Van Dyck, who labored assiduously in the completion of the translation of the Bible from the Hebrew and Greek languages, which was commenced by the compassionated of God, Dr. Eli Smith. They had printed from time to time large editions of this Bible with great labor and expense, and sold them out, and then were obliged to set up the types again for a new edition. But Dr. Van Dyck thought it best, in order to find relief from the vast expenditure of time and money necessary to reset the types, to prepare for every page of the Bible a plate of copper, on whose face the letters should be engraved. He therefore proceeded to New York, and undertook in co-operation, with certain men skilled in the electrotyping art, to make plates exactly corresponding to the pages of the Holy Book, and he has sent to us a specimen page taken from the first plate of the vowelled Testament, and on comparison with the page printed here, we find it an exact copy of the Beirût edition which is printed in the same type with our journal. We regard it as far clearer and better than the sheets printed from movable types, and we congratulate Dr. Van Dyck, and wish him all success in this enterprise."

Such statements as these derive their value from the fact that they appear in the official paper of a Mohammedan government, and are a testimony to the value of the Word of God.

The next article is a literal translation of an address delivered in June, 1867, at the Annual Examination of the Beirût Female Seminary. This Seminary was the first school in Syria for girls, which was established on the paying principle, and in the year 1867 its income from Syrian girls who paid their own board and tuition was about fifteen hundred dollars in gold. It commenced with six pupils, and now has fifty boarders. A crowded assembly attended the examination in the year above mentioned, and at its close, several native gentlemen made addresses in Arabic. The most remarkable address was made by a Greek Priest, Ghubrin Jebara, the Archimandrite and agent of the Patriarch. When it is remembered that in the days of Bird, Goodell and Fisk, the Greek clergy were among the most bitter enemies of the missionaries, it will be seen that this address indicates a great change in Syria. Turning to the great congregation of three or four hundred people who were assembled in the

American Chapel, Greeks, Maronites, Mohammedans, Catholics and Protestants, he said:

"You know my friends, into what a sad state our land and people had fallen, morally, socially and intellectually. We had no schools, no books, no means of instruction, when God in His Providence awakened the zeal of good men far across two seas in distant America, of which many of us had never heard, to leave home and friends and country to spend their lives among us, yes even among such as I am. In the name of my countrymen in Syria, I would this day thank these men, and those who sent them. They have given us the Arabic Bible, numerous good books, founded schools and seminaries, and trained our children and youth. But for the American Missionaries the Word of God would have well nigh died out of the Arabic language. But now through the labors of the lamented Eli Smith and Dr. Van Dyck, they have given us a translation so pure, so exact, so clear and so classical as to be acceptable to all classes and all sects. But for their labors, education would still be where it was centuries ago, and our children would still have continued to grow up like wild beasts. Is there any one among us so bigoted, so ungrateful, as not to appreciate these benevolent labors; so blind as not to see their fruits? True, other European Missionaries have come here from France and Italy, and we will not deny their good intentions. But what have they brought us? And what have they taught? A little French. They tell us how far Lyons is from Paris, and where Napoleon first lived, and then they forbid the Word of God, and scatter broadcast the writings of the accursed infidel Voltaire. But these Americans have come thousands of miles, from a land than which there is no happier on earth, to dwell among such as we are, yes, I repeat it, such as I am, to translate God's word, to give us schools and good books, and a goodly example, and I thank them for it. I thank them and all who are laboring for us. I would thank Mr. Mikhaiel Araman, the Principal of this Female Seminary, who is a son of our land, and Miss Rufka Gregory, the Preceptress, who is a daughter of our own people, for the wonderful progress we have witnessed during these three days among the daughters of our own city and country, in the best kind of knowledge. Allah grant prosperity to this Seminary, and all its teachers and pupils, peace and happiness to all here present to-day and long life to our Sultan Abdul Aziz."

As my object in giving these extracts from Arab writers and orators of the present day, is to give some idea of the change going on in Syrian public sentiment with regard to education, the dignity of woman, and the abolition of superstitious social usages, I cannot do better than to translate from the official journal of Daûd Pasha, late governor of Mt. Lebanon, an article on the customs of the Lebanon population. This paper was styled "Le Liban," and printed both in Arabic and French in July, 1867. It gives us a glimpse of the civilizing and Christianizing influences which are at work in Syria.

"In Mount Lebanon there exist certain customs, which had their origin in kindly feeling and sympathy, but have now passed beyond the limits of propriety, and lost their original meaning. For example, when one falls sick, his relatives and friends at once begin to pour in upon him. The whole population of the town will come crowding into the house, each one speaking to the sick a word of comfort and encouragement, and then sitting down in the sick room. The poor invalid must respond to all these salutations, and even be expected to rise in bed and bow to his loving friends. Then the whole company must speak a word to the family, to the wife and children, assuring them that the disease is but slight, and the sick man will speedily recover. Then they crowd into the sick room (and *such* a crowd it is!) and the family and servants are kept running to supply them with cigars and narghîlehs, by means of which they fill the room with a dense and suffocating smoke. Meantime, they talk all at once and in a loud voice, and the air soon becomes impure and suffocating, and all these things as a matter of course injure the sick man, and he becomes worse. Then the childish doctors of the town are summoned, and in they come with grave faces, and a great show of wisdom, and each one begins to recount the names of all the medicines he has heard of, and describes their effects in working miraculous cures. Then they enter into ignorant disputes on learned subjects, and talk of the art of medicine of which they know nothing save what they have learned by hearsay. One will insist that this medicine is the best, because his father used it with great benefit just before he died, and another will urge the claims of another medicine, of a directly opposite character, and opinions will clash, and all in the presence of the sick man, who thus becomes agitated and alarmed. He takes first one medicine and then its opposite, and then he summons other doctors and consults his relatives. Then all the old women of the neighborhood take him in hand and set at naught all that the doctors have advised, give him medicines of whose properties they are wholly ignorant, and thus they hasten the final departure of their friend on his long last journey. And if he should die, the whole population of the town assembles at once at the house, and the relatives, friends, and people from other villages come thronging in. They fill the house with their screams and wails of mourning. They recount the virtues of the departed with groans and shrieks, and lamentations in measured stanzas. This all resembles the customs of the old Greeks and Romans who hired male and female mourners to do their weeping for them. After this, they proceed at once to bear the corpse to the grave, without one thought as to proving whether there be yet life remaining or not, not leaving it even twelve hours, and never twenty-four hours. It is well known that this custom is most brutal and perilous, for they may suppose a living man to be dead, and bury him alive, as has, no doubt, often been done. Immediately after the burial, the crowd return to the house of the deceased, where a sumptuous table awaits them, and all the relatives, friends, and strangers eat their fill. After eight days, the wailing, assembling, crowding, and eating are repeated, for the consolation of the distracted relatives. And these crowds and turbulent proceedings occur, not simply at Syrian funerals, but also at marriages and births, in case the child born is a *boy*, for the Syrians are fond of exhibiting their joy and sorrow. But it should be remembered, that just as in civilized lands, all these demonstrations of joy and sorrow are tempered by moderation and wisdom, and subdued by silent acquiescence in the Divine will, so in uncivilized lands, they are the occasion for giving the loose rein to passion and tumult and violent emotion. How much in conformity with true faith in God, and religious principle, is the quiet, well-ordered and moderate course of procedure among civilized nations!

"So in former times, the man was everywhere the absolute tyrant of the family. The wife was the slave, never to be seen by others. And if, in conversation, it became necessary to mention her name, it would be by saying this was done by my wife 'ajellak Allah.' But now, there is a change, and woman is no longer so generally regarded as worthy of contempt and abuse, and the progress being made in the emancipation and elevation of woman, is one of the noblest and best proofs of the real progress of Lebanon in the paths of morality and civilization."

This is the language of the official paper of the Lebanon government. Yet how difficult to root out superstitious and injurious customs by official utterances! At the very time that article was written, these customs continued in full force. A woman in Abeih, whose husband died in 1866, refused to allow her house or her clothes to be washed for more than a whole year afterward, just as though untidiness and personal uncleanliness would honor her deceased husband!

CHAPTER XIV.

BEDAWIN ARABS.

THERE is one class of the Arab race, of which little or nothing has been said in the preceding pages, for the simple reason that there is little to be said of missionary work or progress among them. We refer to the Bedawin Arabs. The true sons of Ishmael, boasting of their descent from him, living a wild, free and independent life, rough, untutored and warlike, plundering, robbing and murdering one another as a business; roaming over the vast plains which extend from Aleppo to Baghdad, and from Baghdad to Central Arabia, and bordering the outskirts of the more settled parts of Syria and Palestine; ignorant of reading and writing, and yet transacting extensive business in wool and live-stock with the border towns and cities; nominally Mohammedans, and yet disobeying every precept of Moslem faith and practice; subjects of the Ottoman Sultan, and yet living in perpetual rebellion or coaxed by heavy bribes into nominal submission; suffering untold hardships from their life of constant exposure to winter storms and summer heats; without proper food, clothing or shelter, and utterly destitute of medical aid and relief, and yet despising the refinements of civilized life, and regarding with contempt the man who will sleep under a roof; they constitute a most ancient, attractive class of men, interesting to every lover of his race, and especially to the Missionary of the Cross.

European missionaries can do little among them. To say nothing of the rough, nomadic, unsettled and perilous life they lead, any European would find himself so much an object of curiosity and suspicion among them, and the peculiar Bedawin pronunciation of the Arabic so different from the correct pronunciation, that he would be constantly embarrassed. Native missionaries, on the other hand, can go among them freely, and if provided with a supply of vaccine virus and simple medicines, can have the most unrestrained access to them. During the last ten years, several native colporteurs have been sent among the Bedawin, and lately the Native Missionary Society in Beirût has sent out one of its teachers as a missionary to the Arabs. There is little use in taking books among them, as very few can make use of them. Mr. Arthington of Leeds, England, has been making earnest efforts to induce the Bedawin to send their children to schools in the towns, or allow schools to be opened among their own camps. We have tried every means to induce their leading Sheikhs to send their sons and daughters to Beirût for instruction, but the Arabs all dread sending their children to any point within the jurisdiction of the Turks, lest they be suddenly seized by the Turks as hostages for the good behavior of their parents. The latter course, *i. e.*, sending teachers to live among them, to migrate with them and teach their children as it were "on the wing," seems to be the one most practicable, as soon as teachers can be trained. Until the Turkish government shall compel the Bedawin to settle down in villages and till the soil, there can be little done in the way of instructing them. And when that step is taken, it is quite doubtful whether the Moslem government will not send its Khoteebs or religious teachers, and compel them all to embrace the religion of Islam. If that should be done, Christian teachers will have but little opportunity of opening schools among them.

One of the leading tribes of the Bedawin is the Anazy, who are more numerous, powerful and wealthy than any other Kobileh of the Arabs. Their principal Sheikh on the Damascus border is Mohammed ed Dûkhy, the warlike and successful leader of ten thousand Arab horsemen, of the Weled Ali. He is now an officer of the Turkish government, with a salary of ten thousand dollars a year, employed to protect the great Haj or Pilgrim Caravan, which goes annually from Damascus to Mecca. He furnishes camels for the Haj, and a powerful escort of horsemen, and is under bonds to keep the Arabs quiet.

In Feburary, 1871, he came to Beirût on business, and was the guest of a Maronite merchant, who brought him at our invitation to visit the Female Seminary, the College and the Printing Press. After looking through the Seminary, examining the various departments, and inquiring into the course of study, he turned to the pupils and said, "Our Bedawin girls would learn as much in six months as you learn in two years." I told him we should like to see the experiment tried, and that if he would send on a dozen Bedawin girls, we would see that they had every opportunity for improvement. He said, "Allah only knows the future. Who knows but it may yet come to pass?" The Sheikh himself can neither read nor write, but his wife, the Sitt Harba, or Lady Spear, who came from the vicinity of Hamath, can read and write well, and she is said to be the only Bedawìyeh woman who can write a letter. With this in view we prepared an elegant copy of the Arabic Bible, enclosed in a waterproof case made by the girls of the Seminary, and presented it to him at the Press. He expressed great interest in it, and asked what the book contained. We explained the contents, and he remarked, "I will have the Sitt Harba read to me of Ibrahim, Khalil Allah, (the Friend of God), and Ismaeel, the father of the Arabs, and Neby (prophet) Moosa, and Soleiman the king, and Aieesa, (Jesus,) the son of Mary." The electrotype apparatus deeply interested him, but when Mr. Hallock showed him the steam cylinder press, rolling off the sheets with so great rapidity and exactness, he stood back and remarked in the most deliberate manner, "the man who made that press can conquer anything but death!" It seemed some satisfaction to him that in the matter of *death* the Bedawin was on a level with the European.

From the Press, the Sheikh went to the Church,

and after gazing around on the pure white walls, remarked, "There is the Book, but I see no pictures nor images. You worship only God here!" He was anxious to see the *Tower Clock*, and although he had lost one arm, and the other was nearly paralyzed by a musket shot in a recent fight in the desert, he insisted on climbing up the long ladders to see the clock whose striking he had heard at the other end of the city, and he gazed long and admiringly at this beautiful piece of mechanism. On leaving us, he renewedly thanked us for *The Book*, and the next day he left by diligence coach for Damascus.

In the summer we sent, at Mr. Arthington's expense, a young man from the Beirût Medical College, named Ali, as missionary to itinerate among the Bedawin, with special instructions to persuade the Arabs if possible to send their children to school. He remained a month or two among them, by day and by night, sleeping by night outside the tents with his horse's halter tied to his arms to prevent its being stolen, and spending the evenings reading to the assembled crowd from the New Testament. He was present as a spectator at a fight between Mohammed's men and the Ruella Arabs east of the Sea of Galilee, in which the Ruella were defeated, but Mohammed's son Faûr was wounded, and Ali attended him. The Sitt Harba told Ali that a papist named Shwiry, in Damascus, had taken the Arabic Bible from them! So Ali gave them another. This Bible-hating spirit of the Papacy is the same the world over. How contemptible the spirit of a man *professing* the name of Christian, and yet willing to rob the only woman among the Bedawin who can read, of the word of everlasting life! The whole family of the Sheikh were interested in reading an illustrated book for children of folio size, styled "Lilies of the Field," which we printed in Beirût last year. When Ali set out on this journey, I gave him a letter to the Sheikh, reminding him of his visit to Beirût, and urging again upon him the sending of his children to school. The Sheikh sent me the following reply, written by his wife, the Sitt Harba, and sealed with his own signet ring. I value the letter highly as being written by the only Bedawin woman able to write:

To his excellency the most honored and esteemed, our revered Khowadja Henry Jessup, may his continuance be prolonged! Amen.

After offering you the pearls of salutation, and the ornaments of pure odoriferous greeting, we would beg to inform you that your epistle reached us in the hand of Ali Effendi, and we perused it rejoicing in the information it contained about your health and prosperity. You remind us of the importance of sending our sons and daughters to be educated in your schools. Ali Effendi has urged us very strongly to this course; and has spent several weeks with us among the Arabs. He has read to the children from The Book, and tried to interest them in learning to read. He has also gone from tent to tent among our Bedawin, talking with them and urging upon them this great subject. He constantly read to them that which engaged their attention, and we aided him in urging it upon them. Inshullah (God grant) that there may soon be a school among the Arabs themselves. We Bedawin do not understand the language nor the ways of Europeans, and we should like to have one like Ali Effendi, who knows our way of talking and living, come to teach us and our children. We would also inform you that the book with pictures, which you sent to the Sitt Harba, has reached her, and she has read it with great pleasure, and asks of God to increase your good. She sends salams to you and to the Sitt, and all your family.

And may you live forever! Salam.

MOHAMMED DUKHY.

29 Jemady Akhar }
1289 of the Hegira }

"Postscript.—There has been a battle between us and the Ruella tribe, and the Ruellas ate a defeat. Ali Effendi was present and will give you the particulars."

At the date of this writing, Ali has been again to Mohammed's camp, taking books and medicines, and has done his utmost to prepare the way for opening schools among the Bedawin in their own camps. Ali has brought another letter from Sitt Harba, in which she gives her views with regard to the education of the Bedawin. I sent several written questions to her in Arabic, to which she cheerfully gave replies. The following is the substance of her answers:

I. The Bedawin Arabs ought to learn to read and write, in order to learn religion, to increase in understanding, and to become acquainted with the Koran. They profess to be Moslems, but in reality have no religion.

II. The reason why so few of the Bedawin know how to read, is because it is out of their line of business. They prefer fighting, plundering, and feeding flocks and herds. Reading and books are strange and unknown to them.

III. If they wished to learn to read, the true time and place would be in the winter, when they migrate to the East in the Jowf, where they are quiet and uninterrupted by government tax-gatherers.

IV. I learned to read in the vicinity of Hums. My father brought for my instruction a Khoteeb or Moslem teacher, who taught me reading. His name was Sheikh Abdullah. The Sheikh Mohammed taught me writing.

V. The Bedawin esteem a boy better than a girl, because the boy may rise to honor, but the girl has nothing to expect from her husband, and his parents and relatives, but cursing and abuse.

VI. A man may marry four wives. If one of them ceases bearing children, and she be of his family, he makes a covenant of fraternity with her, and he supports her in his own camp, but she is regarded simply as a sister. If she be of another family, he sends her home, and pays her what her friends demand.

VII. The girls and women have no more religion than the boys and men. They never pray nor fast, nor make the pilgrimage to Mecca. But the old women repeat certain prayers, and visit the ziyaras, mazars, and welys, and other holy places.

VIII. If teachers would come among us, who can live as we do, and dwell in our camps, and travel with us to the desert, they could teach the great part of our children to read, especially if they understood the art of medicine.

Ali spent several weeks among them, sleeping in the camp, and attending upon their sick. The camp was on the mountains east of the Sea of Galilee.

Fevers prevailed through the entire district from Tiberias to Damascus, and Ali devoted himself faithfully to the care of the sick. The Sheikh himself was ill with fever and ague, as were several members of his family. One day Ali prepared an effervescing draught for him, and when the acid and the alkali united, and the mixture effervesced, the Bedawin seated in the great tent screamed and ran from the tent as if the Ruellas were down upon them! What, said they, is this? He pours water into water, and out come fire and smoke! The Sheikh himself was afraid to drink it; so Ali took it himself, and finally, after explaining the principle of the chemical process, he induced both the Sheikh and the Sit Harba to drink the draught. On leaving the encampment, the Sheikh gave Ali a guard, and three Turkish pounds (about $14,) to pay for his medicines and medical services, saying, that as his Bedawin were growing poor since they were forbidden to make raids on other tribes, they could not pay for his services, and he would pay for all. He offered to give him a goat skin bottle of semin (Arab butter) and several sheep, but Ali was unable to carry either, and declined the offer. Ali brought a specimen of Bedawin bread. It is black, coarse, and mixed with ashes and sand. The Bedawin pound their wheat, and knead the coarse gritty flour without sifting, and bake it on the heated earthen ovens.

The Bedawin swarm with vermin. Their garments, their persons, their tents and their mats are literally alive with the third plague of Egypt, *lice!*

Ali soon found himself completely overrun with them, and was almost driven wild. The Sitt Harba urged him to try the Bedawin remedy for cleansing his head. On inquiring what it was, he declared he would rather have the disease than the remedy! After his return to his village in Lebanon, he spent several days in ablutions and purifications before venturing to bring me his report. The Sitt Harba gave him a collection of the nursery rhymes which she and the Bedawin women sing to their little brown babies, and some of them will be found in the "Children's Chapter" of this volume. The Sheikh Mohammed, who can neither read nor write, repeated to Ali the following Kosîdeh or Song, which he composed in Arabic poetry, after his victory over Feisal, of the Ruella tribe, in 1866. The Ruellas had previously driven Mohammed's tribe from one of the finest pasture regions in Howian, and Ed Dukhy regained it after a desperate struggle.

Oh fair and beautiful plain, oh rich green Bedawin pasture,
We had left you, too often stained, with the blood of violent battle;
Ah, dark disastrous day, when brother abandoned his brother,
Though riding the fleetest of mares, and safe from pursuit of the foeman,
He never once turned to inquire, though we tasted the cup of destruction.
Oh fair and beautiful plain, we yesterday fought and regained thee!
I praise and honor His name, who only the victory giveth!
O, Feisal, we've meted to you your deserts in royal measure;
With our spears so burning and sharp, we cut off the necks of your Arabs,
O, Shepherd of Obaid, you fled deserting your pastures,
Biting your finger in pain and regret for your sad disasters—
Savage hyena, come forth, from your lair in the land of Jedaileh,

Howl to your fellow-beasts, in the distant land of Butîna;
Come and eat your fill of the dead in the Plain of Fada,
O, fair and beautiful plain, you belong to the tribe of the victor;
But Feisal is racked with pain, when he hears the battle story,
Our right-handed spearmen have palsied his arm is its strength and power;
A blow fell hard on his breast, from the hand of our Anazy warriors;
Come now, ye who wish for peace, we are ready in honor to meet you!
Our wrongs are all avenged, and our arms are weary of battle.

The Arabic original of these lines breathes the true spirit of poetry, and shows that the old poetic fire still burns in the desert. Feisal now lives in the region adjacent to Mohammed Dûkhy, and they leave a space of several miles between their camps to prevent trespass, and the danger of re-opening the old blood-feud.

I would commend the Arabs of the Desert to the prayerful remembrance of the Women of America. How the gospel is to reach them, is one of the great problems of our day. Their women are sunken to the lowest depths of physical and moral degradation. The extent of their religion is in being able to swear Mohammedan oaths. "Their mouths are full of cursing and bitterness; their feet are swift to shed blood; destruction and misery are in their ways, and the *way of peace* have they not known." Although their hand is against every man, and every man's hand against them, let them feel that there is one class of men who love them and care for them with a disinterested love, and who seek their everlasting welfare!

CHAPTER XV.

"WOMAN BETWEEN BARBARISM AND CIVILIZATION."

THIS is the title of an Arabic article in the "Jenan" for Sept. 1, 1872, written by Frances Effendi Merrash, brother of the Sitt Mariana, whose paper we have translated on a preceding page. It is evident that the Effendi writes from the atmosphere of Aleppo. The more "polite" society of that city is largely made up of that mongrel population, half French and half Arab, which is styled "Levantine" and too often combines the vices of both, with the virtues of neither. It will be seen that the able author is combatting the worst form of French flippant civilization, which has already found its way into many of the towns and cities of the Orient. He says:—

"Inasmuch as woman constitutes a large portion of human kind, and an essential element in society, as well as the leading member of the race in respect to its perpetuation, it becomes necessary both to consider and speak of her character and position, although there are not wanting those who are coarse enough and rude enough to declare woman a worthless part of the creation.

"Woman possesses a nature remarkably impressible and susceptible to influence, owing to the delicacy of her organization and the peculiarities of her structure. Her proper culture therefore calls for the greatest possible skill and care to protect her from those corrupting influences to which she is by nature especially susceptible. We should therefore neither leave her locked in the fetters of the ancient barbarism and rudeness, nor leave her free to the uncontrollable liberty of this modern civilization, for both these extremes bring her into one common evil estate and both have one effect upon her.

"Have you not observed how the customs of ancient rude barbarism corrupted the manners of woman and obliterated all those virtues and excellencies for which she is especially designed by nature? It was deemed most opprobrious for woman to learn to read and write, to say nothing of other arts. It was thought indispensable to bind upon her mouth the fetters of profound silence so that none ever heard her voice but her own coarse husband, and the walls of the enclosure in which she was kept imprisoned. She had no liberty of thought or action. Every woman's thoughts were limited by the thoughts of her husband, and her character was cast in the mould of his, whether that were good or bad. And in addition to this, she always suffered from whatever of rudeness there might be in her rough companion, who availed himself of his superior brute physical strength as a weapon to overcome her moral power. He scourged and cursed and despised her in every possible way, when she was innocent of crime or error. As a result of this course, her own self respect, and the feeling that she was abused and insulted by her companion or partner, led her oftentimes to cast off all shame and modesty, whenever a suitable opportunity presented itself. This grew out of the fact that she no longer regarded herself as the companion of her husband and the sharer of, all his natural and moral rights, his joys and sorrows, but she rather imagined herself his captive and bond slave. She thus sank to the position of a slave-woman who is never allowed peace or rest, and cares nothing for the training of her children or the ordering of her house, since she looks upon herself as a stranger in a home not her own, and we all know how difficult it is for a slave to perform the duties of the free!

" On the other hand, have you not observed how the influence of modern civilization is corrupting the nature of woman and making havoc with her morals?

" There is nothing strange in this, for her delicate nature, when it had escaped from the chains and imprisonment of the mildest barbarism, into the open free arena of civilization, lost its reckoning, and wandered hither and thither in bewilderment according to its own unrestrained passions. Woman thus became like a feather, 'Borne on the tempest wherever it blows, and driven about where no one knows.'

" Now since evil images and objects are far more numerous in this world than those which are good, it becomes evident that the influence of evil upon the mind of woman is stronger and more abiding than the influence of the good, owing to this intense delicacy of texture in her mental constitution. Let us suppose that one man and one woman were placed in a position where they should only see evil deeds, or only good deeds: the woman would leave that place either vastly worse than the man, or vastly better. Now the moral misconduct of woman is far more detrimental to the propagation of the race, than is the misconduct of man. It is therefore better for the woman not to go to the extremes of the modern civilization, whose evils are equal to, yes, and far surpass, its benefits. Have you not noticed that the leaders of modern civilization in our age, have initiated, if not surpassed, all the excesses of riot, and lust and rapine, ever practiced under the barbarism of the ages of antiquity? Do not the women of this age go lower in shamelessness than the women of ancient times? Here we see them veiling their faces with the flimsy gauze of artifice, and befouling the pure waters of life with the turbulent stream of their own vanity. They pollute the purity of real beauty by the foul arts of beautifying, and cry out in loud rude voices in every assembly and gathering. They strut about in vain-glorious conceit, and flaunt their gaudy apparel in indecent boldness. They claim what does not belong to them and meddle with what does not concern them. They do not blush to cloud the precious jewel of modesty with the selfish airs of passion. Nothing is said which they do not hear, nothing occurs which they do not see. They become bold, unblushing and unwomanly.

"Such being the state of things, there can be no doubt that an excess of this kind of civilization for woman amounts to about the same thing as the excess of her rude barbarism in ancient times. The two extremes meet. The dividing line between them then, that is, the middle course, is the proper one for woman to take. To this middle course there must be some natural and legitimate guide. This guide is a sound education, and on this subject we propose at some future time to write, inasmuch as the education of woman is one of the most important of subjects. Woman is the one fountain from which is derived the life of man in its earliest periods. She is the source of all training, and the root of character. Have you not heard that she who rocks the cradle, moves the world?"

It is evident that the author of this paper has not been so happy as to see the noblest type of a sanctified Christian civilization, such as can be seen in the Christian homes of America and England, or even in the truly Christian homes of Syria. Let us hope that the day is not far distant, when even in Aleppo, a pure Christianity shall have taken the place of that semi-barbaric system styled the papacy, which enthralls the intellects and hearts of so many of the *nominal* Christians of the Orient, and when the enslaved inmates of the Moslem hareems shall be set free, not to indulge in the license of a Parisian libertinism, but with that liberty wherewith Christ makes His people free!

THE VALUE SET ON WOMAN'S LIFE IN SYRIA.

The free license allowed to men by the Koran in the beating of their wives, has led the entire population of the East to set a low estimate upon the life of woman. Until recently in Syria women were poisoned, thrown down wells, beaten to death, or cast into the sea, and the government made no inquisition into the matter. According to Mohammedan law, a prosecution for murder must always be commenced by the friends of the victim, and if they do not enter complaint, or furnish witnesses, the murderer is not even arrested. And if he be convicted of the crime, he is released on paying to the relatives of the victim the price of blood, which is fixed at 13,000 piastres, or $520! A man may well "count the cost" before committing murder. This constant compounding of punishment has degraded the popular views of the value of human life, so that formerly the murder of a woman was never punished. In March, 1856, a Druze girl near B'hamdûn married a man of her own choice, instead of marrying the man assigned to her by her family. She was waylaid by her own brother and the rejected suitor, murdered and thrown into a well.

About a year after the massacres of 1860, while the European Commissioners were still in Syria, and Lebanon was beginning to attain something of its wonted quiet, several Turkish soldiers made an assault upon a young Maronite girl from the village of Ain Kesûr, who was carrying a jar of water to the workmen on the Deir el Komr road. Mr. Calhoun was requested by the Relief Committee in Beirût to devote the charity funds distributed in this part of Lebanon, to giving employment to the needy in road-building. This girl was employed to supply the men with water. The brutual soldiers attempted to gag her with a handkerchief, in order to accomplish their design, but she was too strong for them. The struggle was long and violent, but she finally effected her escape, leaving on the road the fragments of the broken jar, her shoes and shreds of calico which they had torn from her clothing. Just at that moment Giurgius el Haddad, Mr. Calhoun's cook, came up, and seeing the broken jar and the clothing, guessed what had happened, and after finding the girl, and hearing her story, started in pursuit of the soldiers to Ainab, whither they had gone, and where a Turkish officer was stationed. He stated the case to the officer, and received in reply a blow on his arm from a heavy cane. The case was reported to the Turkish Colonel in Abeih, who summoned all parties and ordered each of the soldiers to be beaten with forty lashes on the bare back. But word had reached Col. Frazier, the British Commissioner, and he came at once to Abeih in company with Omar Pasha, with order from Fread Pasha, to examine the case *de novo*. The result was that two of the soldiers were condemned by military law to be shot, and were shot at sunset June 5th, in front of the old palace just below Mr. Calhoun's house. The event produced a profound impression, and Druzes and Moslems began to feel that a woman's life and honor were after all of some value.

In April, 1862, when Daûd Pasha was governor of Mt. Lebanon, a Druze, named Hassan, murdered a Druze girl of his own village, supposing that Daûd Pasha would not interfere with the time-honored custom of killing girls! Much to his surprise, however, he was arrested, convicted and hung, and the poor women of all sects in the mountain began to feel that after all they had an equal right to life with the other sex.

In most parts of Syria to-day, the murder of women and girls is an act so insignificant as hardly to deserve notice. Mt. Lebanon and vicinity constitute an exception perhaps, but woman's right to life is one of those rights which have not yet been fully guaranteed in the Turkish Empire.

In October, 1862, the Arabic official newspaper in Beirût, contained a letter from Hums which illustrates this fact. A fanatical wretch from Hamath, one of the infamous Moslem saints, set up the claim that he had received the power to cast out devils by divine inspiration. He found credulous followers among the more ignorant, and went to Hums to practice his diabolical trade. A poor woman had lost her reason through excessive grief at the death of her son. The husband and others of her relatives went to consult the new prophet. He refused to go and see her, stating that he would not condescend to go to the devils, but the devils must come to him. The poor woman was accordingly brought to him, and left to await the opportune moment, when he could cast out the devils, which he declared to be raving within her. After a few days, her father called to inquire about her, and found her growing constantly worse. The Hamathite told him that he must bring a gallon of liquid pitch, to be used as a medicine, and the next day the devils would leave her. The pitch was brought, and after the father had gone, the lying prophet tied a cord around her feet, and drew her up to the ceiling, and while she was thus suspended, thrust a red hot iron rod into one of her eyes, and cauterized her body almost from head to foot! He then placed the pitch on the floor under her head, and set it on fire until the body was "burned to charcoal!" The next day the friends called, expecting to find her restored to her right mind, when the wretch pointed them to the blackened cinder. They exclaimed with horror and asked him the reason of this bloody crime? He replied that on applying the test of burning pitch, one of the devils had gone out of her, tearing out her right eye, and when he forbade the rest from destroying the other eye, they fell upon her and killed her! The body was buried, but the government took not the slightest notice of the fact. The official journal in Beirût simply warned the public against patronizing such a bloody impostor!

CHAPTER XVI.

OPINIONS OF PROTESTANT SYRIANS WITH REGARD TO THE WORK OF AMERICAN WOMEN IN SYRIA.

THE following letters have been addressed to me by prominent native Syrian gentlemen, whose wives have been trained in the American Mission Seminaries and families. They all write in English, and I give their own language.

Mr. Butrus el Bistany, the husband of Raheel, writes me as follows :—

BEIRUT, Oct. 23, 1872.

" It would be superfluous to speak of the efforts of American Missionary ladies in training the females of Syria, and the good done by them.

" The sainted Sarah L. Smith, who was one of the first among them, established the first Female School in Beirût.

" Mrs. Whiting, also, who had no children of her own, trained five girls in her family, all of whom are still living.

" Mrs. De Forest had a very interesting female school in her family, and the girls educated in that school are of the best of those educated by American ladies in Syria.

" The obstacles in those times were very great, and

the people believed that education is injurious to females. But these ladies obtained a few girls to educate gratuitously, and thus made a good impression on the minds of the people, and wrought a change in public opinion, so that year by year the people began to appreciate female education. And as we are now building on the foundation laid by those good ladies and reaping the fruit of their labors, we should pray to be imbued with the same spirit, and try as much as we can to follow their example, and carry on the work with the same spirit, zeal and wisdom as they did."

Mr. Naame Tabet, the husband of Miriam, who was educated by Dr. and Mrs. De Forest, writes as follows:—

BEIRUT, Oct. 21, 1872.

"It affords me unfeigned gratification that you give me an opportunity of recording my impressions in regard to the advantages of female education in this country under the guidance of the light of the Gospel of our Lord and Saviour, such as is exemplified by the American Mission, whose labors in diffusing and disseminating the Scriptures are so conspicuously manifest.

"That example chiefly has had the effect, in this neighborhood, to stir up gigantic efforts to fill the want of female education. The same feeling is extending itself throughout Syria, so that future prospects for the promotion of pure Christian knowledge and true civilization are brilliant and ought surely to encourage the benevolent in persevering in their action."

The Rev. John Wortabet, M. D., Professor of Anatomy in the Syrian Protestant College, and husband of Salome, writes as follows :—

BEIRUT, Oct. 20, 1872.

"Though I was very young when Mrs. Smith, Mrs. Whiting, and Mrs. De Forest began their labors in the cause of Female Education in Syria, I can distinctly recollect that they were the first to initiate that movement which has grown to so vast an extent at the present time. To them belongs the honor of having been the determined and brave pioneers in the important work of raising woman from her degraded position, brought on by ignorance and Mohammedan influence, to one of considerable respect, in a social, intellectual and moral point of view. I do not mean that they achieved then this great and worthy object, but they were first to begin the work, which is still going on, and destined apparently to grow much farther. And it is but just that their names and primary labors be embalmed in the memories of the past.

"Aside from the intrinsic good which they accomplished, and the direct fruits of their labors, and you are as well acquainted with them as I am—they gave the first and best *teachers* for the schools which have sprung up so abundantly since their time. Of the importance of giving well-trained female teachers for female schools, in the peculiar social system of the East, nothing need be said.

"I believe, however, that the main value of these earlier labors was the *impulse* which they gave to the course of Female Education in Syria. Prejudices and barriers, which had become hoary by the lapse of time, have been completely broken down, at least among the Christian Churches of the East."

CHAPTER XVII.

OTHER LABORS FOR WOMEN AND GIRLS IN THIS FIELD.

THE following statements have been chiefly made out from documents furnished to me by those in charge of the various Institutions. I give them in order according to the date of their establishment.

THE IRISH AND AMERICAN UNITED PRESBYTERIAN MISSION IN DAMASCUS.

I have not received official statistics with regard to the work of this Mission in behalf of women, but they have maintained schools for girls and personal labors for the women through a long series of years. Mrs. Crawford, who is thoroughly familiar with the Arabic language, has labored in a quiet and persevering manner among the women of Damascus and Tebrûd, and the fruits of these labors will be seen in years to come. Miss Dales, now Mrs. Dr. Lansing, of Cairo, conducted a school for Jewish girls in Damascus some fifteen years ago, which was well attended.

Mrs. E. Watson, an English lady of great energy and zeal in the cause of female education, after years of labor in North and South America, Greece and Asia Minor, came to Syria in 1858, and commenced a girls' school in her own hired house. She afterwards removed to Shemlan, in Mount Lebanon, where she erected a building at her own expense for a girls' boarding school, and afterwards gave it to the Society for the Promotion of Female Education in the East. She has since, with untiring energy, erected another building for a Seminary for Druze and Christian girls, the former Institution continuing as it has been for many years under the efficient management of Miss Hicks, assisted by Miss Dobbie. She has also recently erected a neat and substantial church edifice in Shemlan.

In Miss Hicks' absence, Mrs. Watson has addressed me the following letter:

SHEMLAN, August 28, 1872.

"Our first school for native girls was commenced in Beirût in 1858. The teachers have been Miss Hicks, Miss Hiscock, Mrs. Walker, Miss Dillon, Miss Jacombs, (now in Sidon,) Miss Stainton, (now in Sidon,) and Miss Dobbie. No native female teachers have been employed except pupils of the school under Miss Hicks' care. Masters Riskullah in Beirût, and Murad, Reshîd and Daûd, in Shemlan, have been connected with the school as teachers of the higher Arabic branches.

"The whole number of boarders under our care up to the present time, is above one hundred. The only teachers in my second boarding school are, my adopted daughter Handûmeh, and Zarifeh Twiney, a pupil of the Prussian Deaconesses. Seventeen or eighteen of our pupils have been, or are now teachers, and ten are married.

"The school directed by Miss Hicks was given over to the Ladies' Society in England, some six or seven years ago, and has been supported by them since. The new school in the upper house is under no society and is not regularly aided by any. There are from twenty-six to twenty-eight boarders under the care of my daughter, Miss Watson, I aiding as I can. Several girls have been supported for the last two years by friends in America and England. We have had ten Druze girls in our school in the upper house. Miss Hicks has had three or four, and a number in her day school. We had also a number in our day school at Aitah, four of whom are married to Druze Sheikhs."

Mr. Elias Suleeby, aided by friends in Scotland, has for a considerable period conducted common schools in a part of Mount Lebanon and the Bukaa, and now the enterprise has been adopted by the Free Church of Scotland, who have sent the Rev. Mr. Ray to be their Superintendent.

Their schools are chiefly for boys, though in all the village schools it is usual for a few of the smaller girls to attend the boys' school. In Suk el Ghurb, however, they have a boarding school containing some twenty-five girls.

THE PRUSSIAN DEACONESSES INSTITUTE IN BEIRUT.

The Orphan House, Boarding School and Hospital with which the Prussian Deaconesses are connected, were established in 1860. The two former are supported by the Kaiserswerth Institution in Germany, and the latter by the Knights of St. John.

In the Orphan House are one hundred and thirty orphan girls, all native Syrians, who are clothed, fed and instructed for four or five years, and often transformed from wild, untutored semi-barbarians to tidy, well behaved and useful young women. They have ordinarily about fifty applicants waiting for a vacancy in order to enter.

The Boarding School is for the education of the children of European residents, Germans, French, Italians, Greeks, Maltese, English, Scotch, Irish, Hungarians, Dutch, Swiss, Danish, Americans and others. The medium of instruction is the French language.

Since the Orphan School began, many of the girls have married, thirty have become teachers, and about twenty of them are living as servants in families.

In August of the year 1861, the Deaconesses had received about 110 orphans. The children entering are received for three years, and the surviving parent or guardian is required to sign a bond, agreeing to leave the child for that period, or if the child is withdrawn before that time, to pay to the Deaconesses all that has been expended upon her.

In the summer of 1861, several of the parents came and tried to remove their children, though they had no means of supporting them, but the contract stood in the way, and they had no money to pay. The Jesuits then came forward and furnished the parents with French gold in Napoleons, and withdrew in one day fifty orphan girls from the institution, sending them, not to an institution of their own, but turning them back upon their wretched parents and friends to be trained in poverty and ignorance. A few days later, thirty more of the girls were removed in the same way, leaving only thirty. The parents had a legal right to remove the children on the payment of the money, but what shall be said of the cruelty of the Jesuits who turned back these wretched children to the destitution and misery of a Syrian orphan? The Jesuits are the same everywhere, unscrupulous and intriguing, counting all means as right, which promote their own end.

THE BRITISH SYRIAN SCHOOLS.

These Schools, so numerous and widely extended, have grown up since the massacre year 1860. I remember well the first arrival of Mrs. Bowen Thompson in Beirût, and her persevering energy in forming her little school for the widows aud orphans of Hasbeiya, Deir el Komr and Damascus.

From that little beginning in 1860, the school increased the following year, until finally other branch schools were organized in Beirût and Lebanon, and then in Damascus and Tyre, until now, the following schedule, furnished to me by the officers of the Institution, will show to what proportions the enterprise has grown. The Memoir of Mrs. Thompson, entitled "The Daughters of Syria,' gives so full a history of these schools, that I need only refer the reader to that volume for all the information desired. Since the lamented death of Mrs. Thompson, the direction of the schools has been entrusted to her sister, Mrs. Mentor Mott. The Central Training School in Beirût was under the care of Mrs. Shrimpton, who labored with great earnestness and wisdom in that important institution until the spring of 1873, when she resigned her position and became connected with the work of Female education under the American mission in Syria. She is aided by English and native teachers. The schools in Zahleh, Damascus, Hasbeiya and Tyre are under the care of English and Scotch ladies, who have certainly evinced the most admirable courage and resolution in entering, in several of these places, upon outpost duty, without European society, and isolated for months together from persons speaking their own language. I believe that such instances as these have demonstrated anew the fact that where woman is to be reached, woman can go, and Christian women from Christian lands, even if beyond the age generally fixed as the best adapted to the easy acquisition of a foreign language, may yet do a great work in maintaining centres of influence at the outposts, and superintending the labors of native teachers. These young native teachers trained in Shemlan, Sidon, Suk el Ghurb and Beirût, cannot go to distant places as teachers, and *ought not to go*, without a home and proper protection provided for them. Such protection *is given* by a European or American woman, who has the independence and the resolution to go where no missionary family resides, and carry on the work of female education. Even at the risk of offending the modesty of the persons concerned, I cannot refrain from putting on record my admiration of the course of Miss Wilson in Zahleh, Miss Gibbon in Hasbeiya, and Miss Williams in Tyre, in making homes for themselves, and carrying on their work far from European society and intercourse.

The British Syrian Schools are doing a good work in promoting Bible education. Many of the native teachers, male and female, have been trained in our Mission Seminaries, and not a few of them are members of our evangelical churches. It has always been my aim, from the time when Mrs. Bowen Thompson first landed in Syria to the present time, to do all in my power to "help those women which labored with me in the gospel."

We are engaged in a common work, surrounded by thousands of needy perishing souls, Mohammedan, Pagan and Nominal Christian. The work is pressing, and the Lord's husbandmen ought to work together, forgetting and ignoring all diversities of nationality, denomination and social customs. There should be no such word as American, English, Scotch or German, attached to any enterprise that belongs to the common Master. The common foe is united in opposition. Let us be united in every practicable way. Let our name be *Christian*, our work one of united sympathy, prayer and coöperation, and let not Christ be divided in His members. I write these words in connection with the subject of the British Syrian

Schools, because I can speak from experience of the value of such coöperation in the past. As Acting Pastor of the Native Evangelical Church in Beirût, to the communion of which I have received so many young teachers and pupils from the various Seminaries and schools, I feel the great importance of this hearty coöperation and unity of action among those who are at the head of the various Protestant Educational Institutions in Syria.

The Emissaries of Rome are laboring with sleepless vigilance to win Syria to the Papacy. Sisters of Charity, Sisters of Nazareth, Jesuits, Lazarists, Capuchins, Dominicans, and Franciscans, monks, nuns and papal legates, are swarming throughout the land. Though notoriously jealous of each other's progress, they are always united in their common opposition to the Evangelical faith, and an open Bible. We have thus not only the old colossal fortresses of Syrian error to demolish, but the new structures of Jesuitical craft to overturn, before Syria comes to Christ.

It has been stated on a preceding page that in 1835, the American wife of an English merchant, Mrs. Alexander Tod, gave a large part of the funds to build the first school-house for girls ever built in Syria. That substantial union has been happily reproduced in the cordial coöperation of the Anglo-American and German communities in Beirût, both in the Church, public charities and educational institutions, up to the present time.

Let us all live in Christ, work for Christ, keep

our eye fixed on Christ, and we shall be with Christ, and Christ with us!

BRITISH SYRIAN SCHOOLS, 1872.

BEIRUT.

No.	Established.	Name.	Scholars.	Teachers.
1	1860	Training Institution,	92	16
2	1863	Musaitebeh,	85	3
3	1868	Blind School, men & boys,	16	2
4	1868	Blind girls' School,	11	1
5	1860	Boys' School,	85	5
6	1861	East Coombe,	120	4
7	1860	Elementary,	30	2
8	1872	Es-Saifeh,	100	4
9	1860	Infant School,	125	3
10	1860	Moslem,	50	4
11	1860	Night School,	—	5
12	1863	Olive Branch,	85	4
		DAMASCUS.		
13	1867	St. Paul's,	170	6
14	1869	Blind School,	15	1
15	1870	Medan,	80	2
16	1867	Night School,	30	1
		LEBANON.		
17	1863	*Ashrafiyeh*	53	3
18	1868	*Ain Zehalteh,*	50	2
19	1869	*Aramoon,*	40	2
20	1863	*Hasbeiya,*	160	3
21	1867	*Mokhtara,*	—	—
22	1868	*Zahleh,*	75	4
		TYRE.		
23	1869	Girls' School,	50	2
	Totals,	. . . . .	1522	79
	Bible Women,	. . . .	7	

MISS TAYLOR'S SCHOOL FOR MOSLEM GIRLS.

This worthy Christian lady from Scotland is doing a quiet yet most effective work in Beirût, with which few are acquainted, yet it is carried on in faith from year to year, and the fruits will no doubt appear one day, in a vast reformation in the order, morality and general improvement of the Moslem families of Beirût.

Ever since the days of Mrs. Sarah L. Smith, and Mrs. Dr. Dodge, Moslem girls have been more or less in attendance upon the schools of the Syria Mission, but the purely Moslem schools of Miss Taylor and of the British Syrian Schools are making a special effort to extend education with every Moslem household.

This school was opened in February, 1868, for the poorest of the poor. It received the name of "The Original Ragged school for Moslem Girls." No one is considered as enrolled, who has not been at least three weeks in regular attendance. The number already received has reached very near five hundred, all Mohammedans, except five Jewish and fifteen Druze girls. Native teachers are also employed, and the pupils are taught reading, writing, geography, and arithmetic. The principal lesson-book is the Bible. The early history of this institution is replete with interest; but it has attracted little public notice hitherto. It has always been a prudential question whether it would not be wiser to proceed with its work in a quiet unobtrusive way, so as not to awake fanatical opposition. But steady and appreciative friends have stood by it from the beginning, and those who know the school best have commended it most earnestly.

CHURCH OF SCOTLAND SCHOOL FOR JEWISH GIRLS IN BEIRUT.

This school has been in operation since 1865. Although established originally for Jewish girls alone, of whom it frequently had fifty in regular attendance, it has also had under instruction, Greek and Moslem girls.

Three European teachers and two native teachers have been connected with it, under the supervision of the Rev. James Robertson, Pastor of the Anglo-American congregation in Beirût.

CHAPTER XVIII.

THE AMOUNT OF BIBLICAL INSTRUCTION GIVEN IN MISSION SCHOOLS.

THERE has been great difference of opinion with regard to the proper position of Education in the Foreign Missionary work. While some have given it the first rank as a missionary agency, others have kept it in the background as being a non-missionary work, and hence to be left to the natives themselves to conduct, after their evangelization by the simple and pure preaching of the gospel. The Syria Mission have been led, by the experience of long and laborious years of labor in this peculiar field, to regard education as one of the most important auxiliaries in bringing the Gospel in contact with the people. Society and sects are so organized and constituted, that while the people of a given village would not receive a missionary as simply a preacher of the Gospel, they will gladly accept a school from his hands, and welcome him on every visit to the school as a benefactor. They will not only receive the daily lessons and instructions of the school-teacher in religious things, but even ask the missionary to preach to them the Word of life. Schools in Syria are entering wedges for Gospel truth.

Our schools are of two classes, the High schools or Seminaries for young men and young women, and the common schools for children of both sexes. In the former, Biblical instruction is the great thing, the chief design of the High schools being to train the young to a correct and thorough acquaintance with Divine truth. The course of Bible instruction conducted by Mr. Calhoun in Abeih Seminary, is, I doubt not, more thorough and constant, than in any College or High School in the United States. While the sciences are taught systematically, the Bible is made the principal text-book, and several hours each day are given to its study. In our common schools, likewise, Bible reading and instruction hold a prominent place. Owing to the paucity of books in the Arabic language proper to be used as reading books, a reading book was prepared by the Mission, consisting almost exclusively of extracts from the Scriptures. In addition to this book, the Psalms of David and the New Testament are used as regular reading books in all the schools. There are daily exercises in reading the Bible and reciting the Catechism. It will be observed from what I have stated, that the amount of spiritual knowledge acquired by the children, in the very process of learning to read, is not small. Being obliged to commit to memory texts, paragraphs, and whole chapters, from year to year, their minds become stored with the precious words of the Sacred Book. Very much depends upon the teacher. When we can obtain pious, praying teachers, the Scripture

الابجدية

ابجد هوّز حطي كلمن سعفص قرشت ثخذ ضظغ

الحركات وما يتعلق بها

ـَ ـً ـُ ـٌ ـْ ء ـٱ ـّ ـــ

ـِ ـٍ

الارقام الهندية

١ ٢ ٣ ٤ ٥ ٦ ٧ ٨ ٩ ٠

Arabic Letters, Vowels and Numerals.

lessons can be given with much more profit and success, and it is our aim to employ only pious teachers where we can get them. And the example of the teacher receives a new auxiliary, as it were, in impressing these lessons on the mind, where the pupils can attend a preaching service on the Sabbath. Sometimes a pressing call comes from a village, where it seems important for strategic reasons, to respond at once. A pious teacher cannot be found, and we send a young man of well-known moral character. But only necessity would oblige us to do this, and a change for the better is always made as soon as practicable.

Bible schools are a mighty means of usefulness. I think nothing strikes a new missionary with more grateful surprise on entering the Syrian Mission-field, than to witness the great prominence given to Biblical instruction, from the humblest village school of little Arab boys and girls, to the highest Seminaries. The examinations in the Scriptures passed by the young men in Abeih, and the girls in the Beirût and Sidon Seminaries, would do credit to the young people in any American community. Bible schools are not merely useful as an entering wedge to give the missionary a position and an influence among the people; they are intrinsically useful in introducing a vast amount of useful Bible knowledge into the minds of the children, and through them to their parents. In countries where the people as a mass are ignorant of reading, they are an absolute necessity, and in any community they are a blessing.

Had all Mission Schools been conducted on the same thorough Biblical basis as those in Syria, there would have been less objection to schools as a part of the missionary work.

THE SPHERE AND MODES OF WOMAN'S WORK IN FOREIGN LANDS.

In this age, when Christian women in many lands are engaging in the Foreign Mission work with so much zeal, it is important to know who should enter personally upon this work, and what are the modes and departments of labor in which they can engage when on the ground.

No woman should go to the Foreign field who has not sound health, thorough education, and a reasonable prospect of being able to learn a foreign language. The languages of different nations differ as to comparative ease of acquisition, but it is well for any one who has the *Arabic* language to learn, to begin as early in life as practicable. It should be borne in mind that the work in foreign lands is a self-denying work, and I know of no persons who are called to undergo greater self-denial than unmarried women engaged in religious work abroad. They are doing a noble work, a necessary work, and a work of lasting usefulness. Deprived in many instances of the social enjoyments and protection of a *home*, they *make* a home in their schools, and throw themselves into a peculiar sympathy with their pupils, and the families with which they are brought into contact. Where several are associated together, as they always should be, the institution in which they live becomes a model of the Christian order, sympathy and mutual help, which is characteristic of the home in Christian lands. Christian women, married and unmarried, can reach a class in every Arabic community from which men are sedulously excluded. They should enter upon the foreign work as a life-work, devote themselves first of all to the mastery of the language of the people, open their eyes to all that is pleasant and attractive among the natives, and close them to all that is unlovable and repulsive, resolved to love the people, and what pertains to them, for Christ's sake who died for them, and to identify themselves with the people in every practicable way. Persons who are incapable of loving or admiring anything that is not American or English had better remain in America or England; and on the other hand, there is no surer passport to the affections of any people, than the disposition to overlook their faults, and to treat them as our brethren and sisters for whom a common Saviour died. Let no missionary of either sex who goes to a foreign land, think that there is nothing to be learned from Syrians or Hindoos, Chinese or Japanese. The good is not all confined to any land or people.

Among the departments of woman's work in foreign lands are the following:—

I. Teaching in established institutions, Female Seminaries, Orphan Houses and High Schools.

II. Acting as Nurses in Hospitals, as is done by

the Prussian Protestant Deaconesses of Kaiserwerth, who are scattered over the East and doing a work of peculiar value.

III. Visiting from house to house, for the express purpose of holding religious conversation with the people *in their own language.* This can only be done in Syria by one versed in the Arabic, and able to speak *without an interpreter.*

Ignorance of the language of the people, is a barrier which no skill of an interpreter can break down, and every woman who would labor with acceptance and success among the women of Syria, must be able to speak to them familiarly in their own mother tongue. Interpreters may be honest and conscientious, but not one person in a thousand can translate accurately from one language to another without previous preparation. And besides, interpreters are not always reliable. There is still living, in the city of Tripoli, an old man named Abdullah Yanni, who acted as interpreter for a Jewish Missionary some forty years ago. He tells many a story of the extraordinary shape which that unsuspecting missionary's discourses assumed in passing through his lips. One day they went through the principal street to preach to the Moslems. A great crowd assembled, and Abdullah trembled, for in those days of darkness Moslems oppressed and insulted Christians with perfect impunity. Said the missionary, "Tell the Moslems that unless they all repent and believe in Christ, they will perish forever." Abdullah translated, and the Moslems gave loud and earnest expression to their delight. They declared, "That is so, that is so, welcome to the Khowadja!" Abdullah had told them that "the Khowadja says, that he loves you very much, and the Engliz and the Moslems are 'sowa sowa,' i. e. together as one."

Abdullah soon found it necessary to tell his confiding friend and employer, that it would not do to preach in that bold manner, for if he should translate it literally, the Moslems would kill both of them on the spot. The missionary replied, "Let them kill us then." Abdullah said, "it may do very well for you, but I am not prepared to die, and would prefer to wait." The very first requisite for usefulness in a foreign land is the language. It might be well, as previously intimated in this volume, that in each of the Female Seminaries, the number of the teachers should be large enough to allow the most experienced in the language to give themselves for a portion of each week to these friendly religious visits. The Arab race are eminently a sociable, visiting people, and a foreign lady is always welcome among the women of every grade of society, from the highest to the lowest.

IV. Holding special Women's Meetings of the Female Church members from week to week in the homes of the different families. The neighboring women will come in, and the native women, who would never take part in a women's prayer-meeting, in the presence of a missionary, will gladly do it with the example and encouragement of one of their own sex. Such meetings have been conducted in Hums and Tripoli, in Beirût, Abeih, Deir el Komr and Sidon, and in Suk el Ghurb, B'hamdûn, Hasbeiya, and Deir Mimas for many years. Mrs. Smith, Mrs. Isaac Bird, Mrs. Thomson, Mrs. Van Dyck, Mrs. Whiting, Mrs. Goodell, Mrs. Dr. Dodge, Miss Williams, Miss Tilden, Mrs. De Forest, Mrs. Calhoun, Mrs. Wilson, Mrs. Ford, Mrs. Foot, Mrs. Eddy, and Mrs. W. Bird, Mrs. Lyons and Mrs. Cheny, Mrs. Bliss, Miss Temple, Miss Mason, Mrs. S. Jessup are among the American Christian women who have labored or are still laboring for the welfare of their sisters in Syria, and younger laborers more recently entered into the work, are preparing to prosecute the work with greater energy than ever. There are other names connected with Woman's Work in Syria as prosecuted by the American Mission, but the list is too long to be enumerated in full. Many of them have rested from their labors, and their works do follow them.

THE BEIRUT FEMALE SEMINARY.

The last Annual Report of the Board of Missions of the Presbyterian Church of the United States, speaks of these two Female Seminaries as follows:

"The Beirût Seminary is conducted by Miss Everett, Miss Jackson and Miss Loring, containing forty boarding and sixty day scholars, where the object is to give an education suited to the wants of the higher classes of the people, to gain a control over the minds of those females who will be most influential in forming society and moulding opinion.

This hold the Papal Sisters of Charity have striven earnestly to gain, and its vantage ground was not to be abandoned to them. The institution is rising in public esteem and confidence, as the number and the class of pupils in attendance testify. The Seminary is close to the Sanctuary, not less in sympathy than in position, and its whole influence is given to make its pupils followers of Christ."

In addition to this brief notice, it should be said that there are in the Beirût Seminary thirty charity boarders, who are selected chiefly from Protestant, Greek and Druze families, to be trained for teachers of a high order in the various girls' schools in the land. A special Normal course of training is conducted every year, and it is believed that eventually young women trained in other schools will enter this Normal Department to receive especial preparation for the work of teaching.

The charity boarders are supported by the contributions of Sabbath Schools and individuals in the United States, with especial reference to their being trained for future usefulness.

After an experience of nearly ten years in conducting the greater part of the correspondence with the patrons of this school, and maintaining their interest in the pupils and teachers whom they were supporting by their contributions, I would venture to make a few suggestions to the Christian Mission Bands, Societies, Bible Classes, Sabbath Schools and individuals who are doing so much for the education of children in foreign lands.

I. Let all contributions for Women's Work and the education of girls, be sent through the Women's Boards of Missions, or if that is not convenient, in the form of a banker's draft on London, payable to the Principal of the Seminary with whom you have correspondence.

II. If possible, allow your donation to be used for the general purposes of the Seminary, without insisting that a special pupil or teacher be assigned to you. But if it be not possible to maintain the interest of your children and youth in a work so distant without some special object, then by all means,—

III. Do not demand too much from your overtaxed sisters in the foreign field in the way of letters and reports. The labors of a teacher are arduous everywhere. But when instruction is given in a foreign language, in a foreign climate, and to children of a foreign nation, these labors are greatly increased. Add then to this toil correspondence with the Board of Missions, the daily study of the language, the work of visiting among the people, and receiving their visits, and you can understand how the keeping up of correspondence with twenty or thirty Sabbath Schools and Societies is a burden which no woman should be called on to bear.

IV. Do not expect sensational letters from your friends abroad. Do not take for granted that the child of ten years of age you are supporting, will develop into a distinguished teacher or Bible woman before the arrival of the next mail. Do not be discouraged if you have to wait and pray for years before you hear good tidings. Should any of the native children ever send you a letter, (and they have about as clear an idea of who you are and where you are, as they have of the satellites of Jupiter,) do not expect from their youthful productions the elegance of Addison or the eloquence of Burke.

V. Pray very earnestly for the conversion of the pupils in Mission Schools. This I regard as the great advantage of the system of having pupils supported by Christians in the home churches, and known to them by name. They are made the subjects of special prayer. This is the precious golden bond which brings the home field near to us, and the foreign field near to you. Our chief hope for these multitudes of children now receiving instruction, is, that they will be prayed for by Christians at home.

THE SIDON FEMALE SEMINARY.

The Annual Report above mentioned, speaks thus of the Sidon Seminary: "It is conducted by Miss Jacombs and Miss Stainton, and has numbered about twenty boarders and six day scholars. The boarders are exclusively from Protestant families, selected from the common schools in all parts of the field, and are in training for the Mission service, as teachers and Bible readers. Four of the graduates of last year are already so employed. One difficulty in the way of reaching with the truth the minds of the women in the numerous villages of the land, will be obviated in part, as the results of this work are farther developed.

"There has been considerable seriousness and some hopeful conversions, in both these seminaries during the past year.

"The work is worthy of the interest taken in it by the Women's Boards of Missions, and by societies and individuals in the church who have co-operated in it."

The Sidon Seminary, as stated on a previous page, was begun in 1862, and has had four European and six native teachers. Of the latter, one was trained in Mrs. Bird's family, one in Shemlan Seminary, three in the Sidon school, and one by Mrs. Watson.

Ten of its graduates have been employed as teachers, and eight are still so engaged.

I annex a list of Girls' Schools now or formerly connected with the Syria Mission.

Location.		No. of Pupils.	No. of Teach'rs	When begun	
Beirut,	Day School,	50	2	1834	
"	Seminary,	50	10	1848	
Sidon,	Seminary,	20	3	1862	
"	Day School,	6	1	1862	
Abeih,	"	60	1	1853	[soon.
Deir el Komr,	"	50	2	1855	To be resumed
Ghorify,	"	40	1	1863	All Druzes.
El Hadeth,	"	40	1	1870	
Shwifat,	"	70	2	1871	
Dibbiyeh,	"	20	1	1868	
B'Hamdûn,	"	30	1	1853	Discontinued.
Meshghara,	"	30	1	1869	Boys and girls,
Ain Anûb,	"	20	1	1870	and 60 boys.
Kefr Shima,	"	40	1	1856	Boys and girls.
Rasheiya el Fokhar,	"	30	1	1869	
Jedaideh,	"	40	1	1870	
El Khiyam,	"	25	1	1868	
Ibl,	"	30	1	1868	
Deir Mimas,	"	15	1	1865	
Kana,	"	35	1	1869	
Hums,	"	40	1	1865	
Safita,	"	30	1	1869	
Hamath,	"	30	1	1872	
Totals . 23		801	36		

This gives a total of twenty-three girls' schools besides the twenty-four boys' schools under the care of the Mission, and three schools where there are both boys and girls. I have kept the name of B'hamdûn in the list, for its historical associations, but the thirty pupils credited to it, will be more than made good in the girl's school about to be resumed in Tripoli under the care of Miss Kip.

The total number of girls is about 800, and the number of teachers 36. The total cost of these twenty-three schools, including the two Seminaries in Beirût and Sidon, is about eight thousand dollars per annum, including rents, salaries of five American and English ladies, and thirty-one native teachers.

The average cost of the common schools in the Sidon field is sixty dollars per annum, and in the Lebanon field it varies from this sum to about twice that amount, owing to the fact that the Deir el Komr and other schools are virtually High Schools.

The teacher in the Sidon field, and in Abeih, and Safita, are graduates of the Sidon Seminary.

It is probable that a High School or Seminary for girls will be opened by Miss Kip in Tripoli during the coming year.

The preceding schedule can give but a faint idea of the struggles and toil, the patient labors, disappointments and trials of faith through which the women of the American Mission have passed during the last forty years, in beginning and maintaining so many of these schools for girls in Syria.

Did I speak of *trials?* The Missionary work has

its trials, but I believe that its joys are far greater. The saddest scenes I have witnessed during a residence of seventeen years in Syria, have been when Missionaries have been obliged to *leave the work* and return to their native land. There are trials growing out of the hardness of the human heart, our own want of faith, the seeming slow progress of the gospel, and the heart-crushing disappointments arising from broken hopes, when individuals and communities who have promised well, turn back to their old errors "like the dog to his vomit" again. But of joys it is much easier to speak, the joy of preaching Christ to the perishing,—of laboring where others will not labor,—of laying foundations for the future,—of feeling that you are doing what you can to fulfil the Saviour's last command,—of seeing the word of God translated into a new language,—a christian literature beginning to grow,—children and youth gathered into Schools and Seminaries of learning, and even sects which hate the Bible obliged to teach their children to read it,—of seeing christian families growing up, loving the Sabbath and the Bible, the sanctuary and the family altar.—Then there is the joy of seeing souls born into the kingdom of our dear Redeemer, and churches planted in a land where pure Christianity had ceased to exist,—and of witnessing unflinching steadfastness in the midst of persecution and danger, and the triumphs of faith in the solemn hour of death.

These are a few of the joys which are strewn so thickly along the path of the Christian Missionary, that he has hardly time to think of sorrow, trial and discouragement. Those who have read Dr. Anderson's "History of Missions to the Oriental Churches," and Rev. Isaac Bird's "History of the Syria Mission," or "Bible Work in Bible Lands," will see that the work of the Syria Mission from 1820 to 1872 has been one of conflict with principalities and powers, and with spiritual wickedness in high and low places, but that at length the hoary fortresses are beginning to totter and fall, and there is a call for a general advance in every department of the work, and in every part of the land.

Other agencies have come upon the ground since the great foundation work was laid, and the first great victories won, and in their success it becomes all of God's people to rejoice; but the veterans who fought the first battles, and overcame the great national prejudice of the Syrian people against female education, should ever be remembered with gratitude.

It has been my aim in this little volume to recount the history of Woman's Work in the past. Who can foretell what the future of Christian work for Syrian Women will be?

May it ever be a work founded on the Word of God, aiming at the elevation of woman through the doctrines and the practice of a pure Christianity, striving to plant in Syria, not the flippant culture of modern fashionable society, but the God-fearing, Sabbath-loving, and Bible-reading culture of our Anglo-Saxon ancestors!

A few years ago, a Greek priest named Job, from

one of the distant villages high up in the range of Lebanon, called on me in Beirût. I had spent several summers in his village, and he had sometimes borrowed our Arabic sermons to read in the Greek Church, and now, he said, he had come down to see what we were doing in Beirût. I took him through the Female Seminary and the Church, and then to the Library and the Printing Press. He examined the presses, the steam engine, the type-setting, and type-casting, the folding, sewing, and binding of books, and looked through the huge cases filled with Arabic books and Scriptures, saw all the editions of the Bible and the Testament, and then turned in silence to take his departure. I went with him to the outer gate. He took my hand, and said, "By your leave I am going. The Lord bless your work. Sir, I have a thought; we are all going to be swept away, priests and bishops, Greeks and Maronites, Moslems and Druzes, and there will be nothing left, nothing but the Word of God and those who follow it. That is my thought. Farewell."

May that thought be speedily realized! May the coarseness, brutality and contempt for woman which characterize the Moslem hareem, give way to the refinement, intelligence, and mutual affection which belong to the Christian family!

May the God of prophecy and promise, hasten the time when Nusairy barbarism, Druze hypocrisy, Moslem fanaticism, Jewish bigotry and nominal Christian superstition shall fade away under the glorious beams of the rising Sun of Righteousness!

May the "glory of Lebanon" be given to the Lord, in the regeneration and sanctification of the families of Lebanon!

Too long has it been true, in the degradation of woman, that the "flower of Lebanon languisheth."

Soon may we say in the truly Oriental imagery of the Song of Songs,—"Come with me from Lebanon, look from the top of Amana, from the top of Shenir and Hermon, from the lions' dens, from the mountains of the leopards,"—and behold, in the culture of woman, in society regenerated, in home affection, in the Christian family, what is in a peculiar sense, "a fountain of gardens, a well of living waters, and streams from Lebanon!"

"Is it not yet a very little while, and Lebanon shall be turned into a fruitful field?" When "the reproach of the daughters of Syria," shall be taken away; and when amid the zearas of the Nusairiyeh, the kholwehs of the Druzes, the mosques of the Moslems and the tents of the Bedawin, may be heard the voice of Christ, saying to the poor women of the Arab race, weary and fainting under the burdens of life:

"Daughter be of good comfort,
"Thy faith hath made thee whole,
"Go in peace!"

CHAPTER XIX.

THE CHILDREN'S CHAPTER.

PART I.

Abeih, Mount Lebanon, Sept., 1872.

MY DEAR SON WILLIE :—

It is now eight years since you left Syria, and you were then so young, that you must have forgotten all about the country and the people. I have often promised to tell you more about the Syrian boys and girls, what they eat and wear, and how they study and play and sleep, and the songs their mothers sing to them, and many other things. And now I will try and fulfil my promise.

Here is a little boy at the door. His name is Asaad Mishrik, or "happy sunrise," and his name is well given, for he comes every morning at sunrise with a basket of fresh ripe figs, sweet and cold, and covered with the sparkling dew. This morning when he came, your brother Harry stood by the door looking at the figs with wistful eyes, and I gave him a large one, which disappeared very suddenly. Asaad is a bright-eyed boy, and helps his mother every day.

When he comes in, he says, Subah koom bil khire, "Your morning in goodness." Then Assaf, the cook, answers him, "Yusaid Subahak," "May God make happy your morning." If I come out when he is here, he runs up to kiss my hand, as the Arab children are trained to be respectful to their superiors. When a little Arab boy comes into a room full of older people, he goes around and kisses the hand of each one and then places it on his forehead. Asaad wears a red tarboosh or cap on his head, a loose jacket, and trowsers which are like a blue bag gathered around the waist, with two small holes for his feet to go through. They are drawn up nearly to his knees, and his legs are bare, as he wears no stockings. He wears red shoes pointed and turned up at the toes. When he comes in at the door, he leaves his shoes outside, but keeps his cap on his head.

The people never take off their caps or turbans when entering a house, or visiting a friend, but always leave their shoes at the door. The reason is, that their floors are covered with clean mats and rugs, and in the Moslem houses, the man kneels on his rug to pray, and presses his forehead to the floor, so that it would not be decent or respectful to walk in with dirty shoes and soil his sijjady on which he kneels to pray. They have no foot-mats or scrapers, and it is much cheaper and simpler to leave the shoes, dirt and all at the door. Sometimes we are much embarrassed in calling on the old style Syrians as they look with horror on our muddy feet, and we find it not quite so easy to remove our European shoes. But it must be done, and it is better to take a little extra trouble, and regard their feelings and customs, than to appear coarse and rude.

It is very curious to go to the Syrian schoolhouses, and see the piles of shoes at the door. There are new bright red shoes, and old tattered shoes, and kob kobs, and black shoes, and sometimes yellow shoes. The kob kobs are wooden clogs made to raise the feet out of the mud and water, having a little strap over the toe to keep it on the foot. You will often see little boys and girls running down steps and paved streets on these dangerous kob kobs. Sometimes they slip and then down they go on their noses, and the kob kobs fly off and go rattling over the stones, and little Ali or Yusef, or whatever his name is, begins to shout, Ya Imme! Ya Imme! "Oh, my mother!" and cries just like little children in other countries.

But the funniest part of it is to see the boys when they come out of school and try to find their shoes. There will be fifty boys, and of course a hundred shoes, all mixed together in one pile. When school is out, the boys make a rush for the door. Then comes the tug of war. A dozen boys are standing and shuffling on the pile of shoes, looking down, kicking away the other shoes, running their toes into their own, stumbling over the kob kobs, and then making a dash to get out of the crowd. Sometimes shins will be kicked, and hair pulled, and tarbooshes thrown off, and a great screaming and cursing follow, which will only cease when the Mûallim comes with his "Asa" or stick, and quells the riot. That pile of shoes will have to answer for a good many schoolboy fights and bruised noses and hard feelings in Syria. You would wonder how they can tell their own shoes. So do I. And the boys often wear off each other's shoes by mistake or on purpose, and then you will see Selim running with one shoe on, and one of Ibrahim's in his hand, shouting and cursing Ibrahim's father and grandfather, until he gets back his lost property. Sometimes when men leave their shoes outside the door of a house where they are calling, some one will steal them, and then they are in a sorry plight. Shoes are regarded as very unclean, and when you are talking in polite society, it will never do to speak of them, without asking pardon. You would say, "the other day some one stole my new shoes, ajellak Allah," i e., May-God exalt you above such a vile subject! You would use the same words if you were talking with a Moslem, and spoke of a dog, a hog, a donkey, a girl or a woman.

They do not think much of girls in Syria. The most of the people are very sorry when a daughter is born. They think it is dreadful, and the poor mother will cry as if her heart would break And the neighbors come in and tell her how sorry they are, and condole with her, just as if they had come to a funeral. In Kesrawan, a district of Mount Lebanon near Beirût, the Arab women have a proverb, "The threshold weeps forty days when a girl is born."

There is a great change going on now in Syria in the feelings of the people in regard to girls, but in the interior towns and villages where the light of the Gospel has not shone as yet, and there are no schools, they have the ancient ideas about them up to this very hour.

I knew an old Syrian grandmother in Tripoli who would not kiss her granddaughter for six months after she was born, because she was born a girl! But I know another family in that city of Tripoli that do not treat girls in that style. The father is Mr. Antonius Yanni, a good Christian man, and a member of the Mission Church. He is American Vice Consul, and on the top of his house is a tall flag-staff, on which floats the stars and stripes, on Fourth of July, and the Sultan's birthday, Queen Victoria's birthday, and other great feast days. One day when the Tripoli women heard that "Sitt Karîmeh, Yanni's wife, had another "*bint*," (girl) they came in crowds to comfort her in her great affliction! When Yanni heard of it, he could not restrain himself. He loved his older daughter Theodora very dearly, and was thankful to God for another sweet baby girl, so he told the women that he would have none of this heathenish mourning in his house. He then shouted to his janizary or Cawass, a white bearded old Moslem named Amr, "Amr, haul up the Bandaira el Americanîyeh, (American flag) to show the world how glad I am that I have another daughter." "On my head, on my head, sir," said Amr, and away he went and hauled up the stars and stripes. Now the Pasha's palace is not far away, and soon the Turkish guards saw the flag, and hastened to the Pasha with the news that the American Consul had some great feast day, as his flag was raised. The Pasha, supposing it to be some important national feast day of the American Government which he was so stupid as not to know about, sent his Chief Secretary at once to Mr. Yanni to ask what feast it might be? Yanni received him politely and ordered a narghileh and coffee and sherbet, and after saying "good-morning," and "may you live forever," and "God prolong your days!" over and over and over again, and wishing that Doulet America might ever flourish, the Secretary asked which of the great American festivals he was celebrating that day. Yanni laughed and said, "Effendum, you know how many of the ignorant in Syria are so foolish as to mourn and lament when God sends them a daughter, but I believe that all God's gifts are good, and that daughters are to be valued as much as sons, and to rebuke this foolish notion among the people, I put up my flag as a token of joy and gratitude." "Sebhan Allah! you have done right, sir," .... was the Secretary's reply, and away he went to the Pasha. What the Pasha said, I do not know, but there was probably more cursing than usual that day in the grand palace of Tripoli, for the Mohammedans think the birth of a daughter a special judgment from God.

When a boy is born, there is great rejoicing.

Presents are sent to him, and the people call to congratulate the father, and the whole house is gay and joyous. After a few days a dainty dish called "Mughly" is made and sent around as a present to all of the relatives. It is made of pounded rice, and flavored with rich spices and sugar and put into little bowls, and almonds and other nuts sprinkled over the top. One of these little bowls is sent to each of the friends. But when a girl is born, there is no rejoicing, no giving of presents, and no making of the delicious "mughly."

Here come two little girls bringing earthen pots of milk. They are poor girls, daughters of two of our neighbors who are fellaheen or farmers. One has no shoes, and neither have stockings. They wear plain blue gowns, made of coarse cotton cloth, dyed with indigo, and rusty looking tarbooshes on their heads, and a little piece of dirty white muslin thrown over their heads as a veil to cover their faces with, when men come in sight. One is named Lebeeby and the other Lokunda, which means *Hotel.* They behave very well when they come here, as they have the fear of the big Khowadja before their eyes, but when they are at home running about, they often use dreadful language. Little boys and girls in Syria have some awful oaths which they constantly use. I suppose the poor things do not know the meaning of half the bad words they use. One of the most common is "Yilān Abook" "curse your father!" It is used everywhere and on every side by bad people, and the children use it constantly in their play. When the little girls come into our Schools and Seminaries, it is a long time before they will give up "abook"-ing. One of our friends in America is educating a nice little girl in the Beirût Seminary, and we asked the teacher about her a few days ago. The answer was, "She still lies and swears dreadfully, but she has greatly improved during the past two years, and we are encouraged about her."

Sometimes a boy will say to another Yilan abook, "Curse your father," and another will answer, Wa jiddak, "and your grandfather," and then they will call back and forth like cats and dogs. I saw a Moslem boy near my house standing by the corner to shield himself from the stones another boy was throwing, and shouting wa jid, jid, jid, jid, jidak, "and your great-great-great-great-grandfather," and away went the other boy, shouting as he ran, "and your "great-great-great-great gr-e-at," and I heard no more. And then there are a great many very naughty and vile words which the children use, which I cannot write, and yet we hear them every day. It is very hard to keep our children from learning them, as they talk Arabic better than we do, and often learn expressions which they do not know the meaning of. One of the most common habits is using the name of God in vain. The name of God is Allah, and "O God," is *Yullah*. Then there is *Wullah* and *Bismillah*, "In the name of God," *Hamdlillah*, "Praise to God," *Inshullah*, "If God will." The most awful oaths are Wullah and Billah. The people use *Yullah* at all times and on all occasions. The

Moslems at Prayer.

donkey-drivers and muleteers say *Yullah* when they drive their animals. Some years ago a good man from America, who fears God and would not take his name in vain was travelling in the Holy Land, and came on to Beirût. When he reached there, some one asked him if he had learned any Arabic during his journey. He said yes, he had learned *Bakhshish* for "a present," and *Yullah* for "go ahead." His friend asked him if he had used the latter word much on the way. He said certainly, he had used it all the way. His friend answered, Professor, you have been swearing all the way through the Holy Land. Of course he did not know it and meant no wrong. But it shows that such words are used so commonly in Syria that strangers do not think them bad language, and it also shows that travellers ought to be careful in using the words they learn of muleteers and sailors in Arab land.

In some parts of the country the little boys and girls swear so dreadfully that you can hardly bear to be with them. Especially among the Nusairîyeh, they think that nothing will be believed unless they add an oath. Dr. Post once rebuked an old Sheikh for using the word "Wullah" so often, and argued so earnestly about it that the man promised never to use it again. The old man a moment after repeated it. The doctor said, "will you now pledge me that you will not say 'Wullah' again? He replied, "Wullah, I will."

Sometimes a donkey-driver will get out of patience with his long-eared beast. The donkey will lie down with his load in a deep mud-hole, or among the sharp rocks. For a time the man will kick and strike him and throw stones at him, and finally when nothing else succeeds he will stand back, with his eyes glaring and his fist raised in the air, and scream out, "May Allah curse the beard of your grandfather!" I believe that the donkey always gets up after that,—that is, if the muleteer first takes off his load and then helps him, by pulling stoutly at his tail.

I told you that one of the girls who bring us milk, is named "*Lokunda*," or *Hotel*. She is a small specimen of a hotel, but provides us purer and sweeter cow's milk than many a six-storied hotel on Broadway would do. You will say that is a queer name for a girl, but if you stop and think about many of our English names you would think them queer too. Here in Syria, we have the house of Wolf, the house of "Stuffed Cabbage," Khowadji Leopard, the lady "Wolves," and one of our fellow villagers in Abeih where we spend the summer is Eman ed Deen "faith-of-religion," although he has neither faith nor religion.

Among the boys' names are Selim, Ibrahim, Moosa, Yakob, Ishoc, Mustafa, Hanna, Yusef, Ali, Saieed, Assaf, Giurgius, Faoor, and Abbas. I once met a boy at the Cedars of Lebanon, who was named Jidry, or "Small-Pox," because that disease was raging in the village when he was born. It is very common to name babies from what is happening in the world when they are born. A friend of mine in Tripoli had a daughter born when an American ship was in the harbor, so he called her America. When another daughter was born there was a Russian ship in port, so he called her Russia. There is a young woman in Sûk el Ghurb named Fetneh or Civil War, and her sister is Hada, or Peace. An old lady lately died in Beirût named Feinûs or Lantern. In the Beirût school are and have been girls named Pearl, Diamond, Morning Dawn, Dew, Rose, Only one, and Mary Flea. That girl America's full name was America Wolves, a curious name for a Syrian lamb!

Sometimes children are named, and if after a few years they are sick, the parents change their names and give them new ones, thinking that the first name did not agree with them. A Druze told me that he named his son in infancy *Asaad* (or happier) but he was sickly, so they changed his name to *Ahmed* (Praised) and after that he grew better! He has now become a Christian, and has resumed his first name Asaad.

I once visited a man in the village of Brummana who had six daughters, whom he named *Sun*, *Morning*, *Zephyr breeze*, *Jewelry*, *Agate*, and *Emerald*. I know girls named Star, Beauty, Sugar, One Eyed, and Christian Barbarian. Some of the names are beautiful, as Leila, Zarifeh, Lûlû, Selma, Luciya, Miriam and Fereedy.

All of the men are called Aboo-somebody; i.e. the father of somebody or something. Old Sheikh Hassein, whose house I am living in, is called Aboo Abbas, i.e. the father of Abbas, because his eldest son's name is Abbas. A young lad in the village, who is just about entering the Freshman class in the Beirût College, has been for years called Aboo Habeeb, or the father of Habeeb, when he has no children at all. Elias, the deacon of the church in Beirût was called Aboo Nasif for more than fifty years, and finally in his old age he married and had a son, whom he named Nasif, so that he got his name right after all. They often give young men such names, and if they have no children they call them by the name of the son they might have had. But they will not call a man Aboo Lûlû or Aboo Leila. If a man has a dozen daughters he will never be called from them. They are "nothing but girls." A queer old man in Ghurzûz once tried to name himself from his daughter Seleemeh, but whenever any one called him Aboo Seleemeh, all the fellaheen would laugh as if they would explode, and the boys would shout at him "there goes old Aboo Seleemeh," as if it was a grand joke.

The Moslems and Druzes generally give their children the old unmixed Arabic names, but the Maronites, the Greeks, and the Protestants often use European names. A young lady named Miss Mason was once a teacher in the Sidon Seminary, and spent the summer in the mountain village of Deir Mimas. One of the women of the village liked her name, and named her daughter "Miss Mason," and if you should go there you would hear the little urchins of Deir Mimas shouting Miss Mason! to a little blue-gowned and tarbooshed Arab girl.

What noise is that we hear down in the village,

under the great jowz (walnut) trees by the fountain? It rolls and gurgles and growls and bellows enough to frighten a whole village full of children. But the little Arab boys and girls are playing around, and the women are filling their jars at the fountain just as if nothing had happened. But it is a frightful noise for all that. It is the bellowing of the camels as their heavy loads are being put on. They are kneeling on the ground, with their long necks swaying and stretching around like boa constrictors. These camels are very useful animals, but I always like to see them at a distance, especially in the month of February, for at that time they get to be as "mad as a March hare." They are what the Arabs call "taish," and often bite men severely. In Hums one bit the whole top of a man's head off, and in Tripoli another bit a man's hand off. I once saw a camel "taish" in Beirût, and he was driving the whole town before him. Wherever he came, with his tongue hanging down and a foaming froth pouring from his mouth as he growled and bellowed through the streets, the people would leave their shops and stools and run in dismay. It was a frightful sight. I was riding down town, and on seeing the crowd, and the camel coming towards me, I put spurs to my horse and rode home.

When camels are tied together in a long caravan with a little mouse-colored donkey leading the van, ridden by a long-legged Bedawy, who sits half-asleep smoking his pipe, you would think them the tamest and most innocent creatures in the world, but when they fall into a panic, they are beyond all control. A few years ago a drove of camels was passing through the city of Damascus. The Arabs drive camels like sheep, hundreds and sometimes thousands in a flock, and they look awkward enough. When this drove entered the city, something frightened them, and they began to run. Just imagine a camel running! What a sight it must have been! Hundreds of them went through the narrow streets, knocking over men and women and donkeys, upsetting the shopkeepers, and spilling out their wares on the ground, and many persons were badly bruised. At length a carpenter saw them coming and put a timber across the street, which dammed up the infuriated tide of camels, and they dashed against one another until they were all wedged together, and thus their owners secured them.

In August, 1862, a famous Bedawin Chief, named Mohammed ed Dukhy, in Houran, east of the Jordan, rebelled against the Turkish Government. The Druzes joined him, and the Turks sent a small army against them. Mohammed had in his camp several thousand of the finest Arabian camels, and they were placed in a row behind his thousands of Arab and Druze horsemen. Behind the camels were the women, children, sheep, cattle and goats. When the Turkish army first opened fire with musketry, the camels made little disturbance, as they were used to hearing small arms, but when the Turkish Colonel gave orders to fire with cannon, "the ships of the desert" began to tremble. The artillery thundered, and the poor camels could stand it no longer. They were driven quite crazy with fright, and fled over the country in every direction in more than a Bull Run panic. Some went down towards the Sea of Galilee, others towards the swamps of Merom, and hundreds towards Banias, the ancient Cæsarea Philippi, and onwards to the West as far as Deir Mimas. Nothing could stop them. Their tongues were projecting, their eyes glaring, and on they went. The fellaheen along the roads caught them as they could, and sold them to their neighbors. Fine camels worth eighty dollars, were sold for four or five dollars a head, and in some villages the fat animals were butchered and sold for beef. Some of them came to Deir Mimas, where two of the missionaries lived. The Protestants said to the missionaries, " here are noble camels selling for five and ten dollars, shall we buy? Others are buying." " By no means," they told them. " They are stolen or strayed property, and you will repent it if you touch them." Others bought and feasted on camel steaks, and camel soup, and camel kibby, but the Protestants could not touch them. In a day or two, the cavalry of the Turks came scouring the country for the camels, as they were the spoils of war. Then the poor fellaheen were sorry enough that they had bought and eaten the camels, for the Turks made them pay back double the price of the beasts, and the Protestants found that "honesty was the best policy."

The camel is very sure footed, but cannot travel on muddy and slippery roads. The Arabs say " the camel never falls, but if he falls, he never gets up again." They carry long timbers over Lebanon, on the steep and rocky roads, the timber being balanced on the pack saddle, one end extending out on front, and the other behind. Sometimes the timber begins to swing about, and down the camel goes over the precipice and is dashed to pieces.

The Arabs say that a man once asked a camel, "What made your *neck* so crooked?" The camel answered, "My neck? Why did you ask about my neck? Is there anything else straight about me, that led you to notice my neck?" This has a meaning, which is, that when a man's habits are all bad, there is no use in talking about *one* of them.

Perhaps you will ask, did you ever eat camel's flesh? Certainly. We do not get it in Beirût, as camels are too expensive along the sea-coast to be used as food, but in the interior towns, like Hums and Hamath, which border on the desert or rather the great plains occupied by the ten thousands of the Bedawin, camel's meat is a common article in the market. They butcher fat camels, and young camel colts that have broken their legs, and sometimes their meat is as delicious as beef steak. But when they kill an old lean worn-out camel, that has been besmeared with pitch and tar for many years, and has been journeying under heavy loads from Aleppo to Damascus until he is what the Arabs call a "basket of bones," and then kill him to save his life, or rather his beef, the meat is not very delicate.

The Arab name for a camel is "Jemel" which

means *beauty!* They call him so perhaps because there is no beauty in him. You will read in books, that the camel is the "ship of the desert." He is very much like a ship, as he carries a heavy cargo over the ocean-like plains and "buraries" or wilds of the Syrian and Arabian deserts. He is also like a ship in making people sea-sick who ride on his back, and because he has a strong odor of tar and pitch like the hold of a ship, which sometimes you can perceive at a long distance.

PART II.

Perhaps you would like to take a ride with me some day, and visit some of the missionary stations in Syria. What will you ride? The horses are gentle, but you would feel safer on a donkey. Mules are sometimes good for riding, but I prefer to let them alone. I never rode a mule but once. I was at Hasbeiya, and wished to visit the bitumen wells. My horse was not in a condition to be ridden, so I took Monsûr's mule. It had only a jillal or pack saddle, and Monsûr made stirrups of rope for me. My companions had gone on in advance, and when I started, the mule was eager to overtake them. All went well until we approached the little stream which afterwards becomes the River Jordan. The ground was descending, and the road covered with loose stones. The rest of our party were crossing the stream and the mule thought he would trot and come up with them. I tried to hold him in with the rope halter, but he shook his head and dashed on. About the middle of the descent he stumbled and fell flat upon his nose. I went over his head upon my hands, but my feet were fast in the rope stirrups. Seeing that he was trying to get up, I tried to work myself back into the saddle, but I had only reached his head, when he sprang up. I was now in a curious and not very safe situation. The mule was trotting on and I was sitting on his head holding on to his ears, with my feet fast in the rope stirrups. A little Arab boy was passing with a tray of bread upon his head and I shouted to him for help. He was so amused to see a Khowadja with a hat, riding at that rate on a mule's head, that he began to roar with laughter and down went his tray on the ground and the Arab bread went rolling among the stones. It was a great mercy that I did not fall under the brute's feet, but I held on until he got the other side of the Jordan, when a man ran out from the mill and stopped him. Monsûr now led him by the halter and I reached the bitumen wells in safety.

You can mount your donkey and Harry will ride another, and I will ride my horse, and we will try a Syrian journey. As we cannot spare the time to go from Beirût to Tripoli by land, I have sent Ibrahim to take the animals along the shore, and we will go up by the French steamer, a fine large vessel called the "Ganges." We go down to the Kumruk or Custom House, and there a little Arab boat takes us out to the steamer. In rough weather it is very dangerous going out to the steamers, and sometimes little boats are capsized, but to-night there is no danger. You are now on the deck of the steamer. What a charming view of Beirût and Mount Lebanon. Far out on the point of the cape are the new buildings of the Syrian College, and next is the Prussian Hospital and then the Protestant Prussian Deaconesses Institution with 130 orphans and 80 paying pupils. There is the house of Dr. Thomson and Dr. Van Dyck and Dr. Post, and the Turkish Barracks, and Mrs. Mott's school, and our beautiful Church, with its clock tower, and you can hear the clock strike six. Then next to the Church is the Female Seminary with its 100 pupils, and the Steam Printing Press, where are printed so many books and Scriptures every year in the Arabic language. Those tall cypress trees are in the Mission Cemetery where Pliny Fisk, and Eli Smith, and Mr. Whiting, and a good many little children are buried. Near by are the houses of Dr. Bliss and Dr. Lewis and our house, and you can see mosques and minarets and domes and red-tiled roofs, and beautiful arched corridors and green trees in every direction. Do you see the beautiful purple tints on the Lebanon Mountains as the sun goes down? Is it not worth a long journey to see that lofty peak gilded and tinted with purple and pink and yellow as the sun sinks into the sea?

What a noise these boatmen make! I doubt whether you have ever heard such a screaming before.

Now you can imagine yourself going to sleep in

the state-room of this great steamer, and away we go. The anchor comes up clank, clank, as the great chain cable is wound up by the donkey engine, and now we move off silently and smoothly. In about five hours we have made the fifty miles, and down goes the anchor again in Tripoli harbor. At sunrise the Tripoli boatmen come around the steamer. We are two miles off from the shore and a rough north wind is blowing. Let us hurry up and get ashore before the wind increases to a gale, as these North winds are very fierce on the Syrian coast. Here comes Mustafa, an old boatman, and begs us to take his felûca. We look over the side of the steamer and see that his boat is large and clean and agree to take it for twelve piastres or fifty cents for all of us and our baggage. Then the other boatmen rush up and scream and curse and try to get us to take their boats, but we say nothing and push through them and climb down the steps to the boat. The white caps are rolling and the boat dances finely. Mustafa puts up a large three-cornered sail, Ali sits at the rudder, and with a stroke or two of the oars we turn around into the wind and away we dash towards the shore. The Meena (port) is before us, that white row of houses on the point; and back among the gardens is the city of Tripoli. In less than half an hour we reach the shore, but the surf is so high that we cannot go near the pier, so they make for the sand beach, and before we reach it, the boat strikes on a little bar and we stop. Out jump the boatmen, and porters come running half naked from the shore and each shouts to us to ride ashore on his shoulders. They can carry you and Harry with ease, but I am always careful how I sit on the shoulders of these rough fellows. There is Ibrahim on the shore with our animals, and two mules for the baggage. We shall take beds and bedsteads and cooking apparatus and provisions and a tent. Ibrahim has bought bread and potatoes and rice and semin (Arab butter) aud smead (farina) and candles, and a little sugar and salt, and other necessaries. We will accept Aunt Annie's invitation to breakfast, and then everything will be ready for a start.

What is the matter with those boys in that dark room? Are they on rockers? They keep swinging back and forth and screaming at the top of their voices all at once, and an old blind man sits on one side holding a long stick. They all sit on the floor and hold books or tin cards in their hands. This is a Moslem school, and the boys are learning to read and write. They all study aloud, and the old blind Sheikh knows their voices so well that when one stops studying, he perceives it, and reaches his long stick over that way until the boy begins again. When a boy comes up to him to recite, he has to shout louder than the rest, so that the Sheikh can distinguish his voice. There, two boys are fighting. The Sheikh cannot and will not have fighting in his school, and he calls them up to him. They begin to scream and kick and call for their mothers, but it is of no use. Sheikh Mohammed will have order. Lie down there you Mahmoud! Mahmoud lies down, and the Sheikh takes a stick like a bow with a cord to it, and winds the cord around his ankles. After twisting the cord as tight as possible, he takes his rod and beats Mahmoud on the soles of his feet, until the poor boy is almost black in the face with screaming and pain. Then he serves Saleh in the same way. This is the *bastinado* of which you have heard and read. When the Missionaries started common schools in Syria, the teachers used the bastinado without their knowledge, though we never allow anything of the kind. But the boys behave so badly and use such bad language to each other, that the teacher's patience is often quite exhausted. I heard of one school where the teacher invited a visitor to hear the boys recite, and then offered to whip the school all around from the biggest boy to the smallest, in order to show how well he governed the school! They do not use the alphabet in the Moslem schools. The boys begin with the Koran and learn the *words by sight*, without knowing the letters of which they are composed.

Here come two young men to meet us. Fine lads they are too. One is named Giurgius, and the other Leopold. When they were small boys, they once amused me very much. Mr. Yanni, who drew up his flag on the birth of Barbara, sent Giurgius his son, and Leopold his nephew to the school of an old man named Hanna Tooma. This old man always slept in the afternoon, and the boys did not study very well when he was asleep. I was once at Yanni's house when the boys came home from school.

They were in high glee. One of them said to his father, our teacher slept all the afternoon, and we appointed a committee of boys to fan him and keep the flies off while the rest went down into the court to play, and when he moved we all hushed up until he was sound asleep again. But when he *did* wake up, he took the big "Asa" and struck out right and left, and gave every boy in the school a flogging. The father asked, but why did he flog them all? Because he said he knew some of us had done wrong, and he was determined to hit the right one, so he flogged us all!

See the piles of fruit in the streets! Grapes and figs, watermelons and pomegranates, peaches, pears, lemons and bananas. At other seasons of the year you have oranges, *sweet lemons*, plums, and apricots. There is fresh fruit on the trees here every week in the year. Now we are passing a lemonade stand, where iced lemonade is sold for a cent a glass, cooled with snow from the summit of Mount Lebanon 9000 feet high. Grapes are about a cent a pound and figs the same, and in March you can buy five oranges or ten sweet lemons for a cent. Huge watermelons are about eight or ten cents a piece. We buy so many pounds of milk and oil and potatoes and charcoal. The prickly pear, or subire, is a delicious fruit, although covered with sharp barbed spines and thorns. It is full of hard large woody seeds, but the people are very fond of the fruit. Sheikh Nasif el Yazijy was a famous Arab poet and scholar, and a young man once brought him a poem to be corrected. He told him to call in a few days and get it. He came again and the Sheikh said to him. "Your poem is like the Missionary's prickly pear!" "The Missionary's prickly pear?" said the young poet. "What do you mean?" "Why said the Sheikh." Dr. —— a missionary, when he first came to Syria, had a dish of prickly pears set before him to eat. Not liking to eat the seeds, he began to pick them out, and when he had picked out all the seeds, there was nothing left! So your poem. You asked me to remove the errors, and I found that when I had taken out all the errors, there was nothing left."

It is about time for us to start. We will ride through the orange gardens and see the rich fruit bending the trees almost down to the ground. Steer your way carefully through the crowd of mules, pack horses, camels and asses loaded with boxes of fruit hastening down to the Meena for the steamer which goes North to-night.

Here is Yanni, with his happy smiling face coming out to meet us. We will dismount and greet him. He will kiss us on both cheeks and insist on our calling at his house. The children are glad to see you, and the Sitt Karîmeh asks, how are "the preserved of God?" that is, the *children.* Then the little tots come up to kiss my hand, and Im Antonius, the old grandmother, comes and greets us most kindly. It was not always so. She was once very hostile to the Missionaries. She thought that her son had done a dreadful deed when he became a Protestant.

Although she once loved him, she hated him and hated us. She used to fast, and make vows, and pray to the Virgin and the saints, and beat her breast in agony over her son. She had a brother and another son, who were like her, and they all persecuted Yanni. But he bore it patiently without an unkind word in return for all their abuse. At length the brother Ishoc was taken ill. Im Antonius brought the pictures and put them over his head and called the priests. He said, "Mother, take away these idols. Send away these priests. Tell my brother Antonius to come here, I want to ask his forgiveness." Yanni came. Ishoc said to him, "Brother, your kindness and patience have broken me down. You are right and I am wrong. I am going to die. Will you forgive me?" "Yes, and may God forgive and bless you too." "Then bring your Bible and read to me. Read about some *great* sinner who was saved." Yanni read about the dying thief on the cross. "Read it again! Ah, that is my case! I am the chief of sinners." Every day he kept Yanni reading and praying with him. He loved to talk about Jesus and at length died trusting in the Saviour! The uncle Michaiel, was also taken ill, and on his death-bed would have neither priest nor pictures, and declared to all the people that he trusted only in the Saviour whom Yanni had loved and served so well. After that Im Antonius was softened and now she loves to hear Yanni read the Bible and pray.

The servant is coming with sherbet and sweetmeats and Arabic coffee in little cups as large as an egg-shell. Did you notice how the marble floors shine! They are scrubbed and polished, and kept clean by the industrious women whom you see so gorgeously dressed now. These good ladies belong to the Akabir, or aristocracy of Tripoli, but they work most faithfully in their housekeeping duties. But alas, they can neither read nor write! And there is hardly a woman in this whole city of 16,000 people that can read or write! I once attended a company of invited guests at one of the wealthy houses in Tripoli, and there were thirty Tripolitan ladies in the large room, dressed in the most elegant style. I think you never saw such magnificence. They were dressed in silks and satins and velvets, embroidered with gold thread and pearls, and their arms and necks were loaded with gold bracelets and necklaces set with precious stones, and on their heads were wreaths of gold and silver work sparkling with diamonds, and fragrant with fresh orange blossoms and jessamine. Many of them were beautiful. But not one of them could read. The little boys and girls too are dressed in the same rich style among the wealthier classes, and they are now beginning to learn. Many of the little girls who were taught in Sada's school here thirteen years ago, are now heads of families, and know how to read the gospel.

Ibrahim comes in to say that we must hurry off if we would reach Halba to sleep to-night. So we bid Yanni's family good-bye. We tell them "Be Khaterkum." "By your pleasure," and they say

"Ma es Salameh" "with peace."—Then they say, "God smooth your way," and we answer, "Peace to your lives." Saieed the muleteer now says "Dih, Ooah," to his mules, and away we ride over the stony pavements and under the dark arches of the city, towards the East. We cross the bridge over the River Kadisha, go through the wheat and barley market, and out of the gate Tibbaneh, among the Moslems, Maronites, Bedawin, Nusairîyeh, Gypsies, and Greeks, who are buying and selling among the Hamath and Hums caravans.

Do you see those boys playing by the stone wall? They are catching scorpions. They put a little wax on a stick and thrust it into the holes in the wall, and the scorpions run their claws into the wax when they are easily drawn out, and the boys like to play with them. The sting of the scorpion is not deadly, but it is very painful, something like being stung by half a dozen hornets.

Here come a company of Greek priests, with the Greek bishop of Akkar. The priests are all Syrians but the bishop is from Greece, and knows but little Arabic. The priests are very ignorant, for they are generally chosen from among the lowest of the people.

When the former Greek Bishop died in Tripoli, in 1858, his dead body was dressed in cloth of gold, with a golden crown on his head, and then the corpse was set up in a chair in the midst of the Greek Church, with the face and hands uncovered so that all the people could see him. The fingers were all black and bloated, but the men, women and children crowded up to kiss them. When the body was taken from the city to Deir Keftin, three miles distant, the Greek mountaineers came down in a rabble to get the blessing from the corpse. And how do you think they got the blessing? They attacked the bearers and knocked off pieces of the coffin, and then carried off the pall and tore it in pieces, fighting for it like hungry wolves. A number of people were wounded. After the burial they dug up the earth for some distance around the tomb, and carried it off to be used as medicine. A little girl brought a piece of the bishop's handkerchief to my house, hearing that some one was ill, saying that if we would burn it and drink the ashes in water, we would be instantly cured.

The Syrians have a good many stories about their priests, which they laugh about, and yet they obey them, no matter how ignorant they are. Abû Selim in the Meena used to tell me this story: Once there was a priest who did not know how to count. This was a great trial to him, as the Greeks have so many fasts and feasts that it is necessary to count all the time or get into trouble. They have a long fast called *Soum el kebîr*, and it is sometimes nearly sixty days long. One year the fast commenced, and the priest had blundered so often that he went to the bishop and asked him to teach him some way to count the days to the Easter feast. The bishop told him it would be forty days, and gave him forty kernels of "hummus," or peas, telling him to put them into his pocket and throw one out every day, and when they were all gone, to proclaim the feast! This was a happy plan for the poor priest, and he went on faithfully throwing away one pea every day, until one day he went to a neighboring village. In crossing the stream he fell from his donkey into the mud, and his black robe was grievously soiled. The good woman of the house where he slept, told him to take off his robe and she would clean it in the night. So after he was asleep she arose and washed it clean, but found to her sorrow that she had destroyed the peas in the priest's pocket. Poor priest, said she, he has lost all his peas which he had for lunch on the road! But I will make it up to him. So she went to her earthen jar and took a big double handful of hummus and put them into the priest's pocket, and said no more. He went on his way and threw out a pea every morning for weeks and weeks. At length, some of his fellaheen heard that the feast had begun in another village, and told the Priest. Impossible, said he. My pocket is half full yet. Others came, and said, will you keep us fasting all the year? He only replied, look into my pocket. Are you wiser than the Bishop? At length some one went and told the Bishop that the priest was keeping his people fasting for twenty days after the time. And then the story leaked out, and the poor woman told how she had filled up the pocket, and the bishop saw that there was no use in trying to teach the man to count.

See the reapers in the field, and the women gleaning after them, just as Ruth did so many thousand years ago! On this side is a "lodge in a garden of cucumbers."

Now we come down upon the sea-shore again, and on our right is the great plain of Akkar, level as a floor, and covered with fields of Indian corn and cotton. Flocks and herds and Arab camps of black tents are scattered over it. Here is a shepherd-boy playing on his "zimmara" or pipe, made of two reeds tied together and perforated. He plays on it hour after hour and day after day, as he leads his sheep and goats or cattle along the plain or over the mountains. You do not like it much, any more than he would like a melodeon or a piano. When King David was a shepherd-boy he played on such a pipe as this as he wandered over the mountains of Judea.

Now we turn away from the sea and go eastward to Halba. Before long we cross the river Arka on a narrow stone bridge, and pass a high hill called "Tel Arka." Here the Arkites lived, who are mentioned in Genesis x: 17. That was four thousand two hundred years ago. What a chain of villages skirt this plain! The people build their villages on the hills for protection and health, but go down to plough and sow and feed their flocks to the rich level plain. Now we cross a little stream of water, and look up the ravine, and there is Ishoc's house perched on the side of the hill opposite Halba. Ishoc and his wife Im Hanna, come out to meet us, and he helps us pitch the tent by the great fig tree near his house. We unroll the tent, splice the tent-pole, open the bag of tent pins, get the mallet, and although the wind is blowing hard, we will drive the pegs so deep that there will be no danger of its blowing over.

Abû Hanna, or Ishoc, is a noble christian man, one of the best men in Syria. He has suffered very much for Christ's sake. The Greeks in the village on the hill have tried to poison him. They hired Nusairy Mughlajees to shoot him. They cut down his trees at night, and pulled up his plantations of vegetables. They came at night and tore up the roof of his house, and shot through at him but did not hit him. But the Mohammedan Begs over there always help him, because he is an honest man, and aids them in their business and accounts. When the Greeks began to persecute him, they told him to fire a gun whenever they came about his house, and they would come over and fight for him. They even offered to go up and burn the Greek village and put an end to these persecutions. But Ishoc would not let them. He said, "Mohammed Beg, you know I am a Christian, not like these Greeks who lie and steal and kill, but I follow the words of our Lord Jesus Christ, who said, 'Love your enemies,' and I do not wish to injure one of them." The Begs were astonished at this, and went away, urging him if there were any more trouble at night to fire his gun and they would come over from Halba at once.

I love this good man Ishoc. His pure life, his patience and gentleness have preached to these wild people in Akkar, more than all the sermons of the missionaries.

Would you like to see Im Hanna make bread for our supper? That hole in the ground, lined with plaster, is the oven, and the flames are pouring out. They heat it with thorns and thistles. She sits by the oven with a flat stone at her side, patting the lumps of dough into thin cakes like wafers as large as the brim of your straw hat. Now the fire is burning out and the coals are left at the bottom of the oven, as if they were in the bottom of a barrel. She takes one thin wafer on her hand and sticks it on the smooth side of the oven, and as it bakes it curls up, but before it drops off into the coals, she pulls it out quickly and puts another in its place. How sweet and fresh the bread is! It is made of Indian corn. She calls it "khubs dura." Abu Hanna says that we must eat supper with them to-night. They are plain fellaheen, and have neither tables, chairs, knives nor forks. They have a few wooden spoons, and a few plates. But hungry travellers and warm-hearted friendship will make the plainest food sweet and pleasant.

Supper is ready now, and we will go around to Abû Hanna's house for he has come to tell us that "all things are ready." The house is one low room, about sixteen by twenty feet. The ceiling you see is of logs smoked black and shining as if they had been varnished. Above the logs are flat stones and thorns, on which earth is piled a foot deep. In the winter this earth is rolled down with a heavy stone roller to keep out the rain. In many of the houses the family, cattle, sheep, calves and horses sleep in the same room. The family sleep in the elevated part of the room along the edge of which is a trough into which they put the barley for the animals. This is the "medhwad" or manger, such as the infant Jesus was laid in. We will now accept Im Hanna's kind invitation to supper. The plates are all on a small tray on a mat in the middle of the floor, and there are four piles of bread around the edge. There is one cup of water for us all to drink from, and each one has a wooden spoon. But Abû Hanna, you will see, prefers to eat without a spoon. After the blessing is asked in Arabic, Abû Hanna says, "tefudduloo," which means help yourselves. Here is kibby, and camel stew, and Esau's pottage, and olives, and rice, and figs cooked in dibbs, and chicken boiled to pieces, and white fresh cheese, and curdled milk, and fried eggs.

Kibby is the Arab plum pudding and mince pie and roast beef all in one. It is made by pounding meat in a mortar with wheat, until both are mixed into a soft pulp and then dressed with nuts and onions and butter, and baked or roasted in cakes over the fire. Dr. Thomson thinks that this dish is alluded to in Prov. 27: 22, "Though thou shouldest bray a fool in a mortar among wheat with a pestle, yet will not his foolishness depart from him." That is, put the fool into Im Hanna's stone mortar with wheat and pound him into kibby, and he would still remain a fool! It takes something besides pounding to get the folly out of foolish men.

You see there are no separate plates for us. We all help ourselves from the various dishes as we prefer. Abû Hanna wants you to try the "mejeddara," made of "oddis." It is like thick pea soup, but with a peculiar flavor. This is what Jacob made the pottage of, when he tempted Esau and bought his birthright. I hope you will, like it, but I do not. After seventeen years of trying, I am not able to enjoy it, but Harry will eat all he can get, and the little Arab children revel in it. You make poor work with that huge wooden spoon. You had better try Abû Hanna's way of eating. Many better men than any of us have eaten in that way, and I suppose our Saviour and his disciples ate as Abû Hanna eats. He tears off a small piece of the thin wafer-like bread, doubles it into a kind of three cornered spoon, dips it into the rice, or picks up a piece of kibby with it, and then eats it down, spoon and all! Im Hanna says I am afraid those little boys do not like our food, so she makes a spoon and dips up a nice morsel of the chicken, and comes to you and says "minshan khatri," for my sake, eat this, and you open your mouth and she puts it in. That is the way our Saviour dipped the "sop" and put it into the mouth of Judas Iscariot to show the disciples which one it was. Giving the sop was a common act, and I have no doubt Jesus had often given it to John and Peter and the other disciples, as a kindly act, when they were eating together.

Im Hanna is fixing the lamp. It is a little earthen saucer having a lip on one side, with the wick hanging over. The wick just began to smoke and she poured in more olive oil, and it burns brightly again. Do you remember what the prophet Isaiah (42: 3) said, "a bruised reed shall he not break, and smoking flax shall he not quench." This is quoted in Matt. 12 of our Lord Jesus. The word flax means *wick*. It is "fetileh" in Arabic, and this is just what Im Hanna has been doing. She saw the wick smoking and flickering, and instead of blowing it out and quenching it, she brought the oil flask, and gently poured in the clear olive oil and you saw how quickly the flame revived. So our Lord would have us learn from Him. When the flame of our faith and love is almost dead and nothing remains but the smoking flickering wick, He does not quench it, and deal harshly with us, but he comes in all gentleness and love and pours in the oil of His grace, and then our faith revives and we live again.

PART III.

Here come some little Bedawin gypsy children. One is laughing at my hat. He never saw one before and he calls me "Abû Suttle," the "father of a Pail," and wonders why I carry a pail on my head. The people love to use the word Abû, [father] or Im, [mother]. They call a musquito Abû Fas, the father of an axe. The centipede is "Im Arbă wa Arb-ain,"

" The mother of forty-four legs." The Arabic poet Hariri calls a *table* the " father of assembling ;" *bread*, the " father of pleasantness ; a *pie*, " the mother of joyfulness," *salt*, the father of help," *soap* the " father of softness ;" Death is called by the Arab poets, " Father of the Living," because all the living are subject to him.

After breakfast we will start for Safita. You see that snow-white dome on the hill-top! and another on the next hill under that huge oak tree, and then another and another. These are called Nebi or Ziarat or Wely. Each one contains one or more tombs of Nusairy saints or sheikhs, and the poor women visit them and burn lamps and make vows to the saints who they think live in them. They know nothing of Christ, and when they feel sad and troubled and want comfort they enter the little room under the white dome, and there they call, " O Jāfar et Tîyyar hear me! O Sheikh Hassan hear me!"

This is just as the old Canaanite women used to go up and worship on every high hill, and under every green tree, thousands of years ago, and these poor Nusairîyeh are thought to be the descendants of the old Canaanites.

Here come men on horseback to visit that " ziyara." Up they go to the little room with the white dome, and all dismount. The old sheikh who has charge, comes out to meet them. They are pilgrims and have to make vows and bring offerings. One had a sick son and he once vowed that if his son got well he would bring a sheep and a bushel of wheat as an offering to this shrine. So there is the sheep on one of the horses, and that mule is bringing the wheat. If the old sheikh has many such visitors he will grow rich. Some of them do. And yet the people laugh at these holy places, and tell some strange stories about them. One of the stories is as follows :—

Once upon a time there was a great Sheikh Ali, a holy man, who kept a holy tomb of an ancient prophet. The tomb was on a hill under a big oak tree, and the white dome could be seen for miles around. Lamps were kept burning day and night in the tomb, and if any one extinguished them, they were miraculously lighted again. Men with sore eyes came to visit it and were cured. The earth around the tomb was carried off to be used as medicine. Women came and tied old rags on the limbs of the tree, as vows to the wonderful prophet. Nobody knew the name of the prophet, but the tomb was called "Kobr en Nebi," or "tomb of the prophet." A green cloth was spread over the tomb under the dome, and incense was sold by the sheikh to those who wished to heal their sick, or drive out evil spirits from their houses. Pilgrims came from afar to visit the holy place, and its fame extended over all the land. Sheikh Ali was becoming a rich man, and all the pilgrims kissed his hand and begged his blessing. Now Sheikh Ali had a faithful servant named Mohammed, who had served him long and well. But Mohammed was weary of living in one place, and asked permission to go and seek his fortune in distant parts. So Sheikh Ali gave him his blessing and presented him with a donkey, which he had for many years, that he might ride when tired of walking. Then Mohammed set out on his journey. He went through cities and towns and villages, and at last came out on the mountains east of the Jordan in a desert place. No village or house was in sight and night came on. Tired, hungy and discouraged poor Mohammed lay down by his donkey on a great pile of stones and fell asleep. In the morning he awoke,.and alas his donkey was dead. He was in despair, but his kindly nature would not let the poor brute lie there to be devoured by jackals and vultures, so he piled a mound of stones over its body and sat down to weep.

While he was weeping, a wealthy Hajji or pilgrim came along, on his return from Mecca. He was surprised to see a man alone in this wilderness, and asked him why he was weeping? Mohammed replied, O Hajji, I have found the tomb of a holy prophet, and I have vowed to be its keeper, but I am in great need. The Hajji thanked him for the news, and dismounted to visit the holy place, and gave Mohammed a rich present. After he had gone Mohammed hastened to the nearest village and bought provisions and then returned to his holy prophet's tomb. The Hajji spread the news, and pilgrms thronged to the spot with rich presents and offerings. As money came in Mohammed brought masons and built a costly tomb with a tall white dome that could be seen across the Jordan. He lived in a little room by the tomb, and soon the miraculous lights began to appear in the tomb at night, which Mohammed had kindled when no one was near. He increased in fame and wealth, and the Prophet's tomb became one of the great shrines of the land.

At length Sheikh Ali heard of the fame of the new holy place in the desert, and as his own visitors began to fall off, decided to go himself and gain the merit of a visit to the tomb of that famous prophet. When he arrived there with his rich presents of green cloth, incense and money, he bowed in silence to pray towards Mecca, when suddenly he recognized in the holy keeper of the tomb, his old servant Mohammed. "Salam alaykoom" said Sheikh Ali. "Alaykoom es Salam," replied Mohammed. When he asked him how he came here, and how he found this tomb, Mohammed replied, this "tomb is a great "sirr" or mystery, and I am forbidden to utter the secret." "But you *must* tell *me*," said Sheikh "Ali, for I am a father to you." Mohammed refused and Ali insisted, until at length Mohammed said, "my honored Sheikh, you remember having given me a donkey. It was a faithful donkey, and when it died I buried it. This is the tomb of that donkey!" "Mashallah! Mashallah!" said Sheikh Ali. The will of Allah be done! Then they ate and drank together, and renewed the memory of their former life, and then Sheikh Mohammed said to Sheikh Ali, "My master, as I have told you the 'sirr' of my prophet's tomb, I wish to know the secret of yours." "Impossible," said Ali, "for that is one of the ancient mysteries, too sacred to be mentioned by mortal lips." "But you *must* tell me, even as I have told you." At length the old Sheikh Ali stroked his snowy beard, adjusted his white turban, and whispered to Mohammed, "and my holy place is the *tomb of that donkey's father!*" "Mashallah," said Mohammed, "may Allah bless the beard of the holy donkeys!"

The people tell this story, which shows, that they ridicule and despise their holy places, and yet are too superstitious to give them up. The great thing with the sheiks who keep them is the *piastres* they make from the visitors.

As we go up the hill to Safita, you see the tall, beautiful Burj, or Crusader's tower, built as were many of the castles and towers whose ruins you see on the hills about here, by the French and English eight hundred years ago, to keep down the wild and rebellious people. The Protestant Church is at the east. These are two watch towers. One was built for warriors who fought with sword and spear, and the other for the simple warfare of the gospel. You may depend upon it, we shall have a welcome here. It is nearly sunset, and the people are coming in from their fields and pastures and vineyards. Daûd and Nicola, and Michaiel, Soleyman, Ibrahim, and Yusef, Miriam, Raheel and Nejmy and crowds of others with a throng of little ragged boys and girls, come running to greet us. "Praise God we have seen you in peace!" "Ehelan wa Sehelan," "Welcome and Welcome!" "Be preferred!" "Honor us with your presence!" "How is your state?"

Inshallah you are all well!" "How are those you left behind?" How are the preserved of God?" "I hope you are not wearied with the long ride, this hot day?" "From whence have you come, in peace?" "What happy day is this to Safita!" and we answer as fast as we can, and dismount and pitch the tent in front of the church door, in the little plot of ground next to the houses of some of the brethren. The church is built of cream colored limestone, the same color as the great Burj, and contrasts strongly with the houses of the people. Did you ever see such houses? They are hardly high enough to stand up in, and are built of roundish boulders of black trap-rock, without lime, and look as if the least jar would tumble them all down. Each house has but one room, and here the cattle, goats and donkeys all sleep in the same room. The people are poorer than any fellaheen (peasants) you ever saw. There is not a chair or table in the village, unless the Beshoor family have them. They are the only wealthy people here, and in years past they have oppressed the Protestants in the most cruel manner. Beshoor had a lawsuit with the people about the land of the village. It belonged to them, and he wanted it. So he brought Government horsemen and drove them off their lands and took the crops himself. They thought they would try a new way to get justice. The Government officials were all bribed, so there was no hope there. So they decided to turn Protestants and get aid in that way. They did not know what the Protestant religion was, but had some idea that it would help them. Down they went to Tripoli to the missionaries with a list of three hundred persons who wanted to become Angliz or Protestants. The people sometimes call us Angliz, or English, others call us "Boostrant" or "Brostant," but the common name is "Injiliyeen" or people of the Enjeel, or Evangel, that is, the Evangelicals.

Dr. Post and your Uncle Samuel came up to Safita to look into the matter. They found the people grossly ignorant and living like cattle, calling themselves Protestants and knowing nothing of the gospel. So they sent a teacher and began to teach them. When the people found that the missionaries did not come to distribute money, some of them went back to the Greeks. But others said no; this new religion is more than we expected. The more we hear, the more we like it. We shall live and die Protestants. Then Beit Beshoor became alarmed. They said, if this people get a school, have a teacher, and read the Bible, we cannot oppress them. They must be kept down in ignorance. So they began in earnest. The Protestants were arrested and dragged off to Duraikish to prison. Women and children were beaten. Brutal horsemen were quartered on their houses. That means, that a rough fellow, armed with pistols and a sword came to the house of Abû Asaad, and stayed two weeks. He made them cook chickens, and bring eggs and bread and everything he wanted every day, and bring barley for his horse. The poor man had no barley and had to buy, and the Greeks would make him pay double price for it. When he could get no more he was beaten and his wife insulted, and so it was in almost every Protestant house. They began to love the Gospel, and the men who knew how to read, would meet to read and pray together. One evening, all the Protestants met together in one of the houses. Their sufferings were very great. Their winter stores had been plundered, their olives gathered by Beit Beshoor, and they talked and prayed over their trouble. It was a dark, cold, rainy night, and the wind blew a gale. While they were talking together, a man came rushing in crying, run for your lives! the horsemen are here! Before they could get out, a squad of wild looking wretches were at the door. The men fled, carrying the larger children and the women carrying the babies, and off they went into the wilderness in the storm and darkness. Some women were seized and tied by ropes around their waists, to the horsemen, and marched off for miles to prison. The men who were caught were put in chains. Some time later they got back home again. But they would not give up the Gospel. Beshoor sent men who told them they could have peace if they would only go back to the Greek Church. But he offered peace quite too late. They had now learned to love the Gospel, and it was worth more to them than all the world beside. One night they were assembled in a little low black house, when some men came to the door and threw in burning bundles of straw and then shut the door, so that they were almost stifled with the smoke. They sent a messenger to Beirût. The case was laid before the Pasha, and he telegraphed to have the Protestants let alone. But Beshoor cared for nothing. A Nusairy was hired to shoot Abû Asaad, the leading Protestant. His house was visited in the daytime, and the man saw where Abû Asaad's bed was placed. In the night he came stealthily upon the roof, dug a hole through, and fired three bullets at the spot. But see how God protects his people! That evening Abû Asaad said to his wife; the floor is getting damp in the corner, let us remove the bed and mat to the other side. They did so, and when the man fired, the bullets went into the ground just where Abû Asaad had slept the night before! He ran out and saw the assassins and recognized one of them as the servant of Beshoor's son. The next day he complained to the Government and they refused to hear him because he did not bring witnesses!

But the poor people would not give up. Every day they went to their fields, carrying their Testaments in their girdles and at noontime would read and find comfort. Their children were half naked and half starved. When word reached Beirût, the native Protestant women met together and collected several hundred piastres (a piastre is four cents) for the women and girls of Safita. They made up a bale of clothing, and sent with it a very touching and kind letter, telling their poor persecuted sisters to bear their trials in patience, and put all their trust in the Lord Jesus. That aid, together with the con-

Safita.

tributions made by the missionaries and others in Beirût, gave them some relief, and the kind words of sympathy strengthened their hearts. The school was kept up amid all these troubles. One of the boys was taught in Abeih Seminary, and two of the girls were sent to the Beirût Female Seminary.

You would have been amused to see those girls when they first reached Beirût. They walked barefoot from Safita down to Tripoli, about forty miles, and then Uncle S. took them on to Beirût. He bought shoes for them, and hired two little donkeys for them to ride, but they preferred to walk a part of the way, and would carry their shoes in their hands and run along the sandy beach in the surf, far ahead of the animals. I rode out to meet them, and they were a sorry sight to see. Uncle S. rode a forlorn-looking horse, and two ragged men from Safita walked by his side, followed by two ragged fat-faced girls riding on little donkeys. The girls were almost bewildered at the city sights and scenes. Soon we met a carriage, and they were so frightened that they turned pale, and their donkeys were almost paralyzed with fear. One of the little girls, when asked if she knew what that was, said it was a mill walking.

The first few days in school they were so homesick for Safita that they ran away several times. They could not bear to be washed and combed and sent to the Turkish bath, but wanted to come back here among the goats and calves and donkeys. One night they went to their room and cried aloud. Rufka, the teacher, asked them what they wanted?

They said, pointing to the white beds, "We don't like these white things to sleep on. We don't want to stay here. There are no calves and donkeys, and the room is so light and cold!" The people here in Safita think that the cattle help to keep the room warm. In the daytime they complained of being tired of sitting on the seats to study, and wished to *stand up and rest.* One was 11 and the other 12 years old, and that was in 1865.

One of them, Raheel, fell sick after a time, and was much troubled about her sins. Her teacher Sara, who slept near her, overheard her praying and saying, "Oh Lord Jesus, do give me a new heart! I am a poor sinner. Do you suppose that because I am from Safita, you cannot give me a new heart? O Lord, I *know* you can. Do have mercy on me!"

Who are those clean and well dressed persons coming out of the church? Our dear brother Yusef Ahtíyeh, the native preacher, and his wife Hadla, and Miriam, the teacher of the girls' school. Yusef is one of the most refined and lovely young men in Syria. What a clear eye he has, and what a pleasant face! He too has borne much for his Master. In 1865, when he left the Greek Church, he was living with his brother in Beirût. His brother turned him out of the house at night, with neither bed nor clothing. He came to my house and staid with me some time. He said it was hard to be driven out by his brother and mother, but he could bear anything for Christ's sake. Said he, "I can bear cursing and beating and the loss of property. But my mother is weeping and wailing over me. She thinks I am a heretic and am lost forever. Oh, it is hard to bear, the 'persecution of tears!'" But the Lord gave him grace to bear it, and he is now the happy spiritual guide of this large Protestant community, and the Nusairy Sheikhs look up to him with respect, while that persecuting brother of his is poverty-stricken and sick, and can hardly get bread for his children.

Miriam, the teacher, is a heroine. Her parents were Greeks, but sent her to school to learn to read. She learned in a short time to read the New Testament, and to love it, and to keep the Sabbath day holy. The keeping of the Sabbath was something new in Safita. The Nusairîyeh have no holy day at all, and the Greeks have so many that they keep none of them. They work and buy and sell and travel on the Sabbath as on other days, and think far more of certain saint's days than of the Sabbath. When Miriam was only seven years old, her father said to her one Sabbath morning, "go with me to the hursh (forest) to get a donkey load of wood." She replied, "my father, I cannot go, it is not right, for it is God's day." The father went without her, and while cutting wood, his donkey strayed away, and he had to search through the mountains for hours, so that he did not reach home until twelve o'clock at night, and then without any wood. He said he should not go for wood on Sunday any more.

But a few Sundays after, it was the olive season, and Miriam's mother told her to go out with the women and girls to gather olives. They had been at work during the week, and the mother thought Miriam ought to go on Sunday with the rest. But Miriam said, "don't you remember father's losing the donkey, and what he said about it? I cannot go." "Then," said her mother, "if you will not work, you shall not eat." "Very well, ya imme, I will not eat. If I keep the Lord's day, He will keep me." Away went the mother to the olive orchard, and Miriam went to the preaching and the Sunday School. At evening, when the family all came home, Miriam read in her New Testament and went to bed without her supper. The next morning she said, "Mother, now I am ready to gather olives. Didn't I tell you the Lord would keep me?"

After this Miriam's father became a Protestant, and allowed the missionaries to send her to the Seminary in Sidon, where she was the best girl in the school. When she went home in the vacation in 1869, new persecutions were stirred up against the Protestants. The Greek Bishop, with a crowd of priests and a body of armed horsemen, came to the village, to compel all the Protestants to turn back to the old religion. The armed men went to the Protestant houses and seized men and women and dragged them to the great Burj, in which is the Greek church. Miriam's father and mother were greatly terrified and went back with them to the Greeks. They then called for Miriam. "Never," said she to the Bishop, "I will never worship pictures and pray to saints again. You may cut me in pieces, but I will not stir one step with them." The old Bishop turned back, and left her to herself. Near by was a man named Abû Isbir, who was so frightened that he said, "yes, I will go back, don't strike me!" But his wife, Im Isbir, was not willing to give up. She rebuked her husband and took hold of his arm, and actually dragged him back to his house, to save him the shame of having denied the Gospel. He stood firm, and afterwards united with the Church.

Here comes Im Isbir. Poor woman, she is a widow now. Her husband died and left her with these little children, and last night her valuable cow died, and she is in great distress. Yusef, the preacher, says she is the most needy person in Safita. You would think so from the ragged appearance of the children. They are like the children in Eastern Turkey, whom Mr. Williams of Mardin used to describe, whose garments were so ragged and tattered that there was hardly cloth enough to *make borders for the holes!* They dig up roots in the fields for food, and now and then the neighbors give them a little of their coarse corn bread. The Greeks tell her to turn back to them and they will help her, but she says, "when one has found the light, can she turn back into the darkness again?" Yusef wishes us to walk in and sit down, as the people are anxious to see us. He lives in the church from necessity. He cannot get a house in the village, excepting these dark cavern-like rooms with damp floors, and so the missionaries told him to occupy one half of the church room. A curtain divides it into two rooms, and on Sunday the curtain is drawn, his things are piled up on one side, and the women and girls sit in that part, while the men and boys sit on the other side. All sit on mats on the floor. Is that cradle hanging from the ring in the arch between the two rooms, kept there on Sunday? Yes, and when I preached here last June, Yusef's baby was swinging there during the whole service. One of the women kept it swinging gently, by pulling a cord, which hung down from it. It did not disturb the meeting at all. No one noticed it. They have calves and cows, donkeys and goats in their own houses at night, and sleep sweetly enough, so that the swinging of a hanging cradle in the inside of the church is not thought to be at all improper.

Do you see that shelf on the wall? It reminds me of a little girl named Miriam who once came to your Aunt Annie in Deir Mimas to ask about the Sidon school, whither she was going in a few weeks. She told Miriam that she would have to be thoroughly washed and combed every day, and would sleep on a *bedstead*. Then Miriam asked permission to see a bedstead, as she did not know what it could be. The next night, about midnight, Miriam's mother heard something drop heavily on the floor, and then a child crying. She went across the room, and there was Miriam sitting on the mat. "What is the matter, Miriam?" she asked. Miriam said, "mother, the Sit told me I was to sleep on a bedstead in Sidon school, and I thought I would practice beforehand, so I tried to sleep on the shelf, and tumbled off in my sleep!"

Abû Asaad says the Nusairy Sheikh who was arrested some months ago has been poisoned. Poisoning used to be very common in Syria. If we should call at the house of a Nusairy, and he brought coffee for us to drink, he would take a sip himself out of the cup before giving it to us, to show that it was not poisoned. Once Uncle S. and Aunt A. were invited out to dine in Hums at the house of the deacon of the church. His mother is an ignorant woman, and had often threatened to kill him. When they had eaten, they suddenly were taken ill, and suffered much from the effects of it. It was found that the mother had put poison into the food, intending to kill her son, the missionaries, and the other invited guests, but through the mercy of God none of them were seriously injured.

Michaiel says that they have only half a crop of corn this year, as the *locusts* devoured the other half in the spring. You remember I sent you some locusts' wings once, in a letter. When they appear in the land, the Pashas and Mudirs and Kaimakams give orders to the people to go out and gather the eggs of the locusts as soon as they begin to settle down to bury themselves in the earth. The body of the female locust is like the spawn of a fish, filled with one mass of eggs. Each man is obliged to bring so many ounces of these eggs to the Pasha and have them weighed and then burned. A tailor of Beirût brought a bag of them, and as it was late, put them in his shop for the night and went home. He was unwell for a few days and when he went to his shop again, opened the door, and thousands of little black hopping creatures, like imps, came like a cloud into his face. They had hatched out in his absence.

This is a fearful land for lying; in these mountains around us, you cannot depend on a word you hear. The people say that in the beginning of the world, Satan came down to the earth with seven bags of lies, which he intended to distribute in the seven kingdoms of the earth. The first night after he reached the earth he slept in Syria, and opened one of the bags, letting the lies loose in the land. But while he was asleep, some one came and opened all the other bags! so that Syria got more than her share!

An old man in Beirût once said, "Sir, you must be careful what you believe, and whom you trust in this country. If there are twenty-four inches of hypocrisy in the world, twenty-three are in Syria." This man was a native of great experience. I think he was rather severe on his countrymen. Yet the people have had a hard training. The Nusairîyeh all lie. They do not even pretend to tell the truth. The Druze religion teaches the people that it is right to lie to all except Druzes. The Moslems are better than either of these two classes, but they lie without a blush, and you must be very careful how you believe them.

Among the Maronite and Greek sects, their

priests tell the people that they can forgive sins. When a man lies or steals or does anything else that is wicked, he pays a few piastres to the priest, who gives him what they call absolution or forgiveness. So the people can do what they please without fear, as the priest is ready to forgive them for money. These sects call themselves Christian, but there is very little of Christianity among them. A Greek in Tripoli once told me that there was not a man in the Greek church in Tripoli who would not lie, excepting *one* of the priests.

Leaving Safita, we will go back on a different road, crossing directly to the sea-shore, and then along the coast to Tripoli. Here is a little abject village, and the people look as abject as the village. Their neighbors laugh at them for their stupidity, and tell the following story: They have no wells in the village, and the little fountain is not sufficient for their cattle, so they water them from the Ramet or pool, which is filled by the rains and lasts nearly all summer. One year the water in the Ramet began to fail, and there was a quarrel between the two quarters of the village, as to which part should have the first right to the water. Finally they decided to divide the pool into two parts, by making a fence of poles across the middle of it. This worked very well. One part watered their cattle on one side and the other part on the other side. But one night there was a great riot in the village. Some of the men from the north side saw a south-sider dipping up water from the north side and pouring it over the fence into the other part of the pool. Of course this made no difference, as the fence was nothing but open lattice work, but the people were too stupid to see that, so they fought and bruised one another for a long time.

In another village, *Aaleih*, near Beirût, the people were formerly so stupid that the Arabs say that once when the clouds came up the mountains and settled like a bank of fog under the cliff on which their village is built, they thought it was the sea, and went to fish in the clouds!

So you see the Syrians are as fond of humorous stories as other people.

PART IV.

But here we are coming upon a gypsy camp. The Arabs call them Nowar, and you will find that the Arab women of the villages are careful to keep an eye on their little children when the gypsies are around. They often steal children in the towns and cities, when they can find them straying away from home at dusk, and then sell them as servants in Moslem families. Last year we were all greatly interested in a story of this kind, which I know you will be glad to hear.

After the terrible massacre in Damascus in 1860, thousands of the Greek and Greek Catholic families migrated to Beirût, and among them was a man named Khalil Ferah, who escaped the fire and sword with his wife and his little daughter Zahidy. I remember well how we were startled one evening in 1862, by hearing a crier going through the streets, "child lost! girl lost!" The next day he came around again, "child lost!" There was great excitement about it. The poor father and mother went almost frantic. Little Zahidy, who was then about six years old, was coming home from school with other girls in the afternoon, and they said a man came along with a sack on his back, and told Zahidy that her mother had sent him to buy her some sugar plums and then take her home, and she went away with him. It is supposed that he decoyed her away to some by-road and then put her into the great sack, and carried her off to the Arabs or the gypsies.

The poor father left no means untried to find her. He wrote to Damascus, Alexandria, and Aleppo, describing the child and begged his friends everywhere to watch for her, and send him word if they found her. There was one mark on the child, which, he said, would be certain to distinguish her. When she was a baby, and nursing at her mother's breast, her mother upset a little cup of scalding hot coffee upon the child's breast, which burned it to a blister, leaving a scar which could not be removed. This sign the father described, and his friends aided him in trying to find the little girl. They went to the encampments of the gypsies and looked at all the children, but all in vain. The father journeyed by land and by sea. Hearing of a little girl in Aleppo who could not give an account of herself, he went there, but it was not his child. Then he went to Damascus and Alexandria, and at length hearing that a French Countess in Marseilles had a little Syrian orphan girl whose parents were not known, he sent to Marseilles and examined the girl, but she was *not his child.* Months and years passed on, but the father never ceased to speak and think of that little lost girl. The mother too was almost distracted.

At length light came. Nine years had passed away, and the Beirût people had almost forgotten the story of the lost Damascene girl. Your uncle S. and your Aunt A. were sittin ; in their house one day, in Tripoli, when Tannoos, the boy, brought word that a man and woman from Beirût wished to see them. They came in and introduced themselves. They were Khalil, the father of the little lost girl, and his sister, who had heard that Zahidy was in Tripoli, and had come to search for her. The mother was not able to leave home.

It seems that a native physician in Tripoli, named Sheikh Aiub el Hashim, was an old friend of the father and had known the family and all the circumstances of the little girl's disappearance, and for years he had been looking for her. At length he was called one day to attend a sick servant girl in the family of a Moslem named Syed Abdullah. The poor girl was ill from having been beaten in a cruel manner by the Moslem. Her face and arms were tattooed in the Bedawin style, and she told him that she was a Bedawin girl, and had been living here for

Women Weeping at the Tomb.

some years, and her name was Khodra. While examining the bruises on her body, he observed a peculiar scar on her breast. He was startled. He looked again. It was precisely the scar that his friend had so often described to him. From her age, her features, her complexion and all, he felt sure that she was the lost child. He said nothing, but went home and wrote all about it to the father in Beirût. He hastened to Tripoli bringing his sister, as he being a man, could not be admitted to a Moslem hareem. Then the question arose, how should the sister see the girl! They came and talked with your uncle, and went to Yanni and the other Vice Consuls, and at length they found out that the women of that Moslem family were skillful in making silk and gold embroidery which they sold. So his sister determined to go and order some embroidered work, and see the girl. She talked with the Moslem women, and with their Bedawy servant girl, and made errands for the women to bring her specimens of their work, improving the opportunity to talk with the servant. She saw the scar, and satisfied herself from the striking resemblance of the girl to her mother, that she was the long-lost Zahidy.

The father now took measures to secure his daughter. The American, Prussian, English and French Vice Consuls sent a united demand to the Turkish Pasha, that the girl be brought to court to meet her father, and that the case be tried in the Mejlis, or City Council. The Moslems were now greatly excited. They knew that there were not less than twenty girls in their families who had been stolen in this way, and if one could be reclaimed, perhaps the rest might, so they resolved to resist. They brought Bedawin Arabs to be present at the trial, and hired them to swear falsely. When the girl was brought in, the father was quite overcome. He could see the features of his dear child, but she was so disfigured with the Bedawin tattooing and the brutal treatment of the Moslems, that his heart sank within him. Yet he examined her, and took his oath that this was his daughter, and demanded that she be given up to him. The Bedawin men and women were now brought in. One swore that he was the father of the girl, and a woman swore that she was her mother. Then several swore that they were her uncles, but it was proved that they were in no way related to the one who said he was her father. Other witnesses were called, but they contradicted one another. Then they asked the girl. Poor thing, she had been so long neglected and abused, that she *had forgotten her father*, and the Moslem women had threatened to kill her if she said she was his daughter, so she declared she was born among the Bedawin, and was a Moslem in religion. Money had been given to certain of the Mejlis, and they finally decided that the girl should go to the Moslem house of Derwish Effendi to await the final decision.

The poor father now went to the Consuls. They made out a statement of the case and sent it to the Consuls General in Beirût, who sent a joint dispatch to the Waly of all Syria, who lives in Damascus, demanding that as the case could not be fairly tried in Tripoli, the girl be brought to Beirût to be examined by a Special Commission. The Waly telegraphed at once to Tripoli, to have the girl sent on by the first steamer to Beirût. The Moslem women now told the girl that orders had come to have her killed, and that she was to be taken on a steamer as if to go to Beirût, but that really they were going to throw her into the sea, and that if she reached Beirût alive they would cut her up and burn her! So the poor child went on the steamer in perfect terror, and she reached Beirût in a state of exhaustion. When she was rested, a Commission was formed consisting of the Moslem Kadi of Beirût who was acting Governor, the political Agent, Delenda Effendi, the Greek Catholic Bishop Agabius, the Maronite Priest Yusef, and the agent of the Greek Bishop, together with all the members of the Executive Council.

Her father, mother and aunt were now brought in and sat near her. She refused to recognize them, and was in constant fear of being injured. The Kadi then turned to her and said, "do not fear, my child. You are among friends. Do not be afraid of people who have threatened you. No one shall harm you." The Moslem Kadi, the Greek Catholic priests, and others having thus spoken kindly to her, the father and mother stated the history of how the little girl was lost nine years ago, and that she had a scar on her breast. The scar was examined, and all began to feel that she was really their own daughter. The girl began to feel more calm, and the Kadi told her that her own mother wanted to ask her a few questions.

Her mother now went up to her and said, "My child, don't you remember me?" She said "no I do not." "Don't you remember that *your name was once Zahidy*, and I used to call you, and you lived in a house with a little yard, and flowers before the door, and that you went with the little girls to school, and came home at night, and that one day a man came and offered you sugar plums and led you away and carried you off to the Arabs? Don't you know *me*, my *own daughter?*" The poor girl trembled; her lips quivered, and she said, "Yes, I *did* have another name. I *was* Zahidy. I did go with little girls. Oh, ya imme! My mother! you *are* my mother," and she sprang into her arms and wept, and the mother wept and laughed, and the Moslem Kadi and the Mufti, and the priests and the Bishops and the Effendis and the great crowd of spectators wiped their eyes, and bowed their heads, and there was a great silence.

After a little the Kadi said, "it is enough. This girl *is* the daughter of Kahlil Ferah. Sir, take your child, and Allah be with you!"

The father wiped away the tears and said, "Your Excellency, you see this poor girl all tattooed and disfigured. You see how ignorant and feeble she is. If she were not my child, there is nothing about her to make me wish to take her. But she is my own darling child, and with all her faults and infirmities, I love her." The whole Council then arose and congratulated the father and mother, and a great crowd accompanied them home. Throngs of people came to see her and congratulate the family, and after a little the girl was sent to a boarding school.

I can hardly think over this story even now without tears, for I think how glad I should have been to get back again a child of mine if it had been lost. And I have another thought too about that little lost girl. If that father loved his daughter so as to search and seek for her, and expend money, and travel by land and sea for years, in trying to find her, and when at length he found her, so forlorn and wretched and degraded, yet loved her still because she was *his daughter*, do you not think that Jesus loves us even more? We were lost and wretched and forlorn. A worse being than Bedawin gypsies has put his mark on our hearts and our natures. We have wandered far, far away. We have served the world, and forgotten our dear Heavenly Father. We have even refused to receive Him when he has come near us. Yet Jesus came to seek and to save us. And when he found us so degraded and sinful and disfigured, He loved us still, because we are His own children. Don't you think that the little lost Damascene girl was thankful when she reached her home, and was loved and kindly treated by father and mother and relatives and friends? And ought we not to be very thankful when Jesus brings us home, and calls us "dear children" and opens the gate of heaven to us?

This story of the lost Damascene child calls to my mind a little song which the Maronite women in Lebanon sing to their babies as a lullaby. The story is that a Prince's daughter was stolen by the Bedawin Arabs, and carried to their camp. She grew up and was married to a Bedawin Sheikh and had a little son. One day a party of muleteers came to the camp selling grapes, and she recognized them as from her own village. She did not dare speak to them, so she began to sing a lullaby to her baby, and motioned to the grape-sellers to come near, and when the Bedawin were not listening, she would sing them her story in the same tone as the lullaby.

THE LULLABY.

Sleep, baby sleep! a sleep so sweet and mild,
Sleep, my Arab boy, my little Bedawin child!
Aside to the grape-sellers . . . . . Once I was a happy girl,
The Prince Abdullah's daughter.
Playing with the village maids,
Bringing wood and water.
Suddenly the Bedawin
Carried me away;
Clothed me in the Aba robe
And here they make me stay.
Sleep, baby sleep! a sleep so sweet and mild,
Sleep, my Arab boy, my little Bedawin child!
Aside . . . . . Ye sellers of grapes hear what I say.
I had dressed in satin rich and gay.
They took my costly robes away,
And dressed me in Aba coarse and grey.
I had lived on viands costly and rare,
And now raw camel's flesh is my fare.

Sleep, baby sleep! a sleep so sweet and mild,
Sleep, my Arab boy, my little Bedawin child!
Aside . . . . . Oh seller of grapes, I beg you hear,
Go tell my mother and father dear,
That you have seen me here to-day.
Just by the Church my parents live,
The Bedawin stole me on Thursday eve.
Let the people come and their sister save,
Let them come with warriors bold and brave,
Lest I die of grief and go to my grave.

The grape-sellers then go home, and the warriors come and rescue her, and take her home.

We will stop here a moment and make a pencil sketch of this Arab camp, but we must be very careful not to let them see us writing. They have a great fear of the art of writing, a superstitious idea that a person who writes or sketches in their camp, is writing some charm or incantation to bring mischief upon them. I once heard of a missionary who went to an Arab village to spend the night. The people were all Maronites, and grossly ignorant. He pitched his tent and sat down to rest. Presently a crowd of rough young men came in and began to insult him. They demanded bakhshish, and handled his bedding and cooking utensils in a very brutal manner, and asked him if he had any weapons. He bethought himself of one weapon and began to use it. He took out a pencil and paper, and began to make a sketch of the ringleader. He looked him steadily in the eye, and then wrote rapidly with his pencil. The man began to tremble and slowly retreated and finally shouted to his companions, and off they all went. Shortly after, they sent a man to beg Mr. L. not to cut off their heads! Their priests teach them that the Protestants have the power of working magic, and that they draw a man's portrait and take it with them, and if the man does anything to displease them, they cut off the head of the picture and the man's head drops off! Mr. L. sent them word that they had better be very careful how they behaved. They did not molest him again.

Here we are near Tripoli, at the Convent of the *Sacred Fish*. What a beautiful spot! This large high building with its snow-white dome, and the great sycamore tree standing by this circular pool of crystal water, make a beautiful scene. What a crowd of Moslem boys! They have come all the way from Tripoli, about two miles, to feed the Sacred Fish. They are a gay looking company, with their red, green, blue, yellow, white and purple clothes, and their bright red caps and shoes, and some of them with white turbans. They come out on feast days and holidays to play on this green lawn and feed the fish. The old sheikh who keeps this holy place, has great faith in these fish. He says they are all good Moslems, and are inhabited by the souls of Moslem saints, and there is one black fish, the Sheikh of the saints, who does not often show himself to spectators. There are hundreds if not thousands of fish, resembling the dace or chubs of America. He says that during the Crimean war, many of the older ones went off under the sea to Sevastopol and fought the Russian infidels, and some of them came back wounded.

The people think that if any one eats these fish he will die immediately. That I *know* to be false, for I have tried it. When the American Consul was here in 1856, his Moslem Kawasses caught several of the fish, and brought them to Mr. Lyons' house. We had them cooked and ate them, but found them coarse and unpalatable. That was sixteen years ago, and we have not felt the evil effects yet.

This poor woman has a sick child, and has come to get the Sheikh to read the Koran over it and cure it. The most of the Syrian doctors are ignorant quacks, and the people have so many superstitions that they prefer going to saints' tombs rather than call a good physician. There is a Medical College in Beirût now, and before long Syria will have some skilful doctors. I knew an old Egyptian doctor in Duma named Haj Ibrahim, who was a conceited fellow. He used to bleed for every kind of disease. An old man eighty years of age was dying of consumption, and the Haj opened a vein and let him bleed to death. When the man died, he said if he had only taken a little more blood, the old man would have recovered. I was surprised by his coming to me one day and asking for some American newspapers. I supposed he wished them to wrap medicines in and gave him several New York Tribunes. A few days after he invited us to eat figs and grapes in his vineyard and we stopped at his house. He said he was very thankful for the papers. They had been very useful. I wondered what he meant, and asked him. He showed me a jar in the corner in which he had dissolved the papers into a pulp in oil and water, and had given the pulp as medicine to the people! He said it was a powerful medicine. He supposed that the English printed letters would have some magic influence on diseases.

One of the Moslem lads carries a short iron spear as a sign that he is going to be a derwish. Dr. De Forest once found himself surrounded in a Moslem village by a troop of little Moslems, each of them with an iron-headed spear in his hand. A Moorish Sheikh, or Chief, had been for some two years teaching the Moslems of the place the customs of their holy devotees, and in consequence all the boys had become derwishes, or Moslem monks. He was a shrewd old Sheikh. He knew that the true way to perpetuate his religion was to *teach the children.* He had taught them the Moslem prayers and prostrations, and to keep certain moral precepts. How glad we should be if these boys would come and sit down by us while we talk to them of Jesus! There they come. See how their eyes sparkle, as I speak to them. They have never heard about the gospel before. But I must speak in a low tone, as the old Sheikh is coming and he looks down upon us as infidel dogs! Perhaps some of them will think of these words some day, and put their trust in our Divine Saviour.

Many of the people seem to think that the missionary's house is like the Cave of Adullam, where David lived, (1 Sam. xxii: 2) when "every one that was in distress, and every one that was in debt, and every one that was discontented, gathered themselves unto him." It makes it very hard to deal with the people, to have so many of them come to us with improper motives. They come and say they love the gospel and want instruction, and have endured persecution, when suddenly you find that they want money, or to be protected from punishment, or to get office, or to get married to some improper person, or something else that is wrong.

Once a sheikh from Dunnîyeh in Lebanon came to Tripoli, and declared himself a Protestant. He was very zealous, and wanted us to feel that he was too good a man to be turned away, as he was wealthy and of a high family. He was armed with a small arsenal of weapons. He had a servant to carry his gun and pipe, and came day after day to read books, and talk on religion. He said that all he needed was the protection of the American Consul, and then he would make his whole village Protestants. We told him we could have nothing to do with politics. If he wanted to become a Christian, he must take up his cross and follow Christ. He said that was just what he wanted to do, only he wished to benefit the cause by bringing others to follow Him. He seemed very earnest, but there was something dark and mysterious in his ways, and we were afraid of him. Now the Arabs have a proverb, "No tree is cut down but by *one of its own limbs*," i. e. the axe handle, and we thought a native only could understand a native, so we took the famous convert around to see Yanni. He went into Yanni's office, and Mr. L. and myself sat out in the garden under the orange trees. After a few minutes Yanni called out, "Come in, be preferred, your excellencies! I have found it all out. I understand the case." We went in and climbed up upon the platform, next the desk in the office. The Maronite candidate for the church sat smiling, as if he thought he would now be received at once. Yanni went on, "I understand the case exactly. This man is a son of a Sheikh in Dunnîyeh. He is in a deadly quarrel with his father and brothers about the property, and says that if we will give him the protection of the American Consulate, he will go home, kill his father and brothers, seize all the property, and then come down and join the church, and live in Tripoli!" We were astounded, but the brutal fellow turned to us and said, "yes, and I will then make all the village Protestants, and if I fail, then cut my head off!" We told him that if he did anything of that kind, we would try to get him hung, and the American Consulate would have nothing to do with him. "Very well," said he, "I have made you a *fair offer*, and if you don't accept it, I have nothing more to say." We rebuked him sharply, and gave him a sermon which he did not relish, for he said he was in haste, and bade us a most polite good morning He was what I should call an Adullamite.

A Greek priest in the village of Barbara once took me aside, to a retired place behind his house, and told me that he had a profound secret to tell me. He wished to become a Protestant and make the whole village Protestant, but on one condition, that I would get him a hat, a coat, and pantaloons, put a flag-staff on his house, and have him appointed American Consul. I told him the matter of the hat, coat and pantaloons he could attend to at but slight expense, but I had no right to make Consuls and erect flagstaffs. Then he said he could not become Protestant.

In 1866, a man named Yusef Keram rebelled against the Government of Lebanon and was captured and exiled. The day he was brought into Beirût, a tall rough looking mountaineer called at my house. He was armed with a musket and sword, besides pistols and dirks. After taking a seat, he said, "I wish to become Angliz and American." "What for," said I. "Only that I would be honored with the honorable religion." "Do you know anything about it?" "Of course not. How should I know?" "Don't you know better than to follow a religion you know nothing about?" "But I can learn." "How do you know but what we worship the devil?" "No matter. Whatever you worship, I will worship." I then asked him what he came for. He said he was in the rebel army, was captured, escaped and fought again, and now feared he should be shot, so he wanted to become Angliz and American. I told him he need have no fear, as the Pasha had granted pardon to all. "Is that so?" "Yes, it is." On hearing this he said he had business to look after, and bade me good evening.

But you will be tired of hearing about the Adullamites. If those who came to David were like the discontented and debtors who come to us, he must have been tired too. So many suspicious characters come to us, that we frequently ask men, when they come professing great zeal for the gospel, whether they have killed anybody, or stolen, or quarrelled with any one? And it is not always easy to find out the truth. If fifty men turn Protestants in a village, perhaps five or ten will stand firm, and the rest go back, and frequently all go back.

But the rain is coming down and we will hasten to the Meena to Uncle S.'s house, where we can rest after this wearisome and hasty journey from Safita. For your sake I am glad that we took comfortable bedding and bedsteads with us. It costs a few piastres more to hire a baggage animal, but it is cheaper in the end. At one time I was going on a hard journey, and I thought I would be economical, so I took only my horse and a few articles in my khurj or saddle bags, with a little boy to show me the road and take care of my horse. When I reached the village, I stopped at the house of a man said to be a Protestant. He lived in the most abject style, and I soon found by his bad language towards his family and his neighbors that he needed all the preaching I could give him that evening. There was only one room in the house, and that was small. By nine o'clock the mother and the children had laid down on a mat to sleep, and the neighbors who came in were beginning to doze. I was very weary with a long ride on a hot August day, and asked mine host where I should lie down to sleep. He led me to a little elevated platform on the back side of the room, where a bed was spread for me. The dim oil lamp showed me that the bed and covering were neither of them clean, but I was too weary to spend much time in examining them, and after spreading my linen handkerchief over the pillow, I tried to sleep. But this could not be done. Creeping things, great and small, were crawling over me from head to foot. There was a hole in the wall near my head, and the bright moonlight showed what was going on. Fleas, bugs, ants, (attracted by the bread in my khurj,) and more horrible still, swarms of lice covered the bed, and my clothing. I could stand it no longer. Gathering up my things, and walking carefully across the floor to keep from stepping on the sleeping family, I reached the door. But it was fastened with an Arab lock and a huge wooden key, and could only be opened by a violent shaking and rattling. This, with the creaking of the hinges, woke up my host, who sprung up to see what was the matter. I told him I had decided to journey on by moonlight. It was then one o'clock in the morning, and on I rode, so weary, that when I reached Jebaa at ten o'clock, I was obliged to go to bed. I did not recover from the onset of the vermin for weeks.

I have known missionaries to travel without beds, tents or bedsteads, and to spend weary days and sleepless nights, so as to be quite unfitted for their great work of preaching to the people. If you ever grow up to become a missionary, I hope you will live as simply as you can, but be careful of your health and try to live as long as you can, for the sake of the people you are working for, and the Lord who sends you forth. It is not good economy for a missionary to become a martyr to studying Arabic, or to poor food, or to exhausting modes of travelling. One can kill himself in a short time, if he wishes, on missionary ground, but he could have done that at home without the great expense of coming here to do it, and besides, that is not what a missionary goes out for. He ought to live as long as he can'. He should have a dry house, in a healthy location, good food, and proper conveniences for safe travelling.

How pleasant it is to hear that sweet toned bell! Let us climb up to the roof and read the inscription on it. "From little Sabbath School Children in America to the Mission Church in Tripoli, Syria." It was sent in 1862 by the children in Fourth Avenue Church, New York, and in Newark, Syracuse, Owego, Montrose and other places.

The Moslems abhor bells. They say bells draw together evil spirits. We are not able yet to have a bell in Hums, on account of the Moslem opposition. They do not use bells, but have men called Muezzins stationed on the little balconies around the top of the tall minarets, to call out five times a day to the people to come to prayer. They select men and boys with high clear voices, and at times their voices sound very sweetly in the still evening. They say, "There is no God but God." That is true. Then they add, "and Mohammed is the Apostle of God," and that is not true. As the great historian Gibbon said; these words contain an "eternal truth and an eternal lie."

The Moslems are obliged to pray five times every day, wherever they may be. At home, in their shops, in the street, or on a journey, whenever the appointed time arrives, they fall on their knees, and go through with the whole routine of prayers and bodily prostrations. One day several Moslems called on us in Tripoli, at the eighth hour of the day (about 2 o'clock P. M.), and after they had been sitting some time engaged in conversation, one of them arose and said to his companions, "I must pray." They all asked, "Why? It is not the hour of prayer." "Because," said he, "when I went to the mosque at noon to pray, I had an ink-spot on my finger nail, and did not perceive it until after I came out, and hence my prayer was of no account. I have just now scraped it off, and must repeat my noon prayer." So saying, he spread his cloak upon the floor, and then kneeling upon it with his face towards Mecca, commenced his prayers, while his companions amused themselves by talking about his ceremonial strictness. One of them said to me, "He thinks he is holy, but if you could see the *inside* of him, you would find it black as pitch!" He kept his head turned to hear what was being said, and after he had finished, disputed a remark one of them had made while he was praying. Such people worship God with their lips, while their hearts are far from him.

Moslems have a great horror of swine. They

think us barbarians to eat ham or pork. In February, 1866, the Moslems of Beirût were keeping the Fast of Ramadan. For a whole month of each year they can eat and drink nothing between sunrise and sunset, and they become very cross and irritable. In Hums, some Moslems saw a dog eating a bone in Ramadan, and killed him because he would not keep the fast. They fast all day and feast all night. Ramadan is really a great nocturnal feast, but it is hard for the working people to wait until night before beginning the feast. During that fast of 1866, a Maronite fellah came into Beirût driving a herd of swine to the market. Now of all sights in the world, the sight of swine is to an orthodox Moslem the most intolerable, and especially in the holy month of Ramadan. Even in ordinary times, when swine enter the city, the Moslems gather up their robes, turn their backs and shout, "hub hub," "hub hub," and if the hogs do not hasten along, the "hub hub," is very apt to become a hubbub. On the 28th of that holy month, a large herd entered Beirût on the Damascus road. The Moslems saw them, and forthwith a crowd of Moslem young men and boys hastened to the fray. A few days before, the Maronite Yusef Keram had entered the city amid the rejoicings of the Maronites. These swine, whom the Moslems called "Christian Khanzir," should meet a different reception. Their wrath overcame their prejudice. The Maronite swine-drivers were dispersed and the whole herd were driven on the run up the Assur with shouts of derision, and pelted with stones and clubs. "You khanzir, you Maronite, you Keram, out with you!" and the air rang with shouts mingled with squeals and grunts. I saw the crowd coming. It gathered strength as it approached Bab Yakoob, where the white turbaned faithful rose from their shops and stables to join in the persecution of the stampeding porkers. "May Allah cut off their days! Curses on their grandfather's beard! Curses on the father of their owner! Hub hub! Allah deliver us from their contamination!" were the cries of the crowd as they rushed along. The little boys were laughing and having a good time, and the men were breathing out wrath and tobacco smoke. Alas, for the poor swine! What became of them I could not tell, but the last I saw, was the infuriated crowd driving them into the Khan of Muhayeddin near by, where one knows not what may have happened to them. I hope they did not steal the pork and eat it "on the sly," as the Bedawin did at Mt. Sinai, who threw away the hams the travellers were carrying for provisions, and declared that their camels should not be defiled with the unclean beast! The travellers were very indignant at such a loss, but thought it was too bad to injure the feelings of the devout Moslems, and said no more. What was their horror and wrath to hear the next night that the Bedawin were seen cooking and eating their hams at midnight, when they thought no one would see them!

Do the Syrian people all smoke? Almost all of them. They speak of it as "drinking a pipe," "drinking a cigar," and you would think that they look upon tobacco as being as necessary to them as water. Old and young men, women and even children smoke, smoke while they work or rest, while at home or journeying, and measure distances by their pipes. I was travelling, and asked a man how far it was to the next village. He said about two pipes of tobacco distant! I found it to be nearly an hour, or three miles. The Orientals spend so much time in smoking, that some one has said "the Moslems came into power with the Koran in one hand, and the sword in the other, but will go out with the Koran in one hand and the pipe in the other!"

Here we are on the sandy beach. What myriads of sea shells, and what beautiful colors they have. And here are sponges without number, but they are worthless. There on the sea are the little sloops of the sponge fishers. They are there through the whole summer and the fishers dive down into the sea where the water is from 100 to 200 feet deep, and walk around on the bottom holding their breath, and when they can bear it no longer pull the cord which is tied around the waist, and then their companions draw them up. They do not live long, as it is very hard and unnatural labor. Sometimes they are killed by sharks or other sea monsters. One of them told me that he was once on the bottom, and just about to pick up a beautiful white sponge, when he saw a great monster with huge claws and arms and enormous eyes coming towards him, and he barely escaped being devoured. At another time, the men in the boat felt a sudden jerk on the rope and pulled in, when they found only the man's head, arms and chest on it, the rest of his body having been devoured by some great fish or sea animal. The sponges grow on rocks, pebbles or shells, and some of them are of great value. It is difficult to get the best ones here, as the company who hire the divers export all the good ones to Europe.

PART V.

Word has come that there is cholera in Odessa, so that all the Russian steamers going to Beirût will be in quarantine. It will not be pleasant to spend a week in the Beirût quarantine, so we will keep our baggage animals and go down by land. It is two long days of nine hours each, and you will be weary enough. Bidding good-bye to our dear friends here and wishing them God's blessing in their difficult work among such people, away we go! Yanni and Uncle S. and some of the teachers will accompany us a little way, according to the Eastern custom, and then we dismount and kiss them all on both cheeks, and pursue our monotonous way along the coast, sometimes riding over rocky capes and promontories and then on the sand and pebbles close to the roaring surf.

See how many monasteries there are on the sides of Lebanon! Between Tripoli and Beirût there are about a hundred. The men who live in them are called monks, who make a vow never to marry, and spend their lives eating and drinking the fruits of other men's labors. They own almost all the valuable land in this range of mountains for fifty miles, and the fellaheen live as "tenants at will" on their estates. When a man is lazy or unfortunate, if he is not married, his first thought is to become a monk. They are the most corrupt and worthless vagabonds in the land, and the day must come before long, when the monasteries and convents will be abolished and their property be given back to the people to whom it justly belongs.

We are now riding along by the telegraph wires. It seems strange to see Morse's telegraph on this old Phenician coast, and it will seem stranger still when we reach Beirût, to receive a daily morning paper printed in Arabic, with telegrams from all parts of the world!

In July, a woman came to the telegraph office in Beirût, asking, "Where is the telegraph?" The Clerk, Yusef Effendi, asked her, "Whom do you want, the Director, the Operator, or the Kawass?" She said, "I want Telegraph himself, for my husband has sent me word that he is in prison in Zahleh and wants me to come with haste, and I heard that Telegraph takes people quicker than any one else. Please tell me the fare, and send me as soon as possible! The Effendi looked at her, and took her measure, and then said, "You are too tall to go by telegraph, so you will have to go on a mule." The poor ignorant woman went away greatly disappointed.

Another old woman, whose son was drafted into the Turkish army, wished to send him a pair of new shoes, so she hung them on the telegraph wire. A way-worn foot traveller coming along soon after took down the new shoes and put them on, and hung his old ones in their place. The next day the old lady returned and finding the old shoes, said, "Mushullah, Mohammed has received his new shoes and sent back his old ones to be repaired."

The telegraph has taught all the world useful lessons, and the Syrians have learned one lesson from it which is of great value. When they write letters they use long titles, and flowery salutations, so that a whole page will be taken up with these empty formalities, leaving only a few lines at the end, or in a postscript, for the important business. But when they send a telegram and have to pay for every word, they leave out the flowery salutations, and send only what is necessary.

The following is a very common way of beginning an Arabic letter:

"To the presence of the affectionate and the most distinguished, the honorable and most ingenious Khowadja, the honored, may his continuance be prolonged!"

"After presenting the precious pearls of affection, the aromatic blossoms of love, and the increase of excessive longing, after the intimate presence of the light of your rising in prosperity, we would say that in a most blessed and propitious hour your precious letter honored us," etc.

That would cost too much to be sent by telegraph. Precious pearls and aromatic blossoms would become expensive luxuries at two cents a word. So they have to be reserved, for letters, if any one has time to write them.

Here we come to the famous Dog River. You will read in books about this river and its old inscriptions. If you have not forgotten your Latin, you can read a lesson in Latin which was written here nearly two thousand years ago. There you can see the words.

Imp. Caes. M. Aurelius
Antoninus Pius Felix Augustus
Par. Max. Brit. Max. Germ. Maximus
Pontifex Maximus
Montibus Imminentibus
etc. etc.

This Emperor Marcus Aurelius, must have cut this road through the rocks about the year 173 A. D. But there is another inscription higher up, with arrow-headed characters and several other tablets. They are Assyrian and Egyptian. One of the Assyrian tablets was cut by Sennacherib 2500 years ago, and one of the Egyptian by Sesostris, king of Egypt, 3100 years ago. Don't you feel very young and small in looking at such ancient monuments? All of those men brought their armies here, and found the path so bad along the high precipice overhanging the sea, that they cut a road for their horses and chariots in the solid limestone rock. Just think of standing where Sennacherib and Alexander the Great passed along with their armies!

What a steep and narrow road! We will dismount and walk over this dangerous pass. It is not pleasant to meet camels and loaded mules on such a dizzy precipice, with the high cliff above, and the roaring waves of the sea far below! It is well we dismounted. Our horses are afraid of those camels carrying long timbers balanced on their backs. Let us turn aside and wait until they pass.

Seeing these camels reminds me of what I saw here in 1857. I was coming down the coast from Tripoli and reached the top of this pass, in the narrowest part, just as a caravan of camels were coming from the opposite direction. I turned back a little, and stood close under the edge of the cliff to let the camels go by. They were loaded with huge canvas sacks of tibn, or cut straw, which hung down on both sides, making it impossible to pass them without stooping very low. Just then I heard a voice behind me, and looking around, saw a shepherd coming up the pass with his flock of sheep. He was walking ahead, and they all followed on. I called to him to go back, as the camels were coming over the pass. He said, "Ma ahlaik," or "don't trouble yourself," and on he came. When he met the camels, they were in the narrowest part, where a low stone wall runs along the edge of the precipice. He stooped down and stepped upon the narrow wall, calling all the time to his sheep, who followed close upon his heels, walking in single file. He said, "tahl, tahl," "come, come," and then made a shrill whirring call, which could be heard above the roaring of the waves on the rocks below. It was wonderful to see how closely they followed the shepherd. They did not seem to notice the camels on the one side, or the abyss on the other side. Had they left the narrow track, they would either have been trodden down by the heavily laden camels, or have fallen off into the dark waters below. But they were intent on following their shepherd. They heard his voice, and that was enough. The cameleers were shouting and screaming to their camels to keep them from slipping on these smooth rocks, but the sheep paid no attention to them. They knew the shepherd's voice. They had followed him before, through rivers and thickets, among rocks and sands, and he had always led them safely. The waves were dashing and roaring on the rocks below, but they did not fear, for the shepherd was going on before. Had one of those sheep turned aside, he would have lost his footing and been destroyed and thrown the whole flock into confusion.

You know why I have told you this story. You know that Jesus is the Good Shepherd. He said, "My sheep hear my voice, and I know them and they follow me." Wherever Jesus leads it is safe for us to go. How many boys and girls there are who think they know a better path than the one Jesus calls them to follow. There are "stranger" voices calling on every side, and many a child leaves the path of the Good Shepherd, and turns aside to hear what they would say. If they were truly lambs of Jesus' fold, they would love Him, and follow Him in calm and storm, and never heed the voice of strangers.

I was once travelling from Dûma to Akûra, high up on the range of Lebanon. It was a hot summer's day, and at noon I stopped to rest by a fountain. The waste water of the fountain ran into a square stone birkeh or pool, and around the pool were several shepherds resting with their flocks of sheep and goats. The shepherds came and talked with me, and sat smoking for nearly an hour, when suddenly one of them arose and walked away calling to his flock to follow him. The flocks were all mixed together, but when he called, his sheep and goats began to raise their heads and start along together behind him. He kept walking along and calling, until all his flock had gone. The rest of the sheep and goats remained quietly as though nothing had happened. Then another "Rai," or shepherd, started up in another direction, calling out in a shrill voice, and *his sheep* followed him. They knew their shepherd's voice. Our muleteers were talking all the time, but the sheep paid no attention to them. They knew one voice, and would follow no other.

We will now hasten on to Beirût. You will wish to see the Female Seminary, and the Sabath School and the Steam Printing Press, and many of the Beirût Schools, before we start to Abeih again.

Here is the Female Seminary. There are a hundred girls here, studying Arabic reading and writing, geography, arithmetic, grammar, botany, physiology and astronomy, and a few study English, French and music. But the great study is the *Bible.* I am afraid that very few schools in America have as much instruction in the Bible, as the girls in this Seminary and the Sidon Seminary receive. You would be surprised to hear the girls recite correctly the names of all the patriarchs, kings and prophets of the Old Testament, with the year when they lived, and the date of all the important events of the Old and New Testament History, and the Life of Christ, and the travels of the Apostle Paul, and the prophecies about Christ in the Old Testament, and then recite the whole Westminster Assembly's Catechism in Arabic! I have given out *one hundred and twenty* Bibles and Hymn Books as rewards to children in the schools in Beirût, who have learned the Shorter Catechism perfectly in Arabic.

Five years ago there was a girl in the school who was once very rude and self-willed, and very hard to control. She had a poor bed-ridden brother who had been a cripple for years, and was a great care to the family. They used to carry him out in the garden in fine weather and lay him on a seat under the trees, and sometimes his sister would come home from the school and read to him from the Bible, to which he listened with great delight. Not long after this he died, and his sister was sent for to come home to the funeral. On reaching home she found a large crowd of women assembled from all that quarter of the city, shrieking and wailing over his death, according to the Oriental custom. When A. the little girl came in, one of the women from an aristocratic Greek family was talking in a loud voice and saying that it was wrong for any person to go from the house of mourning to another house before first going home, because one going from a house of mourning would carry an *evil influence* with her. A. listened and then spoke out boldly before the seventy women, "How long will you hold on to these foolish superstitions? Beirût is a place of light and civilization. Where can you find any such teaching as this in the gospel? It is time for us to give up such superstitions." The old woman asked, "Where did that girl learn these things? Truly she is right. These things *are* superstitions, but they will not die until *we old women die.*" It required a great deal of courage in A. to speak out so boldly, when her own brother had died, but all felt that she spoke the truth, and no one rebuked her.

Near by the house of A. is another beautiful house surrounded by gardens, and ornamented in the most expensive manner. A little girl from this family was attending the school in 1867. Her name was Fereedy. She was a boarder and the best behaved girl in the school. One day during vacation, her mother came to Rufka and said, "What have you done to my little daughter Fereedy? She came home last Saturday with her sister, and at once took the whole care of the little children, so that I had no trouble with them. And when night came she put her little sisters to bed and prayed with them all, and then in the morning she prayed with them again. I never saw such a child. She is like a little angel." The mother is of the Greek sect, and the little girl was only twelve years old.

And here is a story about another of the superstitions of the fellaheen, and what a little girl taught the people about them. This little girl named L. went with her father to spend the summer in a mountain village, where the people had a strange superstition about an oak tree. One day she went out to walk and came to the great oak tree which stood alone on the mountain side. You know that the Canaanites used to have idols under the green trees in ancient times. When L. reached the tree, she found the ground covered with dead branches which had fallen from the tree. Now, wood is very scarce and costly in Syria, and the people are very poor, so that she wondered to see the wood left to rot on the ground, and asked the people why they did not use it for fuel. They said they dared not, as the tree belonged to Moses the Prophet, and he protected the tree, and if any one took the wood, they would *fall dead*. She said, "Moses is in heaven, and does not live in oak trees, and if he did, he is a good man, and would not hurt me for burning up old dry sticks." So she asked them if she might have the wood? They said, "yes, if you *dare* to take it, for we are afraid to touch it." So she went to the tree and gathered up as much as she could carry, and took it home. The people screamed when they saw her, and told her to drop it or it would kill her, but on she went, and afterwards went back and brought the rest. She then talked with the ignorant women, and her father told them about the folly of their superstitions, and read to them in the Bible about Moses, and they listened with great attention. I have often thought I should like to go to that village, and see whether the people now leave the dead branches under Moses' oak, or use them for fuel during the heavy snow storms of winter.

PART VI.

Here we are, home again at Abeih. Here are Asaad and Khalîl, and several others. I asked Khalîl one day to write out for me a list of all the games the boys play in Abeih, and he brought me a list of *twenty-eight* different ones, and said there were many more.

I. The first is called Khatim or the Ring. A boy puts a ring on the back of his hand, tosses it and catches it on the back of his fingers. If it falls on the middle finger, he shakes it to the forefinger, and then he is Sultan, and appoints a Vizier, whom he commands to beat the other boys. Then the boys all sing,

Ding, dong, turn the wheel,
Wind the purple thread :
Spin the white and spin the red,
Wind it on the reel :
Silk and linen as well as you can,
Weave a robe for the Great Sultan.

II. Killeh. Like the game of shooting marbles.

III. Owal Howa. The same as leap frog.

IV. Biz Zowaia. Cat in the corner.

V. Taia ya Taia. All the boys stand in a row, and one in front facing them, who calls out Taia ya Taia. They all then run after him and hit him. He then hops on one foot as if lame, and catches one of them, who takes his place.

VI. El Manya. Hig tig.

VII. Bil Kobbeh. A circle of boys stand with their heads bowed. Another circle stand outside, and on a given signal try to mount on the backs of the inner circle of boys. If they succeed they remain standing in this way; if not, the boy who failed must take the inside place.

VIII. Ghummaida. Blind-man's-buff.

IX. Tabeh. Base ball and drop ball.

X. Kurd Murboot or Tied Monkey. A rope is tied to a peg in the ground, and one boy holds it fast. The others tie knots in their handkerchiefs and beat him. If he catches them without letting go his hold on the rope, they take his place.

XI. Shooha or Hawk. Make a swing on the limb of a tree. A boy leans on the swing and runs around among the boys, until he catches one to take his place.

XII. Joora. Shooting marbles into a joora or hole in the ground.

XIII. Khubby Mukhzinak. "Pebble pebble." One boy goes around and hides a pebble in the hand of one of the circle and asks "pebble, pebble, who's got the pebble." This is like "Button, button."

Then there are other games like chequers and "Morris," chess, and games which are used in gambling, which you will not care to hear about.

Sometimes when playing, they sing a song which I have translated:

> I found a black crow,
> With a cake in his maw,
> I asked him to feed me,
> He cried caw, caw.
>
> A chicken I found
> With a loaf of bread—
> I asked him to feed me,
> He cried, enough said.
>
> And an eagle black
> With a beam on his back
> Said from Egypt I come
> And he cried clack, clack.

So you see the Arab boys are as fond of plays and songs as American boys. They have scores of songs about gazelles, and pearls, and Sultans, and Bedawîn, andGhouls, and the "Ghuz," and the Evil Eye, and Arab mares and Pashas.

A few days ago a Druze, named Sheikh Ali, called upon me and recited to me a strange song, which reminded me of the story of "Who killed Cock Robin," and "The House that Jack built." In some of the Arab villages where fleas abound, the people go at times to the tennûr or oven, (which is like a great earthen jar sunken in the ground,) to shake off the fleas into the fire. The story which I have translated goes thus: A brilliant bug and a noble flea once went to the oven to shake off the ignoble fleas from their garments into the fire. But alas, alas, the noble flea lost his footing, fell into the fire and was consumed. Then the brilliant bug began to weep and mourn, saying,

> Alas! Ah me!
> The Noble Flea!
> While he was thus weeping,
> And his sad watch keeping,
> A glossy raven overhead,
> Flew swiftly down and gently said,
> Oh my friend, oh brilliant bug,
> Why are you weeping on the rug?
> The bug replied, O glossy raven,
> With your head all shorn and shaven,
> I am now weeping,
> And sad watch keeping,
> Over, Ah me!
> The Noble Flea.
> The raven he,
> Wept over the flea,
> And flew to a green palm tree—
> And in grief, *dropped a feather,*
> Like snow in winter weather.
> The palm tree said my glossy raven,
> Why do you look so craven,
> Why did you drop a feather,
> Like snow in winter weather?
> The raven said,
> The flea is dead!
> I saw the brilliant bug weeping,
> And his sad watch keeping,
> Alas, Alas, Ah me!
> Over the Noble Flea.
> Then the green Palm tree,
> Wept over the noble flea.
> Said he, The flea is dead!
> And *all his branches shed!*

The Shaggy Wolf he strayed,
To rest in the Palm tree's shade:
He saw the branches broken,
Of deepest grief the token,
And said, Oh Palm tree green,
What sorrow have you seen?
What noble one is dead,
That you your branches shed?
He said, O Wolf so shaggy,
Living in rocks so craggy,
I saw the glossy raven,
Looking forlorn and craven,
Dropping down a feather,
Like snow in winter weather.
He saw the brilliant bug weeping,
And his sad watch keeping,
Alas, Alas, Ah me!
Over the Noble Flea!
Then the Wolf in despair
Shed his shaggy hair.
Then the River clear and shining,
Saw the wolf in sorrow pining,
Asked him why in sad despair,
He had shed his shaggy hair?
Said the Wolf, Oh River shining,
I in sorrow deep am pining,
For the Palm tree I have seen,
Shedding all his branches green,
And he saw the glossy raven,
Looking so forlorn and craven,
As he dropped a downy feather,
Like the snow in winter weather,
He saw the brilliant bug weeping,
And his sad watch keeping,
Alas, Alas, Ah me,
Over the Noble Flea!
Sadly then the shining River,
Dried its waters up forever.
Then the Shepherd with his sheep,

Asked the River once so deep,
What great grief, oh shining river,
Dried your waters up forever?
Said the River once so shining,
I in sorrow deep am pining,
Since I saw the wolf's despair,
When he shed his shaggy hair,
For the Palm tree he had seen,
Shedding all his branches green,
And he saw the glossy raven,
Looking so forlorn and craven,
As he dropped a downy feather,
Like the snow in winter weather
He saw the brilliant bug weeping,
And his sad watch keeping.
Alas, Alas, Ah me!
Over the Noble Flea!
Then the Shepherd in sorrow deep,
Tore the horns from all his sheep,
Sadly bound them on his head,
Since he heard the flea was dead.
Then the Shepherd's mother dear,
Asked him why in desert drear,
He had torn in sorrow deep,
All the horns from all his sheep,
Sadly bound them on his head,
Just as though a friend was dead?
Said he, 'tis because the River,
Dried his waters up forever,
Since he saw the Wolf's despair,
When he shed his shaggy hair,
For the Palm tree he had seen,
Shedding all his branches green,
For he saw the glossy raven,
Looking so forlorn and craven,
As he dropped a downy feather,
Like the snow in winter weather.
He saw the brilliant bug weeping,
And his sad watch keeping,

Alas, Alas, Ah me!
Over the Noble Flea!
Mother sad began to cry,
Thrust her needle in her eye;
Could no longer see her thread,
Since she heard the flea was dead
Then the Father grave and bland
Hearing this, *cut off his hand;*
And the daughter, when she hears,
In despair, *cuts off her ears;*
And through the town deep grief is spread,
Because they heard the flea was dead.

THE NURSERY RHYMES OF THE ARABS.

Who is that singing in such a sweet plaintive voice in the room beneath our porch? It is the Sit Leila, wife of Sheikh Abbas, saying a lullaby to her little baby boy, Sheikh Fereed. We will sit on the porch in this bright moonlight, and listen while she sings:

Whoever loves you not,
My little baby boy;
May she be driven from her house,
And never know a joy!
May the "Ghuz" eat up her husband,
And the mouse her oil destroy!

This is not very sweet language for a gentle lady to use to a little infant boy, but the Druze and Moslem women use this kind of imprecation in many of their nursery songs. Katrina says that many of the Greek and Maronite women sing them too. This young woman Laia, who sits here, has repeated for me not less than a hundred and twenty of these nursery rhymes, songs for weddings, funeral wails, etc. Some of the imprecations are dreadful.

They seem to think that the best way to show their love to their babies, is to hate those who do not love them.

Im Faris says she has heard this one in Hasbeiya, her birthplace:

O sleep to God, my child, my eyes,
Your heart no ill shall know;
Who loves you not as much as I,
May God her house o'erthrow!
May the mosque and the minaret, dome and all,
On her wicked head in anger fall!
May the Arabs rob her threshing floor,
And not one kernel remain in her store.

The servant girl Nideh, who attends the Sit Leila, thinks that her turn has come, and she is singing,

We've the white and the red in our baby's cheeks,
In pounds and tons to spare;
But the black and the rust,
And the mould and the must,
For our neighbor's children are!

I hope she does not refer to *us* for we are her nearest neighbors. But in reality I do not suppose that they actually mean what they sing in these Ishmaelitic songs. Perhaps they do when they are angry, but they probably sing them ordinarily without thinking of their meaning at all.

Sometimes snakes come down from the ceilings of these earth-roofed houses, and terrify the people. At other times government horsemen come and drag them off to prison, as they did in Safita. These things are referred to in this next song which Nideh is singing:

> If she love you not, my boy,
> May the Lord her life destroy!
> Seven mules tread her down,
> Drag her body through the town!
> Snakes that from the ceiling hang,
> Sting her dead with poison fang!
> Soldiers from Damascus city,
> Drag her off and shew no pity!
> Nor release her for a day,
> Though a thousand pounds she pay!

That is about enough of imprecations, and it will be pleasanter to listen to Katrina, for she will sing us some of the sweetest of the Syrian Nursery Songs.

> Sleep, my moon, my baby sleep!
> The Pleiades bright their watches keep.
> The Libra shines so fair and clear,
> The stars are shining, hush my dear!

There is not much music in the tunes they sing to these words. The airs generally are plaintive and monotonous, and have a sad and weary sound.

Here is another:

> My boy, my moon, I bid you good morrow!
> Who wishes you peace shall know no sorrow;
> Whom you salute, his earth is like heaven,
> His care relieved, his sin forgiven!

She says that last line is extravagant, and I think as much. The next one is a Moslem lullaby.

> O Lord of the heavens, Knowing and Wise,
> Preserve my Ali, the light of my eyes!
> Lord of high heaven, Compassionate!
> Keep my dear boy in every state!

This one is used by the women of all the sects, but in all of the songs the name is changed to suit the name of the baby to whom the mother is singing:

Ali, your eyes are sleeping,
But God's eyes never sleep:
Their hours of lonely weeping
None can forever keep.
How sweet is the night of health.
When Ali sleeps in peace!
Oh may such nights continue,
Nor ever, ever cease!

Among all the scores of nursery songs, I have heard only a very few addressed to *girls*, but some of these are beautiful. Hear Katrina sing this one:

Lûlû dear the house is bright,
With your forehead's sunny light;
Men your father honor now
When they see your lovely brow.
If father comes home sad and weary,
Sight of you will make him cheery.

The "fuller's soap" mentioned in Malachi 3: 2, is the plant called in Arabic "Ashnan or Shenan," and the Arabs sometimes use it in the place of soap. The following is another song addressed to a baby girl:

Come Cameleer, as quick as you can,
And make us soap from the green "Shenan,"
To bathe our Lûlû dear;
We'll wash her and dress her,
And then we'll caress her,
She'll sleep in her little sereer. (cradle)

This song is sung by the Druze women to their baby girls:

Your eye is jet black, and dark are its lashes,
Between the arched brows, like a crescent it flashes;
When painted with "kohl" 'tis brighter by far,
Than the full-orbed moon or the morning star.

The following is supposed to be addressed by a Druze woman to her neighbor who has a daughter of marriageable age, when she is obliged to veil her face:

Hide your daughter, veil her face,
Neighbor, do not tarry:
For my Hanna is of age,
Says he wants to marry.
When I asked about his choice,
Said he was not needy:
But that if he ever wed,
He thought he'd like Fereedy.

The next one is also Druze and purely Oriental:

Two healths, one health,
Four healths more:
Four sacks of sesamé seed,
Scattered on the floor;
Pick and count them one by one.
Reckon up their number;
For every seed wish Hassan's health,
Sweetly may he slumber!

The Druze women delight in nothing so much as to have their sons ride fine horses:

My Yusef, my cup of sherbet sweet,
My broadcloth red hung over the street,
When you ride the blood mare with sword and pistol,
Your saddle is gold and your stirrups crystal.

Katrina says that this little song is the morning salutation to baby boys:

Good morning now to you, Little boy!
Your face is like the dew, Little boy!
There never was a child, so merry and so mild,
So good morning once again, Little boy!

This song is sung by the Druze women to their babes:

O Sparrow of Paradise,
Hush him to sleep?
Your feathers are "henna."
Watch him and keep!
Bring sleep soft and sweet
Upon your white wings!
For Hassan the pet
And his mother who sings!

The apples of Damascus are noted throughout Syria, though we should regard them as very poor fruit:

What's he like? If any ask us,
Flowers and apples of Damascus;
Apples fragrant on the tray,
Roses sweet with scent of May.

Laia says that the next one is sung by the Druze women to their baby boys:

I love you, I prize you, and for you I wish,
A hundred oak trees in the valley;
A hundred blood mares all tied in the court,
And ready for foray or sally.
Mount your horse, fly away, with your scarf flowing free,
The chiefs of the tribe will assemble;
Damascus, Aleppo, and Ghutah beside,
At the sound of your coming will tremble.

Nejmeh says that the Bedawin women who come to Safita, her native place, often sing the following song:

Come little Bedawy, sit on my lap,
Pretty pearls shine in your little white cap,
Rings are in your ears,
Rings are in your nose,
Rings upon your fingers,
And "henna" on your toes.

They use the "henna" to dye their hands, feet and finger nails, when a wedding or festive occasion occurs in the family.

Katrina recalls another little song which she used to sing to Harry:

Welcome now, my baby dear,
Whence did you come?
Your voice is sweet,
What little feet!
Make yourself at home!

Nideh, the Druze girl down stairs is ready with another song. She is rocking little Sheikh Fereed in his cradle, and says:

In your cradle sleep my boy,
Rest from all your labor;
May El Hakim, heaven's God,
Ever be your neighbor!

It makes me feel sad to hear a poor woman praying to a man. This El Hakim was a man, and a bad man too, who lived many hundred years ago, and now the Druzes regard him as their God. But what difference is there between worshipping Hakim as the Druzes do, and worshipping Mary and Joseph as the Greeks and Maronites do. Laia says the Maronites down in the lower part of this village sing the following song:

Hillû, Hillû, Hallelujah!
Come my wild gazelles!
He who into trouble falls
On the Virgin Mother calls;
To Damascus she's departing.
All the mountain monks are starting.
Come my priest and come my deacon,
Bring the censer and the beacon,
We will celebrate the Mass,
In the Church of Mar Elias;
Mar Elias, my neighbor dear,
You must be deaf if you did not hear.

Sit Leila sings:

I love you my boy, and this is the proof,
I wish that you had all the wealth of the "Shoof,"
Hundreds of costly silken bales,
Hundreds of ships with lofty sails,
Hundreds of towns to obey your word,
And thousands of thousands to call you lord!

Katrina is ready to sing again:

I will sing to you,
God will bring to you,
All you need, my dear:
He's here and there,
He is everywhere,
And to you He's ever near.

People say that every baby that is born into the world is thought by its mother to be better than any other ever born. The Arab women think so too, and this is the way they sing it:

One like you was never born,
One like you was never brought;
All the Arabs might grow old,
Fighting ne'er so brave and bold,
Yet with all their battles fought,
One like you they never caught.

Im Faris asks if we would not like to hear some of the rhymes the Arab women sing when playing with their children. Here are some of them. The first one you will think is like what you have already seen in "Mother Goose."

Blacksmith, blacksmith, shoe the mare,
Shoe the colt with greatest care;
Hold the shoe and drive the nail,
Else your labor all will fail;
Shoe a donkey for Seleem
And a colt for Ibraheem.

Sugar cane grows luxuriantly in Syria, and it was first taken from Tripoli, Syria, to Spain, and thence to the West Indies and America. But all they do with it now in Syria, is to suck it. It is cut up in pieces and sold to the people, old and young, who peel it and suck it. So the Arab women sing to their children:

Pluck it and suck it, the green sugar cane,
Whatever is sweet is costly and vain;
He'll cut you a joint as long as a span,
And charge two piastres. Now buy if you can!

Wered says she will sing us two or three which they use in teaching the little Arab babies to "pat" their hands:

Patty cake, baby! Make him dance!
May his age increase and his years advance!
May his life like the rock, long years endure,
Overgrown with lilies, so sweet and pure!

And now the Sit Leila is singing again one of the Druze lullabys:

Tish for two, Tish for two!
A linen shirt with a border blue!
With cloth that the little pedler sells,
For the father of eyes like the little gazelles!
Your mother will weave and spin and twine,
To clothe you so nicely O little Hassein!

Do you hear the jackals crying as they come up out of the valley? Their cry is like the voice of the cat and dog mingled together, and Im Faris knows some of the ditties which they sing to their children about the jackals and their fondness for chickens:

You cunning rogues beware!
You jackals with the long hair!
You ate up the chickens of old Katrin,
And ran away singing like wild Bedawin.

It is not pleasant to have so many fleas annoying us all the time, but we must not be more anxious to keep the fleas out than to get the people in, and as the fellaheen come to see us, they will be likely to *flea* us too. Safita is famous for fleas, so no wonder that Nejmeh knows the following song of the boys about fleas:

I caught and killed a hopping flea,
His sister's children came to me:
One with drum my ears did pierce,
One was fluting loud and fierce,
Then they danced me, made me sing,
Like a monkey in a ring.
Come O Deeby, come I pray,
Bring the Doctor right away!
Peace on your heart feel no alarm,
You have not had the slightest harm.

Laia is never at a loss for something new, and I am amazed at her memory. She will give us some rhyming riddles in Arabic, and we will put them into English as best we may. The first is about the *Ant:*

'Tis black as night,
But it is not night:
Like a bird it has wings,
But it never sings:
It digs through the house,
But it is not a mouse:
It eats barley and grass,
But it is not an ass.

Riddle about a *gun:*

A featherless bird flew over the sea,
A bird without feathers, how can that be?
A beautiful bird which I admire,
With wooden feet and a head of fire!

Riddle on *salt:*

O Arab tribes, so bold and gay,
What little grain have you to-day?
It never on the trees is seen,
Nor on the flowers and wheat so green,
Its source is pure, 'tis pleasant to eat,
From water it comes that is not sweet,
Though from water it comes, and there's water in it,
You put it in water, it dies in a minute.

The door has opened down stairs, and some of Sit Leila's friends have come to see her. The moment they saw the little baby Fereed, they all began to call out, "Ism Allah alayhee," "The name of Allah upon him." They use this expression to keep off the Evil Eye. This superstition is universal throughout Western Asia, Northern Africa, and exists also in Italy and Spain. Dr. Meshaka of Damascus says that those who believe in the Evil Eye, "think that certain people have the power of killing others by a glance of the eye. Others inflict injury by the eye. Others pick grapes by merely looking at them. This power may rest in *one* eye, and one man who thought he had this power, *veiled one eye*, out of compassion for others! The Moslem Sheikhs and others profess to cure the evil eye, and prevent its evil effects by writing mystic talismanic words on papers, which are to be worn. Others write the words on an egg, and then strike the forehead of the evil eyed with the egg."

Whenever a new house is built, the workmen hang up an egg shell or a piece of alum, or an old root, or a donkey's skull, in the front door, to keep off the evil eye. Moslem women leave their children ragged and dirty to keep people from admiring them, and thus smiting them with the evil eye. They think that blue eyes are especially dangerous.

They think that the name of God or Allah is a charm against evil, and when they repeat it, they have no idea of reverence for that Holy Name.

Here is a terrible imprecation against a woman who smites with the Evil Eye:

May her hand be thrust in her mouth,
And her eyes be burned in the fire!
The blessings of Mighty God,
Preserve you from her ire!

An Arab Ploughing.

Nideh sings

> Upon you the name of Allah,
> Around you Allah's eye!
> May the Evil Eye be blinded,
> And never harm my boy!

It is ten o'clock at night, and Katrina, Laia, Wered, and Handumeh say it is time to go. Handumeh insists that we come to her wedding to-morrow. Amîn will go with them to drive away the dogs, and see that no wolves, hyenas, or leopards attack them by the way.

PART VII.

The boys of Abeih are early risers. What a merry laugh they have! What new song is that they are singing now?

There has been a shower in the night and Yusef and Khalil are singing about the rain. We say in English "*it* rains," but the Arabs tell us what "it" refers to. They say "The world rains," "The world snows," "The world is coming down," "The world thunders and lightens." So you will be able to tell your teacher, when he asks you to parse "it rains," that "*it*" is a pronoun referring to "world." Hear them sing:

> Rain, O world, all day and night,
> We will wash our clothing white,
> Rain, O world, your waters shed,
> On my dear grandmother's head.

The sun shines out now, and Khalil says the "world has got well" again, so he sings:

Shines the sun with brightest beam
On the roof of Im Seleem;
Now the bear will dance a reel,
On the roof of Im Khaleel.

The roofs of the houses are low and flat, and on the hill-sides you can walk from the street above upon the roof of the houses below. I once lived in a house in Duma in which the cattle, donkeys, and sheep used to walk on our roof every evening as they came in from pasture. It was not very pleasant to be awakened at midnight by a cow-fight on the roof, and have the stones and dirt rattling down into our faces, but we could get no other house, and had to make the best of it. You can understand then Khalil's song:

The sun is rising all so bright
Upon the Pasha's daughter:
See her toss the tassels blue,
As her mother taught her.
Turn the oxen on the roof
Of the village priest;
He will kill them one and all,
And give the poor a feast.

The boys seem to be in high glee. They all know Handûmeh and her betrothed Shaheen Ma'ttar, so they are swinging and singing in honor of her wedding.

But the time has come for the wedding, and we will go over to Ain Kesûr, about a mile away, and join in the bridal procession. As we come near the house we hear the women inside singing. They have been dressing the bride, and after she is dressed they lead her around and try to make her dance. Perhaps they will let us see how she is dressed. Her head is covered with a head-dress of pink gauze, embroidered with gold thread and purple chenille, and ornamented with pearl beads and artificial flowers, and over all a long white gauze veil trimmed with lace. Her ear-rings are gold filigree work with pendant pearls, and around her neck is a string of pure amber beads and a gold necklace. She wears a jacket of black velvet, and a gilt belt embroidered with blue, and fastened with a silver gilt filigree buckle in the form of a bow knot with pendants. On her finger is a gold ring set with sapphire, and others with turquoises and amethysts. Her dress is of brown satin, and on her arms are solid gold bracelets which cost 1400 piastres or fifty-six dollars. You know Handûmeh is not a rich girl, and her betrothed is a hard working muleteer, and he has had to work very hard to get the money to buy all these things, for it is the custom for the bridegroom to pay for the bride's outfit. The people always lay out their money in jewelry, because it is easily carried, and easily buried in time of civil wars and troubles in the land. Shaheen's brothers and relatives have come to take her to Abeih, but he is nowhere to be seen. It would not be proper for him to come to her house. For weeks she has not been over to Abeih, except to invite us to her wedding, and when

Anna asked her on what day she was to be married, she professed not to know anything about it. They think it is not modest for a bride to care anything about the wedding, and she will try to appear unwilling to go when they are ready to start. The women are singing now:

Dance, our bride so fair,
Dance and never care;
Your bracelets sing, your anklets ring,
Your shining beauty would dazzle a king!
To Damascus your father a journey has made,
And your bridegroom's name is Abû Zeid.

And now the young men outside are dancing and fencing, and they all join in singing:

Dance, my dancer, early and late,
Would I had like you seven or eight;
Two uncles like you, blithe and gay,
To stand at my back in the judgment day!

And now the young men, relatives of the bridegroom, address the brother of the bride, as her father is not living, and they all sing:

O brother of the bride, on a charger you should ride;
A Councillor of State you should be;
Whene'er you lift your voice,
The judgment halls rejoice,
And the earth quakes with fear
From Acre to Ghuzeer.

And now the warlike Druzes, who are old friends of Shaheen and his father, wish to show their good will by singing a wedding song, which they have borrowed from the old wild inhabitants of this land of Canaan:

O brother of the bride, your mare has gnawed her bridle,
Run for the blacksmith, do not be idle.
She has run to the grave where are buried your foes,
And pawed out their hearts with her iron shoes!

But the time has come for the procession to move, and we go along slowly enough. The bride rides a mare, led by one of Shaheen's brothers, and as we pass the fountain, the people pour water under the mare's feet as a libation, and Handûmeh throws down a few little copper coins to the children. The women in the company set up the zilagheet, a high piercing trill of the voice, and all goes merry as a marriage bell. When we reach the house of Shaheen, he keeps out of sight, not even offering to help his bride dismount from her horse. That would never do. He will stay among the men, and she in a separate room among the women, until the hour of the ceremony arrives.

But the women are singing again, and this time the song is really beautiful in Arabic, but I fear I have made lame work of it in the translation:

Allah, belaly, belaly,
Allah, belaly, belaly,
May God spare the life of your sire,
Our lovely gazelle of the valley!
May Allah his riches increase
He has brought you so costly a dowry;
The moonlight has gone from his house,
The rose from his gardens so flow'ry.

Run away, rude men, turn aside,
Give place to our beautiful bride:
From her sweet perfumes I am sighing,
From the odor of musk I am dying.
Come and join us fair maid, they have brought you your dress,
Leave your peacocks and doves, give our bride a caress;
Red silk! crimson silk! the weaver cries as he goes:
But our bride's cheeks are redder blushing bright as the rose.
Dark silk! black silk! hear him now as he sings:
But our bride's hair is black, like the raven's dark wings;
With the light of our eyes with our Handûmeh sweet
No maid of the Druzes can ever compete.
She is worth all the wealth of the Lebanon domain,
All the vineyards and olives, the silk worms and grain.
And no maids of the Christians can with her compare
Tho' shining with pearls and with jewels so rare.

The house is now crowded full, the men being all in one room with Shaheen, and the women in the other room, and the court with the bride Handûmeh. One of Shaheen's brothers comes around with a kumkum, and sprinkles orange flower water in all our faces, and Khalil asks us if we wish the ceremony to take place now? We tell him that he must ask the bride and groom. So Abû Shaheen comes into the court with the old priest Eklemandus, as Shaheen's family belong to the Greek Catholic sect. Handûmeh is really a Protestant, and Shaheen has nothing to do with the priests, but the "old folks" had their way about it. A white curtain hangs across the court, and the bride stands on one side, with her bridesmaid, and all the women and girls, and on the other side is the priest with Shaheen, and all of the men and boys. Then candles were distributed, and lighted, and the old priest adjusted his robes and began to read the marriage service. An assistant stood by his side looking over his shoulder, and responding Amen in a loud and long drawn voice. At length the priest called out to him, "A little shorter there on those Amens. We don't want long Amens at a wedding!" This set the whole crowd laughing, and on he went reading passages of Scripture, prayers and advice to the bride and bridegroom in the most hasty and trifling manner, intoning it through his nose, so that no one could understand what he was saying. While he was reading from the gospel about the marriage at Cana of Galilee, a small boy, holding a lighted candle, came very near burning off the old man's beard, and he called out to him, "Put out your candle! You have tormented my life out of me with that candle." This raised another laugh, and on he read. Then he took two rings, and drawing aside the curtain, placed one on the bride's head, and the other on the bridegroom's head, pronouncing them man and wife, and then gave them each a sip of wine and the ceremony was concluded, all the men kissing Shaheen, and the women Handûmeh. Refreshments were then served to the guests from the village, and a dinner to those from other villages. In the evening there assembled a great company in Shaheen's house, and the hour was given up to story telling. Saleh, whose brother married Shaheen's sister, will begin with the *Story of the Goats and the Ghoul.*

Once there was a Nanny Goat, strong and powerful, with long and strong horns, and once upon a time she brought forth twin kids, fair and beautiful. One was named *Sunaisil*, and the other Rabab. Now the Nanny Goat went out every morning to the pasture, leaving her twin kids in the cave. She shut the door carefully, and they locked it on the inside through fear of the Ghoul, for her neighbor in the next house was a Ghoul who swallowed little children alive. Then at evening when she came home, she would stand outside the door, and sing to her twin kids this little song:

Hearken now Sunaisil,
Come Rabab my dear:
Open to your mother,
Never, never fear.
She has sweet milk in her udder,
Tufts of grass upon her horn;
She'll give you both your supper,
And breakfast in the morn.

The little twin kids would know her voice, open the door in gladness, and eat a hearty supper, and after hearing a nice story from the Anzîyeh, (for so their mother was called), drop off to sweet sleep.

Now all things went on well for some time, until one day the Ghoul neighbor being very hungry for a supper of twin kids, came to the door of the cave and tried to push it open. But it was too strong for her, so she went away in perplexity. At length she thought she would sing to them the very song, which the Nanny Goat sang to them every evening on her return, so she sang it:

Hearken now Sunaisil,
Come Rabab, my dear, etc., etc.

and when they heard this song, they opened the door with gladness to eat their supper, when suddenly the Ghoul sprang upon them with her huge mouth open, and swallowed them both down at once. She then shut the door and fastened it as it was before, and went on her way. At evening the Nanny Goat came home with milk and grass for her twin kids' supper, and knocked at the door and sang:

Hearken now Sunaisil,
Come Rabab my dear, etc., etc.,

as usual, but no one opened the door. Then she knocked and sang again, and at length she gave up all hope of their opening the door, and butted against the door with her horns and broke it open. She then entered the cave but there were no twin kids there. All was still. Then she knew that the Ghoul had eaten them. So she hastened to the house of the Ghoul, and went upon the top of the house, and began to stamp and pound upon the roof. The Ghoul, hearing the stamping upon the roof, called out, whosoever stamps on my roof, may Allah stamp on his roof! The Nanny Goat replied, I am on your roof; I, whose children you have eaten. Come out now, and we will fight it out by butting our heads together. Very well, said the Ghoul, only wait a little until I can make me a pair of horns like you. So the goat waited, and away went the Ghoul to make her horns. She made two horns of dough and dried them in the sun until they were hard, and then came to "butt" with the goat. At the first shock, when the goat butted her with her horns, the horns of dough broke all to pieces; then the goat butted her again in her bowels and broke her in twain, and out jumped Sunaisil and Rabab, frisking and leaping and calling out "ya imme," oh, my mother, Oh, my mother! The Ghoul being dead they had no more fear, and lived long and happy lives with their mother the Anazîyeh.

Did you notice how the little boys listened to Saleh's story of the Goats and the Ghoul? This story is told by the mothers to their little children, all over Syria, in the tents of the Bedawîn and in the houses of the citizens. One of the women, named Noor, (i. e. Light), a sister of the bridegroom, says she will tell the children the story of the Hamam, the Britta, the Wez, and the Hamar, that is, of the Dove, the Duck, the Goose, and the Donkey, if all will sit still on the floor. So all the little boys and girls curl their feet under them and fold their arms, and Noor begins:

Once the Dove, the Duck, the Goose, and the Donkey joined company and agreed to live together. Then they took counsel about their means of living, and said, how long shall we continue in such distress for our necessary food? Come let us plough a piece of ground, and plant each one such seeds as are suited to his taste. So they ploughed a piece of ground and sowed the seed. The Goose planted rice, the Duck planted wheat, the Dove planted pulse, and the Donkey planted barley, and they stationed the Donkey on guard to watch the growing crop. Now when the seeds began to grow and flourish, and the Donkey looked upon it green and bright and waving in the wind, he arose and ate it all, and then went and threw himself into a ditch near by. Then came the Dove, the Goose, and the Duck to survey the growing crop, and lo and behold, it was all eaten up, and the ground was red and barren. Then said they, where is the Donkey whom we set on guard over our crop? They searched near and far, and at length they found him standing in the ditch, and they asked him where are the crops we so carefully planted and set you to watch? Then said the Donkey, the Bedawîn came with their flocks of sheep and pastured them on our crops, and when I tried to resist, they threw me into this ditch. Then they replied, it is false, you have eaten it yourself. He said, I did not. They said, yes, you did, for you are sleek and fat, and the contest waxed hot between them, until at length they all agreed to make each one swear an oath "by the life of the Lake," which was near at hand, and whoever swore the oath, and sprang into the Lake without falling, should be declared innocent. So the Dove went down first and said:

Ham, Ham, Ham, I am the Dove Hamam,
Ham, Ham, Ham, My food is the plain Kotan, (pulse).
Ham, Ham, Ham, If I ate the growing crop,
May I suddenly throw it up!

May Allah tumble me into the Lake,
And none any news of me ever take!

Then the Dove leaped into the Lake, and flew to the limb of a tree on the shore, and was proved innocent.

Then the Duck went down and said:

But, But, But, I am the Butta Duck,
But, But, But, My food is wheat and muck;
But, But, But, If I ate the growing crop,
May I suddenly throw it up!
May Allah tumble me into the Lake,
And none any news of me ever take!

So the Duck leaped into the Lake, and then flew to the limb of a tree on the shore and was proved innocent.

Then the Goose went down and said:

Wez, Wez, Wez, I am the Goose and the Wez,
Wez, Wez, Wez, I eat Egyptian riz, (rice),
Wez, Wez, Wez, If I ate the growing crop,
May I suddenly throw it up!
May Allah tumble me into the Lake,
And none any news of me ever take!

So the Goose leaped into the Lake and then flew to the limb of a tree on the shore and was proved innocent.

Then the Donkey went down and said:

Hak, Hak, Hak, I am the Donkey Jack,
Hak, Hak, Hak, I barley eat by the sack;
Hak, Hak, Hak, If I ate the growing crop,
May I suddenly throw it up!
May Allah tumble me into the Lake,
And none any news of me ever take!

Then the Donkey leaped boldly into the Lake, ıd down he fell, and his feet stuck fast in the mud ıd mire. Then his three companions, seeing him oved guilty of the crime, flew away and left him his fate. Then the Donkey began to "bray" for ercy, and called at the top of his voice:

Whoever will help me out of this plight,
May eat my tail at a single bite!

The Bear heard the braying,
And without long delaying,
He answered by saying:

Long eared Donkey will you pay,
Every word of what you say?
If I save you by my might,
Will you stand still while I bite?

The lying Ass lay still,
And answered, "Yes, I will."

The Bear then gave a fearful roar,
And dragged the Donkey to the shore,
And said, I saved you from your plight,
Now stand still, Donkey, while I bite!

He said: Wait Bruin till I rest,
And "smell the air" from East to West,
And then I'll run with all my might,
And turn my tail for you to bite!

Then Bruin took him at his word,
Away he went swift as a bird,
And called out, now Bruin, I will rest,
I'll smell the air from East to West,
I'm running now with all my might,
I've "turned my tail" for you to bite!

The Bear resolved in grief and pain,
He'd never help an Ass again.

Abû Habeeb, who is just about to enter the col-ge, has a story which all the Arabs know, and love hear. It is called;

The Lion and Ibn Adam, that is, the Lion and Man, the son of Adam.

Once there was a Lion who had a son, and he always charged him, saying, my son, beware of Ibn Adam. But at length the old Lion died, and the young lion resolved that he would search through the world and see that wonderful animal called Ibn Adam, of whom his father had so often warned him. So out he went from his cave, and walked to and fro in the wilderness. At length he saw a huge animal coming towards him, with long crooked legs and neck, and running at the top of his speed. It was a Camel. But when the Lion saw his enormous size and rapid pace, he said, surely, this must be Ibn Adam himself. So he ran towards him and roared a fearful roar. Stop where you are! The Camel stopped, trembling with fear of the Lion. Said the Lion, are you Ibn Adam? No, said the Camel, I am a Camel fleeing from Ibn Adam. Said the Lion, and what did Ibn Adam do to you that you should flee from him? The Camel said, he loaded me with heavy burdens, and beat me cruelly, and when I found a fit chance, I fled from him to this wilderness. Said the Lion, is Ibn Adam stronger than you are? Yes indeed, many times stronger. Then the Lion was filled with terror, lest he too should fall into the hands of Ibn Adam, and he left the Camel to go his way in peace. After a little while, an Ox passed by, and the Lion said, *this* must be Ibn Adam. But he found that he too was fleeing from the yoke and the goad of Ibn Adam. Then he met a Horse running fleet as the wind, and he said, this swift animal must be the famous Ibn Adam, but the Horse too was running away from the halter, the bridle the spur or the harness of the terrible Ibu Adam. Then he met a mule, a donkey, a buffalo and an elephant, and all were running in terror of Ibn Adam. The Lion thought what terrible monster must he be to have struck terror into all these monstrous animals! And on he went trembling, until hunger drove him to a forest to seek for prey to eat. While he was searching through the forest, lo and behold, a Carpenter was at work cutting wood. The Lion wondered at his curious form, and said, who knows but this may be Ibn Adam? So he came near and asked him saying, Are you Ibn Adam? He replied, I am. Then the Lion roared a fearful roar, and said, prepare for battle with the Lion, the king of beasts! Then Ibn Adam said: What do you want of me? Said the Lion, I want to devour you. Very well, said the Carpenter, wait until I can get my claws ready. I will go and take this wood yonder, and then I will return and fight you. If you kill me, eat me, and if I conquer you I will let you go, for we the sons of Adam do not eat the flesh of wild beasts, nor do we kill them, but we let them go. The Lion was deceived by those artful words, for he had seen the Camel and his companions running away, and he thought within himself, now, if Ibn Adam did really eat the flesh of beasts, he would not have let the Camel and the Horse, the Buffalo and the Mule escape into the desert. So he said to the Carpenter, very well, I will wait for you to take the wood, and return with your claws. Not so, said the Carpenter, I am afraid that you will not wait for me. You are a stranger, and I do not trust your word. I. fear you will run away before I return. Said the Lion, it is impossible that the Lion should run away from any one. Said the Carpenter, I cannot admit what you say, unless you will grant me one thing. And what is that, said the Lion. The Carpenter said, I have here a little rope. Come let me tie you to this tree until I return, and then I shall know where to find you. The Lion agreed to this plan, and the Carpenter bound him with ropes to the tree until he and the tree were one compact bundle. Then the Carpenter went away to his shop, and brought his glue pot, and filling it with glue and pitch boiled it over the fire. Then he returned and besmeared the Lion with the boiling mixture from his head to the end of his tail, and applied a torch until he was all in a flame from head to tail, and in this plight the Carpenter left him. Then the Lion roared in agony until the whole forest echoed the savage roar, and all the animals and wild beasts came running together to see what had happened. And when they saw him in this sad plight, they rushed to him and loosed his bonds, and he sprang to the river and extinguished the flames, but came out singed and scarred, with neither hair nor mane. Now when all the beasts saw this pitiable sight, they made a covenant together to kill Ibn Adam. So they watched and waited day and night, until at length they found him in the forest. As soon as he saw them, he ran to a lofty tree, and climbed to its very top, taking only his adze with him, and there awaited his fate. The whole company of beasts now gathered around the foot of the tree, and tried in vain to climb it, and after they walked around and around, at length they agreed that one should stand at the foot of the tree, and another on his back, and so on, until the upper one should reach Ibn Adam, and throw him down to the ground. Now the Lion, whose back was burned and blistered, from his great fear of man demanded that he should stand at the bottom of the tree. To this all agreed. Then the Camel mounted upon the Lion's back, the Horse upon the Camel, the Buffalo upon the Horse, the Bear upon the Buffalo, the Wolf upon the bear, and the Donkey upon the Wolf, and so on in order, until the topmost animal was almost within reach of the Carpenter, Ibn Adam. Now, when he saw the animals coming nearer and nearer, and almost ready to seize him, he shouted at the top of his voice. Bring the glue pot of boiling pitch to the Lion! Hasten! Hasten! Now when the Lion heard of the boiling pitch, he was terrified beyond measure and leaped one side with all his might and fled. Down came the pile of beasts, tumbling in confusion, the one upon the other, and all lay groaning bruised and bleeding, some with broken legs, some with broken ribs, and some with broken heads. But as soon as the clamor of their first agony was over, they all called out to the Lion, why did you leap out and bring all this misery upon us! The Lion replied:

> The story's point he never knew,
> Who never felt the burning glue!

Monsoor, who has just been to Damascus, says that if he can have another pipe, and a cup of Arab coffee, he will tell the story of the famous Jew Rufaiel of Damascus. So he begins:

The story of Rufaiel, the rich Jew of Damascus, and the Moslem Dervish.

Once there lived in Damascus a rich Jew named Rufaiel. He had great wealth in marble palaces and rich silk robes, and well stored bazaars, and his wife and daughters were clad in velvets and satins, in gold and precious stones. He had also great wit and cunning, and often helped his fellow Jews out of their troubles. Now the Pasha of Damascus was a Mohammedan, who had a superstitious fear of the holy Moslem Dervishes, and they could persuade him to tax and oppress the Jews in the most cruel manner. In those days there came to Damascus a holy Dervish who had long, uncombed black hair, and although he was a vile and wicked man, he made the people believe that he was a holy saint, and could perform wonderful miracles. The Pasha held him in great reverence, and invited him often to dinner, and when he came in, he would stoop and kiss the Dervish's feet! And what was most wonderful of all, the Dervish left Damascus every Thursday night after bidding the Pasha farewell, and journeyed to Mecca and returned in the morning and told the Pasha all the Mecca news and what he had seen and heard. This he did every week, though all wise men laughed at him, and said he only went out of the City Gate and slept in the gardens of Damascus!

Now the Dervish was a great enemy of the Jews. He hated them, cursed them, spat upon them, and called them infidel dogs, and he persuaded the Pasha to increase their taxes fourfold. Their sufferings now became very great. They had to sell their houses and furniture to pay the heavy taxes, and many were beaten and thrust into prison. So the leading Jews in their distress came to Rufaiel, and begged him to go to the Pasha and obtain relief for them and their families. He said he would think about the matter. So after they had gone, he called the chief jeweller and pipe maker of the city, and ordered them to make a long pipe of exquisite workmanship, with a stem of rosewood carved and inlaid with pearls, a bowl of pure gold set with diamonds, and a mouth-piece of gold and amber. Then he went one day to call on the Pasha, and made him a present of this elegant pipe, the like of which had never been seen in Damascus. The Pasha was greatly pleased and ordered all in his presence to retire that he might enjoy the society of Rufaiel, the munificent Jew. Then Rufaiel turned to the Pasha and said, "may your Excellency live forever! I have brought you this pipe as a faint token of my high esteem and affection, but I am filled with deepest sorrow that it is not perfect." "Not perfect?" said the Pasha. "In what respect could it be more perfect than what it is?" Said Rufaiel, "you will notice that between the amber and the gold of the mouth-piece a little ring is wanting. This ring was the very gem and excellence of the pipe. It was cut from the Black Stone of the Kaaba in Mecca, and has miraculous properties. But when the pipe was brought from Mecca, the ring was left with Mustafa, the jeweller, who is ready to send it by the first fit opportunity." "Alas," said the Pasha, "but how can we send for it now? The Pilgrim caravan has gone, and there will be none again for a year." "Oh," said Rufaiel, "this is easily arranged. To-day is Thursday, and to-night the holy Dervish will go to Mecca and return to-morrow morning. Your Excellency need only command him to bring the black ring, and before this time to-morrow the pipe will be complete in its beauty and excellency." "El Hamdû Lillah! Praise to Allah! It shall be done!" So when Rufaiel had gone, the Pasha summoned the Dervish, and told him of this wonderful pipe which had come to him from Mecca, and that it only needed the black ring to make it absolutely perfect, and that he was hereby commanded on pain of death to bring the ring from Mecca before Friday at the hour of noon prayer. The Dervish bowed most obeisantly and retired black in the face with rage and despair. But it occurred to him at once that none in Damascus but Rufaiel could have purchased such a pipe. So he left the City Gate, called the Bab Allah, or Gate of God, at sunset, bidding his friends farewell, and walked away in the gardens until night came on

Then, at the sixth hour of the night he returned by another gate, and crept along to the door of the mansion of Rufaiel. The door was opened, and Rufaiel received him with great politeness. The Dervish fell on the floor and kissed his feet and begged for his life. Said he, "give me that black ring which belongs to the Pasha's pipe, and we will be friends forever! Ask what you will and it shall be done to you. Only give me this ring." Said Rufaiel, "you have ruined my people with oppression, and now do you ask a favor?" "Yes," said the Dervish, "and you shall have any favor you ask." So Rufaiel thought to himself a moment, and then said, "I ask one thing. Do you obtain from the Pasha an order on all the tax collectors of Damascus, that when any Jew shall say, *I am one of the Seventy*, the collector shall pass him by, and no tax ever be demanded of him." "Done," said the Dervish, and embracing Rufaiel, he bade him good-night. Then in the morning he hastened in at Bab Allah, and presented the ring to the Pasha, who was so delighted that he granted his request, and orders were given that no tax should ever be collected from any Jew who should say "I am one of the Seventy." Then Rufaiel assembled all the Jews of Damascus, and bade them say to the tax-gatherers whenever they came, "*I am one of the Seventy.*" So the Jews had rest from taxation, all the days of Rufaiel.

Saleh Bû Nusr, one of the best men in Mount Lebanon, and the father of Khalil, who brought us the list of Arab boys' games, has already told us the story of the Goats and the Ghoul, and he says that the savory odor of the egg plant being cooked for the wedding guests, reminds him of the story of the Badinjan or Egg Plant.

Once there was a great Emir or Prince who had a very abject and obsequious servant named Deeb (Wolf). One day Deeb brought to the Emir for his dinner a dish of stewed badinjan, which pleased the Emir so much that he complimented Deeb, and told him that it was the best dinner he had eaten for months. Deeb bowed to the earth and kissed the feet of the Emir, and said, "may God prolong the life of your excellency! Your excellency knows what is good. There is nothing like the badinjan. It is the best of vegetables. Its fruit is good, its leaf is good, its stalk is good, and its root is good. It is good roasted, stewed, boiled, fried, and even raw. It is good for old and young. Your excellency, there is nothing like the badinjan." Now the Emir was unusually hungry, and ate so bountifully of the badinjan that he was made very ill. So he sent for Deeb, and rebuked him sharply, saying, "you rascal, you Deeb, your name is Wolf, and you are rightly named. This badinjan which you praised so highly has almost killed me." "Exactly so," said Deeb, "may your excellency live forever! The badinjan is the vilest of plants. It is never eaten without injury. Its fruit is injurious, its leaf is injurious, its stalk is noxious, and its root is the vilest of all. It is not fit 'ajell shanak Allah,' for the pigs to eat, whether raw, roasted, stewed, boiled or fried. It is injurious to the young and dangerous to the old. Your excellency, there is nothing so bad as the badinjan! Never touch the badinjan!"—"Out with you, you worthless fellow, you Deeb! What do you mean by praising the badinjan when I praise it, and abusing it when it injures me?" "Ah, your excellency," said Deeb, "am I the servant of the badinjan, or the servant of your excellency? I must say what pleases you, but it makes no difference whether I please the badinjan or not."

The wedding party is now over, and the guests are departing. Each one on leaving says, "by your pleasure, good evening!" The host answers, "go in peace, you have honored us." The guests reply, "we have been honored, Allah give the newly married ones an arees," (a bridegroom). They would not dare wish that Shaheen and Handûmeh might some day have a little baby *girl*. That would be thought an insult.

We will walk up the hill to our mountain home, passing the fountain and the great walnut trees. Here comes a horseman. It is Ali, who has been spending a month among the Bedawin Arabs. He will come up and stay with us, and tell us of his adventures. He says that the Sit Harba, the wife of the great Arab Sheikh ed Dukhy, taught him a number of the Bedawin Nursery Songs, and although he is weary with his journey, he will repeat some of them in Arabic.

They are all about camels and spears and fighting and similar subjects, and no wonder, as they see nothing else, and think of nothing else.

To-morrow is the feast day,
We've no "henna" on our hands;
Our camels went to bring it,
From far off distant lands;
We'll rise by night and listen,
The camel bells will ring;
And say a thousand welcomes
To those who "henna" bring.

And here is a song which shows that the Bedawin have the same habit of cursing their enemies, which we noticed in the Druze lullabys:

On the rose and sweetest myrtle,
May you sleep, my eyes, my boy;
But may sharpest thorns and briars,
All your enemies destroy!

Ali says that one of the most mournful songs he heard in the desert was the following:

I am like a wounded camel,
I grind my teeth in pain;
My load is great and heavy,
I am tottering again.
My back is torn and bleeding,
My wound is past relief,
And what is harder still to bear,
None other knows my grief!

The next is a song which the people sung in the villages on the borders of the desert. By "the sea" they mean the Sea of Galilee:

My companions three,
Were fishing by the sea;
The Arabs captured one,
The Koords took his brother,
In one land was I,
My friends were in another.

"Ho, Every one that thirsteth!"

I was left to moan,
In sorrow deep and sad,
Like a camel all alone,
Departing to Baghdad ;
My soul I beg you tell me whether,
Once parted friends e'er met together?

The Bedawin have as low an idea of girls as the Bedawin in the cities, and are very glad when a boy is born. Sometimes when the Abeih girls are playing together, you will hear a little girl call out, "it is very small indeed. Why it is a little wee thing, as small as was the rejoicing the day I was born!" But hear what the Bedawin women sing when a boy is born:

Mashallah, a boy, a *boy!*
May Allah's eye defend him!
May she who sees and says not *the Name*,
Be smitten with blindness and die in shame!

How would you like to live among the Bedawin, and have a dusky Arab woman, clad in coarse garments, covered with vermin and odorous of garlic and oil, to sing you to sleep on a mat on the ground?

Hasten my cameleer, where are you going?
It is eventide, and the camels are lowing:
My house in a bundle I bear on my back,
Whenever night comes, I my bundle unpack.

The next is a song of the pastoral Arabs:

Hasten my guide and lead us away,
For we have fought and lost the day;
To the well we went all thirsty and worn,
The well was dry! and we slept forlorn.

The Bedawin came in battle array,
Attacked us all famished at break of day,
And took all our camels and tents away!

Death enters the Bedawin tents as well as the palaces of kings and the comfortable homes of the people in Christian lands. But what desolation it leaves behind in those dark sorrowing hearts, who know nothing of the love of Jesus and the consolations of the gospel. This is a funeral song the poor Bedawin women sing over the death of a child:

Oh hasten my camel, begone, begone,
Oh haste where your loved ones stay:
There weep and lament. There my "spirit" is gone,
Is gone to a night without day:
Oh Star of the Morning, thou Star of the day,
And Star of the Evening, both hasten away,
And bring me a balm for my wounded heart,
For I from my child, my "spirit" must part.

Soon may the "day dawn, and the day star arise" in their dark hearts, and Jesus the "Bright and Morning Star" be their portion forever!

The next song is about the pilgrimage to Jerusalem. Thousands of Greeks, Armenians and Catholics go to Jerusalem every year to visit the "Holy Places," and get a certificate of the pardon of all their sins. The Greek Patriarch performs a lying imposture called the Holy Fire every year at Greek Easter, by lighting a candle with a match inside a dark room, and declaring that it is miraculously lighted by fire which comes forth from the tomb of Christ! So the poor Greek woman sings to her child:

Oh take me on a pilgrimage,
Jerusalem to see :
The Tomb of Christ and Holy fire,
And Hill of Calvary :
And then I'll to the Convent go,
Ask pardon for my sin :
And say, my Lady, now forgive,
And comfort me again.

The next is really beautiful, and is good enough for any mother to sing to her child. It is a morning song:

Praise to Him who brings the light,
And keeps the birds in darkest night.
God is merciful to all,
Rise ye men and on Him call !
Allah praise in every lot,
He keeps you and you know it not.

And this one too, about the little worms, is curious enough :

Praise to Him who feeds the worms,
In the silent vale !
Provides their portion every day,
Protects them in the dangerous way.
No doubt they praise Him too, and pray,
In the silent vale !

When our good friend Yusef, whom we saw in Safita, asked the Nusairîyeh women to repeat to him their nursery rhymes, they denied that they had any. They were afraid to recite them, lest he write them down and use them as a magic spell or charm against them. When a child is born among them, no one is allowed to take a coal or spark of fire from the house for a week, lest the child be injured. They always hang a little coin around the child's neck to keep off eruptions and diseases from its body.

You must be weary by this time, after Handumeh's wedding and the story telling and the Bedawin songs. Let us retire to rest for the night, thankful for the precious Bible, and the knowledge of Jesus Christ. You are safe indeed in the hands of God, and need not fear the Ghoul nor the Bah'oo. Good night.

Such is life. Yesterday a wedding, and to-day a funeral. Do you hear that terrific wail, those shrieks and bitter cries of anguish? Young Sheikh Milham has died. The Druze and Christian women are gathered in the house, and wailing together in the most piteous manner. It is dreadful to think what sufferings the poor women must endure. They do everything possible to excite one another. They not only call out, "Milham, my pride, my bridegroom, star of my life, you have set, my flower, you have faded," but they remind each other of all the deaths that have occurred in their various families for years, and thus open old wounds of sorrow which time had healed. Yet they have regular funeral songs, and we will listen while they sing in a mournful strain:

Milham Beg my warrior,
Your spear is burnished gold:
Your costly robes and trappings,
Will in the street be sold.
"Where is the Beg who bore me?"
I hear the armor crying—
Where is the lord who wore me?
I hear the garments sighing.

Now Im Hassein from Ainab bursts out in a loud song, addressing the dead body, around which they are all seated on the ground :

Rise up my lord, gird on your sword,
Of heavy Baalbec steel ;
Why leave it hanging on the nail ?
Let foes its temper feel !
Would that the Pasha's son had died,
Not our Barmakeh's son and pride !

Then Lemis answers in another song in which they all join :

Ten thousands are thronging together,
The Beg has a feast to-day ;
We thought he had gone on a visit,
But alas, he has gone to stay.

Then they all scream, and tear their hair and beat their breasts. Alas, they have no light beyond the grave. Who could expect them to do otherwise? The Apostle Paul urges the Christians " not to sorrow even as others which have no hope ! " This is sorrow without hope. The grave is all dark to them. How we should thank our Saviour for having cast light on the darkness of the tomb, and given us great consolation in our sorrows ! Here comes a procession of women from Kefr Metta. Hear them chanting :

I saw the mourners thronging round,
I saw the beds thrown on the ground ;
The marble columns leaning,
The wooden beams careening,

My lord and Sheikh with flowing tears,
I asked what was its meaning?
He sadly beckoned me aside,
And said, To-day *my son* has died!

Then an old woman, a widow, who has been reminded of the death of her husband, calls out to him:

Oh, Sheikh, have you gone to the land?
Then give my salams to my boy,
He has gone on a long, long journey,
And took neither clothing nor toy.
Ah, what will he wear on the feast days,
When the people their festal enjoy?

Now one of the women addresses the corpse:

Lord of the wide domain,
All praise of you is true:
The women of your hareem,
Are dressed in mourning blue.

Then one sings the mother's wail:

My tears are consuming my heart,
How can I from him bear to part.
Oh raven of death, tell me why,
You betrayed me and left him to die?
Oh raven of death begone!
You falsely betrayed my son!
Oh Milham, I beg you to tell,
Why you've gone to the valley to dwell?
From far, far away I have come,
Who will come now to take me back home?

Then rises such a wail as you never heard before. A hundred women all screaming together and then grasping the hands and feet of the corpse, while the men are coming to take it away. The women hug and kiss the corpse, and try to pull it back, while the men drive them off, and carry it out to the bier. Some of the women faint away, and a piercing shriek arises. Then you hear the mother's wail again.

Then one sings the call of the dead man for help:

Oh ransom me, buy me, my friends to-day,
'Tis a costly ransom you'll have to pay,
Oh ransom me, father, whate'er they demand,
Though they take all your money and houses and land.

And another sings his address to the grave-diggers:

Oh cease, grave-diggers, my feelings you shock,
I forbade you to dig, you have dug to the rock;
I bade you dig little, you have dug so deep!
When his father's not here, will you lay him to sleep?

Then a poor woman who has lately buried a young daughter begins to sing:

Oh bride! on the roofs of heaven,
Come now and look over the wall:
Oh let your sad mother but see you,
Oh let her not vainly call!
Hasten, her heart is breaking,
Let her your smile behold;
The mother is sadly weeping,
The maiden is still and cold.

The Druzes believe that millions of Druzes live in China and that China is a kind of heaven. So another woman sings:

Yullah, now my lady, happy is your state!
Happy China's people, when you reached the gate!
Lady, you are passing,
To the palace bright,
All the stars supassing,
On the brow of night!

And now the body is taken to be buried, and the women return to the house, where the wailing is kept up for days and weeks. They have many other funeral songs, of which I will give two in conclusion:

Ye Druzes, gird on your swords,
A great one is dead to-day;
The Arabs came down upon us,
They thought us in battle array,
But they wept when they found us mourning,
For our leader has gone away!

The next is the lament of the mother over her dead son:

The sun is set, the tents are rolled,
Happy the mother whose lambs are in fold;
But one who death's dark sorrow knew,
Let her go to the Nile of indigo blue,
And dye her robes a mourning hue!

And now, my dear boy, our Syrian journey is ended. You have seen and heard many strange things. Whatever is good among the Arabs, try to imitate; whatever is evil, avoid. Perhaps you will write to me some day, and tell me what you think of Syria and the Syrians. Many little boys and girls will read this long letter, but it is your letter, and I have written it for your instruction and amusement.

May the good Shepherd, who gave His life for the sheep, lead you beside the still waters of life, and at last when He shall appear, may He give you a crown of glory which fadeth not away!

THE END.

INDEX.

Crown Buildings, 188, *Fleet Street*,
London, *October*, 1873.

SAMPSON LOW, MARSTON & CO.'S

ANNOUNCEMENTS FOR THE COMING SEASON.

THE AUTHORIZED VERSION OF THE FOUR GOSPELS.

WITH THE WHOLE OF THE

MAGNIFICENT ETCHINGS ON STEEL,

AFTER THE

DRAWINGS BY M. BIDA.

THE drawings, etchings, and engravings have been twelve years in preparation, and an idea of the importance of this splendid work may be gathered from the fact that upwards of twelve hundred and fifty thousand francs, or fifty thousand pounds, have been expended on its production, and it has obtained for MM. Hachette the Diplome d'Honneur at the Vienna Exhibition.

The English edition will contain the whole of the 132 steel etchings, and in addition some very exquisite woodcut ornaments.

The Gospel of St. Matthew	will contain	41	Steel Etchings.
The Gospel of St. Mark	,,	24	,,
The Gospel of St. Luke	,,	40	,,
The Gospel of St. John	,,	27	,,

Size, large Imperial quarto.

It is intended to publish each Gospel separately, and at intervals of from six to twelve months: and in order to preserve uniformity, the price will in the first instance be fixed at £3 3s. each volume. This uniformity of price has been determined on the assumption that purchasers will take the whole of the four volumes as published; but, as it will be seen that the Gospels of St. Matthew and St. Luke contain more etchings and more letterpress than St. Mark and St. John, and are therefore proportionately more costly in production, it must be understood that at the expiration of three months from the first issue of each of these two volumes, the price (if purchased separately) will be raised to four guineas. This extra charge will, however, be allowed at any time to all bona fide purchasers of the four volumes.

The Gospel of St. John, appropriately bound in cloth extra, price £3 3s., will be the first volume issued, and will be ready for publication shortly.

Specimen pages of text and etchings may be seen on application to any bookseller in town and country, who will be happy to register the names of subscribers, either for each Gospel separately, or for the whole of the Gospels as published.

IMPORTANT ANNOUNCEMENT.

DR. SCHWEINFURTH'S TRAVELS AND DISCOVERIES IN CENTRAL AFRICA.

From 1868 to 1871.

Translated by ELLEN E. FREWER. With an Introduction by WINWOOD READE.

ESSRS. SAMPSON LOW & Co. have the pleasure of stating that they have completed arrangements with the celebrated African Traveller, Dr. GEORG SCHWEINFURTH, for the exclusive right to publish his new work, entitled—

THE HEART OF AFRICA.

OR, THREE YEARS' TRAVELS AND ADVENTURES IN THE UNEXPLORED REGIONS OF THE CENTRE OF AFRICA.

This is unquestionably, in a scientific point of view, one of the most valuable contributions to a knowledge of the Natural History, Botany, Geography, and River System of Central Africa that has ever appeared; but its chief interest will consist in the personal adventures of the author amongst unknown tribes, and wanderings in lands hitherto unexplored. The Doctor carries his reader into a veritable wonderland, full of peculiar customs, and where his experiences have been of the most eventful nature. The district explored embraces a wide tract of country extending southward from the Meschera on the Bahr el Ghazal, and betwixt the 10th and 3rd degrees of north latitude.

The present work cannot fail to be of most unusual interest to general readers; inasmuch as it will include adventures in an unknown country amongst cannibals and pygmies, the discovery and exploration of twenty-two hitherto quite unknown rivers, the wonderful land of the Monbuttoo, his reception by King Munza, horrible cannibalism, fights with natives and struggles with wild animals, adventures on rivers, on mountains, and in jungles; and, in short, experiences of the most novel and startling kind that could be imagined in an unknown and savage country.

The work will form two volumes, demy 8vo., of upwards of 500 pages each, and will be illustrated by about 130 woodcuts from drawings made by the author—comprising figures of different races of men; animals, domestic and wild; remarkable fish and snakes; varieties of trees, plants, and fruits; landscapes; forest scenery; watered plains; episodes of the journey; cannibal feasts and dances; fording rivers; villages and huts; night encampments; meetings with chieftains; weapons of war, &c. &c.; with maps and plans.

It is proposed that the work shall be published in England and America (in English), and in the respective languages of Germany, France, Russia, Italy, &c., simultaneously, and arrangements are now in progress for this purpose; and the Publishers hope to have it ready for publication during the present Autumn.

SPECIAL NOTICE.

New Story for Youths by H. M. STANLEY.

"MY KALULU," PRINCE, KING, AND SLAVE.

A Story from Central Africa.

BY HENRY M. STANLEY,

Author of "How I found Livingstone."

Crown 8vo., about 430 pp., with numerous Graphic Illustrations, after Original Designs by the Author. Cloth, 7s. 6d. [*In October*

For the convenience of those who did not care to pay so high a price as 21s. for the original Edition of MR. STANLEY'S *first great Work, it is now offered, in a new and elegant binding, with a revised Introductory Chapter, at 10s. 6d. In this form and at this price it will form an excellent School Prize or Christmas Present.*

HOW I FOUND LIVINGSTONE.

Including Travels, Adventures, and Discoveries in Central Africa, and Four Months' Residence with Dr. Livingstone.

BY H. M. STANLEY.

Numerous Illustrations by Mr. J. B. ZWECKER, Mr. JOHN JELLICOE, and other Artists, from Mr. STANLEY'S own Sketches, with Maps of Route, Physical Features, &c. Twelfth Thousand. New issue, in new binding, gilt edges, extra cloth, 10s. 6d. [*Now ready.*

Magnificent Work on the Pottery of all Ages and all Nations.

HISTORY OF THE CERAMIC ART:

Descriptive and Analytical Study of the Potteries of all Times and of all Nations.

BY ALBERT JACQUEMART.

Author of the "History of Porcelain," "The Wonders of Ceramic," &c.

Two hundred Woodcuts by H. CATENACCI and J. JACQUEMART, 12 Steel-plate Engravings by JULES JACQUEMART, and 1,000 Marks and Monograms. Translated by Mrs. BURY PALLISER. In 1 vol., super royal 8vo., of about 700 pp., cloth extra, gilt edges, 42s. [*Nearly ready.*

In One Volume, Demy 8vo., cloth extra, price about 16s.

THE LAND OF THE WHITE ELEPHANT;

SIGHTS AND SCENES IN SOUTH EASTERN ASIA.

A Personal Narrative of Travel and Adventure in Farther India, embracing the countries of Burma, Siam, Cambodia, and Cochin-China (1871-72).

BY FRANK VINCENT, JUN.

With Map, Plans, and numerous Illustrations. [*Nearly ready.*

New Works by the celebrated French Writer, JULES VERNE.

1.

THE FUR COUNTRY; OR, SEVENTY DEGREES NORTH LATITUDE.

BY JULES VERNE. TRANSLATED BY N. D'ANVERS.

A Story of remarkable Adventures in the Northern Regions of the Hudson's Bay Territory. Crown 8vo. with upwards of 80 very graphic full-page Illustrations. Cloth extra. Uniform in size and style with "Twenty Thousand Leagues under the Sea." Price 10*s*. 6*d*. [*In October*.

2.

FROM THE EARTH TO THE MOON; AND A TRIP ROUND IT.

BY JULES VERNE. TRANSLATED BY L. P. MERCIER.

With numerous characteristic Illustrations. Crown 8vo. Uniform in size and price with the above. Cloth, gilt edges, 10*s*. 6*d*. [*Ready*.

3.

AROUND THE WORLD IN EIGHTY DAYS.

BY JULES VERNE.

Square crown 8vo. With numerous Illustrations. Uniform in size and style with "Meridiana," by the same author. Price 7*s*. 6*d*. [*Nearly ready*.

One Vol., Demy 8vo., cloth, with numerous woodcuts and a map.

THE WILD NORTH LAND:

The Story of a Winter Journey with dogs across Northern North America.

BY CAPTAIN W. F. BUTLER,

Author of "The Great Lone Land." [*In November*.

A WHALING CRUISE TO BAFFIN'S BAY AND THE GULF OF BOOTHIA.

With an Account of the Rescue, by his Ship, of the survivors of the Crew of the "Polaris."

BY CAPTAIN MARKHAM, R.N.

One Volume, demy 8vo., with Map and Illustrations, cloth extra.

Now Ready, in One Volume, demy 8vo., with Maps and Illustrations, cloth extra, 16*s*.

THE THRESHOLD OF THE UNKNOWN REGION.

BY CLEMENTS R. MARKHAM, C.B., F.R.S.

Secretary of the Royal Geographical Society. [*Now ready*.

IN PREPARATION FOR PUBLICATION IN DECEMBER.

In Two Volumes, Royal 8vo., cloth extra, numerous Woodcuts, Maps, and Chromolithographs.

THE SECOND NORTH GERMAN POLAR EXPEDITION IN THE YEARS 1869-70.

Of the Ships "Germania" and "Hansa," under command of Captain Koldeway,

EDITED AND CONDENSED BY H. W. BATES, ESQ.,

Of the Royal Geographical Society.

Important Work on Peru.

TWO YEARS IN PERU; WITH EXPLORATION OF ITS ANTIQUITIES.

BY THOMAS J. HUTCHINSON, F.R.G.S., F.R.S.L., F.A.I.,

Map by DANIEL BARRERA, and numerous Illustrations. In 1 vol., demy 8vo., cloth extra. [*In the press.*

New Work on Morocco.

ADVENTURES IN MOROCCO, AND JOURNEY SOUTH THROUGH THE OASES OF DRAA AND TAFILET.

BY DR. GERHARD ROHLFS. EDITED BY WINWOOD READE.

1 vol., crown 8vo., Map and Portrait of the Author, cloth extra. [*In the press.*

Magnificent Work on China.

ILLUSTRATIONS OF CHINA AND ITS PEOPLE

BY J. THOMSON, F.R.G.S.

Being Photographs from the Author's Negatives, printed in permanent Pigments by the Autotype Process, and Notes from Personal Observation.

*** The complete work will embrace 200 Photographs, with Letterpress Descriptions of the Places and People represented. In four volumes, imperial 4to., price £3 3*s.* each volume. The First Volume, containing Fifty Photographs, was published in the Spring; and the Second Volume, containing Photographs as below, is now ready.

Subscribers ordering the Four Volumes at once will be supplied for £10 10*s.* half of which to be paid on receipt of Vol. I., and balance on completion of the Work. Non-Subscribers' price is £3 3*s.* a Volume.

VOLUME III. is in active preparation, and will be Published before Christmas.

A most beautiful Christmas Present.

WOMAN IN SACRED HISTORY.

BY MRS. HARRIET BEECHER STOWE.

Illustrated with 15 chromo-lithographs and about 200 pages of letterpress forming one of the most elegant and attractive Volumes ever published. Demy 4to., cloth extra, gilt edges, price 25*s*. [*In November.*

NEW WORK BY THE REV. E. H. BICKERSTETH.

One Volume square 8vo., with Numerous very beautiful Engravings, uniform in Character with the Illustrated Edition of Heber's Hymns, &c., price 7s. 6d.

THE REEF, AND OTHER PARABLES.

By the Rev. E. H. BICKERSTETH, M. A., Author of "Yesterday, To-day, and for Ever," &c. [*Nearly Ready.*

CARL WERNER'S NILE SKETCHES,

Painted from Nature during his Travels through Egypt. Facsimiles of Water-colour Paintings executed by Gustave W. Seitz, with Descriptive Text by Dr. E. A. BREHM and Dr. DUMICHEN. Third Series. Imperial folio, in Cardboard Wrapper, £3 10*s*.

Beautiful Work for Winter Evenings. Dedicated, by Permission, to His Royal Highness, Prince Leopold.

ILLUSTRATED GAMES OF PATIENCE.

By the LADY ADELAIDE CADOGAN. Twenty-four Diagrams in Colours, with Descriptive Text. Foolscap 4to., cloth extra, gilt edges, 12*s*. 6*d*.

THE ROYAL PASTRY AND CONFECTIONERY BOOK

(Le livre de Patisserie). By JULES GOUFFE, Chef de Cuisine of the Paris Jockey Club. Translated from the French and adapted to English use by ALPHONSE GOUFFE, Head Pastrycook to Her Majesty the Queen. Illustrated with 10 large Plates printed in Colours, and 137 Engravings on Wood, after the Oil Paintings and Designs of E. RONJAT. Royal 8vo., cloth extra. [*In the Press.*

Important New Work by Professor Guyot.

PHYSICAL GEOGRAPHY.

By ARNOLD GUYOT, Author of "Earth and Man." In 1 Volume, large 4to., 128 pp., numerous coloured Diagrams, Maps and Woodcuts, price 10*s*. 6*d*., strong boards.

HISTORY OF THE AMERICAN AMBULANCE,

Established in Paris during the Siege of 1870-71. Together with the Details of its Method and its Work. By THOMAS W. EVANS, M. D., D. D. S., Ph. D., President of the American International Sanitary Committee, &c., Author of "La Commission Sanitaire des Etats Unis: son Origine, son Organisation et ses Resultats," &c. In 1 Volume, Imperial 8vo., with numerous Illustrations, cloth extra, price 35*s*. [*Now Ready.*

Preparing for publication in one handsome small 4to., cloth gilt edges, price 15s.

PHYNNODDERREE, AND OTHER TALES:

Fairy Legends of the Isle of Man. By EDWARD MCALOE. To be profusely Illustrated with upwards of 120 Engravings on Wood.

THE POSTHUMOUS WORKS AND UNPUBLISHED AUTOGRAPHS OF NAPOLEON III. IN EXILE.

Collected and arranged by COUNT DE LA CHAPELLE, Coadjutor in the last Works of the Emperor at Chislehurst. 1 Volume demy 8vo., cloth extra, 14s. [*Now Ready.*

RECOLLECTIONS OF THE EMPEROR NAPOLEON I.

During the First Three Years of his Captivity on the Island of St. Helena Including the time of his Residence at her father's house, "The Briars." By Mrs. ABELL (late Miss Elizabeth Balcombe). Third Edition. Revised throughout with additional matter by her daugbter, Mrs. CHARLES JOHNSTONE. 1 Volume, demy 8vo. With Steel Portrait of Mrs. Abell, and Woodcut Illustrations. Cloth extra, gilt edges, 10s. 6d. [*Now Ready.*

ENGLISH MATRONS AND THEIR PROFESSION;

With some Considerations as to its Various Branches, its National Value, and the Education it requires. By M. L. F., Writer of "My Life, and what shall I do with it," "Battle of the Two Philosophies," and "Strong and Free." Crown 8vo., cloth extra, 7s. 6d. [*Now Ready.*

"All States among which the regulations regarding women are bad, enjoy scarcely the half of happiness."—ARISTOTLE.

SPECIAL NOTICE.—*The long-desired Map to Mr. King's Work has now been added, and also a Chapter of entirely new matter. (Dedicated to Professor Tyndal.)*

MOUNTAINEERING IN THE SIERRA NEVADA.

By CLARENCE KING. Crown 8vo. Fourth and Cheaper Edition. Cloth extra, with Map and Additional Chapter, 6s. [*Nearly Ready.*

A CHRONICLE OF THE FERMORS; HORACE WALPOLE IN LOVE.

By M. F. MAHONY (Matthew Stradling), Author of "The Misadventures of Mr. Catlyn," "The Irish Bar-sinister," &c. In 2 Volumes, Demy 8vo., with Steel Portrait. [*In the Press.*

MILITARY LIFE IN PRUSSIA.

First Series. The Soldier in Time of Peace. Translated (by permission of the Author) from the German of F. W. Häcklander. By F. E. R. and H. E R. Crown 8vo., cloth extra, 9s. [*Now Ready.*

University Local Examinations.

ST. MARK'S GOSPEL.

With Explanatory Notes. For the Use of Schools and Colleges. By GEORGE BOWKER, late Second Master of the Newport Grammar School, Isle of Wight. 1 Volume, foolscap, cloth. [*In Preparation.*

NEW NOVELS.

Victor Hugo's New Novel.

IN THE YEAR '93 (QUATRE-VINGT TREIZE).

Three Volumes, crown 8vo. [*In Preparation.*

This work, which will he published simultaneously in France, England, and America, is said to surpass in style and dramatic interest anything that Victor Hugo has yet produced.

New Work by the Author of "Lorna Doone."

ALICE LORRAINE;

A Tale of the South Downs. Three Volumes, crown 8vo. [*In Preparation.*

IN THE ISLE OF WIGHT.

Two Volumes, crown 8vo., cloth, 21*s.* [*Now Ready.*

BETTER THAN GOLD.

By Mrs. ARNOLD, Author of "His by Right," "John Hesketh's Charge," "Under Foot," &c. In 3 Volumes, crown 8vo., 31*s.* 6*d.* [*In the Press.*

New Work by Hain Friswell, Author of "The Gentle Life," &c.

OUR SQUARE CIRCLE.

Two Volumes, crown 8vo., cloth, 21*s* [*In the Press.*

New Work of Fiction by Georgiana M. Craik.

ONLY A BUTTERFLY.

One Volume, crown 8vo., cloth, 10*s.* 6*d.* [*Now Ready.*

ARGUS FAIRBAIRNE; OR, A WRONG NEVER RIGHTED.

By HENRY JACKSON, Author of "Hearth Ghosts," &c. Three Volumes, crown 8vo., cloth, 31*s.* 6*d.* [*In the Press.*

New Volume of the John Halifax Series of Girls' Books.

MISS MOORE.

By GEORGIANA M. CRAIK. Small post 8vo., with Illustrations, gilt edges, 4*s.* [*Nearly Ready*

Crown Buildings, 188, *Fleet Street*,
London, *October*, 1873.

A List of Books

PUBLISHING BY

SAMPSON LOW, MARSTON, LOW, & SEARLE.

ALPHABETICAL LIST.

ABBOTT (J. S. C.) History of Frederick the Great, with numerous Illustrations. 8vo. 1*l.* 1*s.*

About in the World, by the author of "The Gentle Life." Crown 8vo. bevelled cloth, 4th edition. 6*s.*

Adamson (Rev. T. H.) The Gospel according to St. Matthew, expounded. 8vo. 12*s.*

Adventures of a Young Naturalist. By LUCIEN BIART, with 117 beautiful Illustrations on Wood. Edited and adapted by PARKER GILLMORE, author of "All Round the World," "Gun, Rod, and Saddle," &c. Post 8vo. cloth extra, gilt edges, new edition, 7*s.* 6*d.*

"The adventures are charmingly narrated."—*Athenæum.*

Adventures of a Brownie. See **Craik, Mrs.**

Adventures on the Great Hunting Grounds of the World, translated from the French of Victor Meunier, with engravings, 2nd edition. 5*s.*

"The book for all boys in whom the love of travel and adventure is strong. They will find here plenty to amuse them and much to instruct them besides."—*Times.*

Alcott, (Louisa M.) Aunt Jo's Scrap-Bag. Square 16mo, 3*s.* 6*d.*

—— **Little Men: Life at Plumfield with Jo's Boys.** By the author of "Little Women." Small post 8vo. cloth, gilt edges, 3*s.* 6*d.* Cheap edition, cloth, 2*s.*; fancy boards, 1*s.* 6*d.*

—— **Little Women.** Complete in 1 vol. fcap. 3*s.* 6*d.* Cheap edition, 2 vols. cloth, 2*s.*; boards, 1*s.* 6*d.* each.

——. **Old Fashioned Girl,** best edition, small post 8vo. cloth extra, gilt edges, 3*s.* 6*d.*; Low's Copyright Series, 1*s.* 6*d.*; cloth, 2*s.*

The *Guardian* says of "Little Women," that it is—"A bright, cheerful, healthy story—with a tinge of thoughtful gravity about it which reminds one of John Bunyan. The *Athenæum* says of "Old-Fashioned Girl"—"Let whoever wishes to read a bright, spirited, wholesome story, get the 'Old Fashioned Girl' at once."

Alcott (Louisa M.) Shawl Straps. Small post 8vo. Cloth extra, gilt edges, 3*s*. 6*d*.

—— **Work, a Story of Experience.** 2 vols. cr. 8vo. 21*s*.

Allston (Captain). *See* **Ready, O Ready.**

Alexander (Sir James E.) Bush Fighting. Illustrated by Remarkable Actions and Incidents of the Maori War. With a Map, Plans, and Woodcuts. 1 vol. demy 8vo. pp. 328, cloth extra, 16*s*.

"This book tells the story of the late war in New Zealand, with its many desperate encounters and exciting personal adventures, and tells that story well."—*Naval and Military Gazette.*

"This is a valuable history of the Maori war."—*Standard.*

Alexander (W. D. S.) The Lonely Guiding Star. A Legend of the Pyrenean Mountains and other Poems. Fcap. 8vo. cloth. 5*s*.

Among the Arabs, a Narrative of Adventures in Algeria, by G. Naphegyi, M. D., A. M. 7*s*. 6*d*.

Andersen (Hans Christian) The Story of My Life. 8vo. 10*s*. 6*d*.

—— **Fairy Tales,** with Illustrations in Colours by E. V. B. Royal 4to. cloth. 1*l*. 5*s*.

Andrews (Dr.) Latin-English Lexicon. 13th edition. Royal 8vo. pp. 1,670, cloth extra. Price 18*s*.

The superiority of this justly-famed Lexicon is retained over all others by the fulness of its Quotations, the including in the Vocabulary Proper Names, the distinguishing whether the Derivative is classical or otherwise, the exactness of the References to the Original Authors, and by the price.

"The best Latin Dictionary, whether for the scholar or advanced student."—*Spectator.*

"Every page bears the impress of industry and care."—*Athenæum.*

Anecdotes of the Queen and Royal Family, collected and edited by J. G. Hodgins, with Illustrations. New edition, revised by John Timbs. 5*s*.

Angell (J. K.) A Treatise on the Law of Highways. 8vo. 1*l*. 5*s*.

Arctic Regions (The). Illustrated. *See* **Bradford.**

—— **German Polar Expedition.** *See* **Koldeway.**

—— **Explorations.** *See* **Markham.**

Around the World. *See* **Prime.**

Art, Pictorial and Industrial, Vol. 1, 1*l.* 11*s.* 6*d.* Vols. 2 and 3, 18*s.* each.

Atmosphere (The). *See* Flammarion.

Aunt Jo's Scrap Bag. *See* Alcott.

Australian Tales, by the "Old Boomerang." Post 8vo. 5*s.*

ACK-LOG Studies. *See* Warner.

Baldwin (J. D.) Prehistoric Nations. 12mo. 4*s.* 6*d.*

—— **Ancient America,** in notes of American Archæology. Crown 8vo. 10*s.* 6*d.*

Bancroft's History of America. Library edition, vols. 1 to 9, 8vo. 5*l.* 8*s.*

—— **History of America,** Vol. X. (completing the Work.) 8vo. 12*s.* [*In the press.*

Barber (E. C.) The Crack Shot. Post 8vo. 8*s.* 6*d.*

Barnes's (Rev. A.) Lectures on the Evidences of Christianity in the 19th Century. 12mo. 7*s.* 6*d.*

Barnum (P. T.) Struggles and Triumphs. Crown 8vo. Fancy boards. 2*s.* 6*d.*

Barrington (Hon. and Rev. L. J.) From Ur to Macpelah; the Story of Abraham. Crown 8vo., cloth, 5*s.*

THE BAYARD SERIES. Comprising Pleasure Books of Literature produced in the Choicest Style as Companionable Volumes at Home and Abroad.

Price 2s. 6d. each Volume, complete in itself, printed at the Chiswick Press, bound by Burn, flexible cloth extra, gilt leaves, with silk Headbands and Registers.

The Story of the Chevalier Bayard. By M. DE BERVILLE.

De Joinville's St. Louis, King of France.

The Essays of Abraham Cowley, including all his Prose Works.

Abdallah; or, the Four Leaves. By EDOUARD LABOULLAYE.

Table-Talk and Opinions of Napoleon Buonaparte.

Vathek: An Oriental Romance. By WILLIAM BECKFORD.

The King and the Commons: a Selection of Cavalier and Puritan Song. Edited by Prof. MORLEY.

Words of Wellington: Maxims and Opinions of the Great Duke.

Dr. Johnson's Rasselas, Prince of Abyssinia. With Notes.

Hazlitt's Round Table. With Biographical Introduction.

The Religio Medici, Hydriotaphia, and the Letter to a Friend. By Sir THOMAS BROWNE, Knt.

Ballad Poetry of the Affections. By ROBERT BUCHANAN.

Coleridge's Christabel, and other Imaginative Poems. With Preface by ALGERNON C. SWINBURNE.

Lord Chesterfield's Letters, Sentences and Maxims. With Introduction by the Editor, and Essay on Chesterfield by M. De St. Beuve, of the French Academy.

Essays in Mosaic. By THOS. BALLANTYNE.

My Uncle Toby; his Story and his Friends. Edited by P. FITZGERALD.

Reflections; or, Moral Sentences and Maxims of the Duke de la Rochefoucauld.

Socrates, Memoirs for English Readers from Xenophon's Memorabilia. By EDW. LEVIEN.

Prince Albert's Golden Precepts.

A suitable Case containing 12 *volumes, price* 31*s.* 6*d.*; *or the Case separate, price* 3*s.* 6*d.*

EXTRACTS FROM LITERARY NOTICES.

"The present series—taking its name from the opening volume, which contained a translation of the Knight without Fear and without Reproach—will really, we think, fill a void in the shelves of all except the most complete English libraries. These little square-shaped volumes contain, in a very manageable and pretty form, a great many things not very easy of access elsewhere, and some things for the first time brought together." —*Pall Mall Gazette.* "We have here two more volumes of the series appropriately called the 'Bayard,' as they certainly are 'sans reproche.' Of convenient size, with clear typography and tasteful binding, we know no other little volumes which make such good gift-books for persons of mature age."—*Examiner.* "St. Louis and his companions, as described by Joinville, not only in their glistening armour, but in their every-day attire, are brought nearer to us, become intelligible to us, and teach us lessons of humanity which we can learn from men only, and not from saints and heroes. Here lies the real value of real history. It widens our minds and our hearts, and gives us that true knowledge of the world and of human nature in all its phases which but few can gain in the short span of their own life, and in the narrow sphere of their friends and enemies. We can hardly imagine a better book for boys to read or for men to ponder over."—*Times.*

Beecher (Henry Ward, D. D.) Life Thoughts. Complete in 1 vol. 12mo. 2*s.* 6*d.*

—— **Sermons Selected.** 12mo. 8*s.* 6*d.*

—— **Norwood, or Village Life in New England.** Crown 8vo. 6*s.*

—— **(Dr. Lyman) Life and Correspondence of.** 2 vols. post 8vo. 1*l.* 1*s.*

Bees and Beekeeping. By the Times' Beemaster. Illustrated. Crown 8vo. New Edition, with additions. 2*s.* 6*d.*

Bell (Rev. C. D.) Faith in Earnest. 18mo. 1*s.* 6*d.*

—— **Blanche Nevile.** Fcap. 8vo. 6*s.*

Bellows (A. J.) The Philosophy of Eating. Post 8vo. 7*s.* 6*d.*

—— **How not to be Sick, a Sequel to Philosophy of Eating.** Post 8vo. 7*s.* 6*d.*

Bickersteth's Hymnal Companion to Book of Common Prayer.

The following Editions are now ready:—

				s.	*d.*
No. 1. A	Small-type Edition, medium 32mo.		cloth limp	0	6
No. 1. B		ditto	roan limp, red edges ..	1	0
No. 1. C		ditto	morocco limp, gilt edges ..	2	0
No. 2.	Second-size type, super-royal 32mo.		cloth limp ..	1	0
No. 2. A		ditto	roan limp, red edges ..	2	0
No. 2. B		ditto	morocco limp, gilt edges ..	3	0
No. 3.	Large-type Edition, crown 8vo.		cloth, red edges ..	2	6
No. 3. A		ditto	roan limp, red edges ..	3	6
No. 3. B		ditto	morocco limp, gilt edges ..	5	6
No. 4.	Large-type Edition, crown 8vo. with Introduction and Notes, cloth, red edges			3	6
No. 4. A		ditto	roan limp, red edges ..	4	6
No. 4. B		ditto	morocco, gilt edges ..	6	6
No. 5.	Crown 8vo. with accompanying Tunes to every Hymn, New Edition			3	0
No. 5. A		ditto	with Chants	4	0
No. 5. B	The Chants separately			1	6

No. 6. Penny Edition.

Fcap. 4to. Organists' edition. Cloth, 7*s.* 6*d.*

*** *A liberal allowance is made to Clergymen introducing the Hymnal.*

☞ The Book of Common Prayer, bound with The Hymnal Companion. 32mo. cloth, 9*d.* And in various superior bindings.

Benedict (F. L.) Miss Dorothy's Charge. 3 vols. 31*s*. 6*d*.

Biart (L.) Adventures of a Young Naturalist. (See *Adventures*.)

Bickersteth (Rev. E. H., M.A.) The Master's Home-Call; Or, Brief Memorials of Alice Frances Bickersteth. 3rd Edition. 32mo. cloth gilt. 1*s*.

"They recall in a touching manner a character of which the religious beauty has a warmth and grace almost too tender to be definite."—*The Guardian*.

—— **The Shadow of the Rock. A Selection of Religious Poetry.** 18mo. Cloth extra. 2*s*. 6*d*.

Bigelow (John) France and Hereditary Monarchy. 8vo. 3*s*.

Bishop (J. L.) History of American Manufacture. 3 vols. 8vo. 2*l*. 5*s*.

—— **(J. P.) First Book of the Law.** 8vo. 1*l*. 1*s*.

Bits of Talk about Home Matters. By H. H. Fcap. 8vo. cloth gilt edges. 3*s*.

Black (Wm.) Uniform Editions:

—— **Kilmeny: a Novel.** Small Post 8vo. cloth. 6*s*.

—— **In Silk Attire.** 3rd and cheaper edition, small post 8vo. 6*s*.

"A work which deserves a hearty welcome for its skill and power in delineation of character."—*Saturday Review*.

"A very charming book."—*Pall Mall Gazette*.

"As a story it is all absorbing."—*Spectator*.

—— **A Daughter of Heth.** 11th and cheaper edition, crown 8vo., cloth extra. 6*s*. With Frontispiece by F. Walker, A.R.A.

"If humour, sweetness, and pathos, and a story told with simplicity and vigour, ought to insure success, 'A Daughter of Heth' is of the kind to deserve it."—*Saturday Review*.

"The special genius of the book is the conception of such a character as Coquette's."—*Spectator*.

"An inviting title, agreeable writing, humour, sweetness and a fresh natural style are combined."—*Pall Mall Gazette*.

"The 'Daughter of Heth' is a novel of real power and promise."—*Standard*.

Black (C. B.) New Continental Route Guides.

—— **Guide to the North of France,** including Normandy, Brittany, Touraine, Picardy, Champagne, Burgundy, Lorraine, Alsace, and the Valley of the Loire; Belgium and Holland; the Valley of the Rhine to Switzerland; and the South-West of Germany, to Italy by the Brenner Pass. Illustrated with numerous Maps and Plans. Crown 8vo., cloth limp. 8*s*. 6*d*.

—— **Guide to Normandy and Brittany,** their Celtic Monuments, Ancient Churches, and Pleasant Watering-Places. Illustrated with Maps and Plans. Crown 8vo., cloth limp, 2*s*. 6*d*.

Black (C. B.) New Continental Route Guides.

—— **Guide to the North-East of France,** including Picardy, Champagne, Burgundy, Lorraine, and Alsace; Belgium and Holland; the Valley of the Rhine, to Switzerland; and the South-West of Germany, to Italy, by the Brenner Pass, with Description of Vienna. Illustrated with Maps and Plans. Crown 8vo., cloth limp. 4*s.* 6*d.*

—— **Paris, and Excursions from Paris.** Illustrated with numerous Maps, Plans, and Views. Small post 8vo. cloth limp, price 2*s.* 6*d.*

—— **Guide to the South of France and to the North of Italy**: including the Pyrenees and their Watering-Places; the Health Resorts on the Mediterranean from Perpignan to Genoa; and the towns of Turin, Milan, and Venice. Illustrated with Maps and Plans. Small post 8vo., cloth limp, 5*s*.

—— **Switzerland and the Italian Lakes.** Small post 8vo. price 2*s.* 6*d.*

Blackburn (H.) **Art in the Mountains**: the Story of the Passion Play, with upwards of Fifty Illustrations. 8vo. 12*s.*

—— **Artists and Arabs.** With numerous Illustrations. 8vo. 7*s.* 6*d.*

—— **Harz Mountains: a Tour in the Toy Country.** With numerous Illustrations. 12s.

—— **Normandy Picturesque.** Numerous Illustrations. 8vo. 16*s.*

—— **Travelling in Spain.** With numerous Illustrations. 8vo. 16*s.*

—— **Travelling in Spain.** Guide Book Edition 12mo. 2*s.* 6*d.*

—— **The Pyrenees.** Summer Life at French Watering-Places. 100 Illustrations by GUSTAVE DORE. Royal 8vo. 18*s.*

Blackmore (R. D.) **Lorna Doone.** New edition. Crown, 8vo. 6*s.*

"The reader at times holds his breath, so graphically yet so simply does John Ridd tell his tale . . . . 'Lorna Doone' is a work of real excellence, and as such we heartily commend it to the public."—*Saturday Review.*

—— **Cradock Nowell.** 2nd and cheaper edition. 6*s.*

—— **Clara Vaughan.** Revised edition. 6*s.*

—— **Georgics of Virgil.** Small 4to. 4*s.* 6*d.*

Blackwell (E.) **Laws of Life.** New edition. Fcp. 3*s.* 6*d.*

Boardman's Higher Christian Life. Fcp. 1*s.* 6*d.*

Bonwick (J.) **Last of the Tasmanians.** 8vo. 16*s.*

Bonwick (J.) Daily Life of the Tasmanians. 8vo. 12*s*. 6*d*.

—— **Curious Facts of Old Colonial Days.** 12mo. cloth. 5*s*.

Book of Common Prayer with the Hymnal Companion. 32mo. cloth. 9*d*. And in various bindings.

Books suitable for School Prizes and Presents. (Fuller description of each book will be found in the alphabet.)

Adventures of a Young Naturalist. 7*s*. 6*d*.
—— on Great Hunting Grounds. 5*s*.
Allcott's Aunt Jo's Scrap-bag. 3*s* 6*d*.
—— Old Fashioned Girl. 3*s*. 6*d*.
—— Little Women. 3*s*. 6*d*.
—— Little Men. 3*s*. 6*d*.
—— Shawl Straps. 3*s*. 6*d*.
Anecdotes of the Queen. 5*s*.
Atmosphere (The). By FLAMMARION. 30*s*.
Bickersteth (Rev. E. H.) Shadow of the Rock. 2*s*. 6*d*.
Butler's Great Lone Land. 7*s*. 6*d*.
—— Cradock Nowell. 6*s*.
—— Clara Vaughan. 6*s*.
Bayard Series (See Bayard.)
Blackmore's Lorna Doone. 6*s*.
Changed Cross (The). 2*s*. 6*d*.
Child's Play. 7*s*. 6*d*.
Christ in Song. 5*s*.
Craik (Mrs.) Adventures of a Brownie. 5*s*.
—— Little Sunshine's Holiday. 4*s*.
Craik (Miss) The Cousin from India. 4*s*.
Dana's Corals and Coral Islands. 21*s*.
—— Two Years before the Mast. 6*s*.
Davies's Pilgrimage of the Tiber. 18*s*.
De Witt (Mad.) An Only Sister. 4*s*.
Erkmann-Chatrian's, The Forest House. 3*s*. 6*d*.
Faith Gartney. 3*s*. 6*d*. cloth; boards, 1*s*. 6*d*.
Favell Children (The). 4*s*.
Favourite English Poems. 300 Illustration. 21*s*.
Franc's Emily's Choice. 5*s*.
—— Marian. 5*s*.
—— Silken Cord. 5*s*.
—— Vermont Vale. 5*s*.
—— Minnie's Mission. 4*s*.

Books for School Prizes and Presents, *continued.*

Gayworthys (The). 3*s.* 6*d.*
Gentle Life, (Queen Edition). 10*s.* 6*d.*
Gentle Life Series. (*See* Alphabet).
Getting on in the World. 6*s.*
Glover's Light of the Word. 2*s.* 6*d.*
Hayes (Dr.) Cast Away in the Cold. 6*s.*
Healy (Miss) The Home Theatre. 3*s.* 6*d.*
Henderson's Latin Proverbs. 10*s.* 6*d.*
Hugo's Toilers of the Sea. 10*s.* 6*d.*
,, ,, ,, 6*s.*
Jack Hazard, by Trowbridge. 3*s.* 6*d.*
Kingston's Ben Burton. 3*s.* 6*d.*
Kennan's Tent Life. 6*s.*
King's Mountaineering in the Sierra Nevada. 6*s.*
Low's Edition of American Authors. 1*s.* 6*d.* and 2*s.* each. 23 Vols. published. *See* Alphabet under Low.
Lyra Sacra Americana. 4*s.* 6*d.*
Macgregor (John) Rob Roy Books. (*See* Alphabet.)
Marigold Manor, by Miss Waring. 4*s.*
Maury's Physical Geography of the Sea 6*s.*
Parisian Family. 5*s.*
Phelps (Miss) The Silent Partner. 5*s.*
Picture Gallery British Art. 12*s.*
—— Sacred Art. 12*s.*
Ready, O Ready. By Captain Allston, R.N. 3*s.* 6*d.*
Reynard the Fox. 100 Exquisite Illustrations. 7*s.* 6*d.*
Sea-Gull Rock. 79 Beautiful Woodcuts. 7*s.* 6*d.*
Stanley's How I Found Livingstone. 21*s.*
Stowe (Mrs.) Pink and White Tyranny. 3*s.* 6*d.*
—— Old Town Folks. Cloth extra 6*s.* and 2*s.* 6*d.*
—— Ministers Wooing. 5*s.*; boards, 1*s.* 6*d.*
—— Pearl of Orr's Island. 5*s.*
—— My Wife and I. 6*s.*
Tauchnitz's German Authors. *See* Tauchnitz.
Tayler (C. B.) Sacred Records. 2*s.* 6*d.*
Titcomb's Letters to Young People. 1*s.* 6*d.* and 2*s.*
Twenty Years Ago. 4*s.*
Under the Blue Sky. 7*s.* 6*d.*
Verne's Meridiana. 7*s.* 6*d.*
—— Twenty Thousand Leagues Under the Sea. 10*s.* 6*d.*
Whitney's (Mrs.) Books. *See* Alphabet.

Bowles (T. G.) The Defence of Paris, narrated as it was Seen. 8vo. 14*s.*

Boynton (Charles B., D.D.) Navy of the United States, with Illustrations of the Ironclad Vessels. 8vo. 2 vols. 2*l.*

Under the Special Patronage of Her Most Gracious Majesty the Queen, the Duke of Argyll, the Marquis of Lorn, &c.

Bradford (Wm.) The Arctic Regions. Illustrated with Photographs, taken on an Art Expedition to Greenland. With Descriptive Narrative by the Artist. In One Volume, royal broadside, 25 inches by 20, beautifully bound in morocco extra, price Twenty-five Guineas.

Bremer (Fredrika) Life, Letters, and Posthumous Works. Crown 8vo. 10*s.* 6*d.*

Brett (E.) Notes on Yachts. Fcp. 6*s.*

Bristed (C. A.) Five Years in an English University. Fourth Edition, Revised and Amended by the Author. Post 8vo. 10*s.* 6*d.*

Broke (Admiral Sir B. V. P., Bart., K.C.B.) Biography of. 1*l.*

Brothers Rantzau. *See* **Erckmann Chatrian.**

Browning (Mrs. E. B.) The Rhyme of the Duchess May. Demy 4to. Illustrated with Eight Photographs, after Drawings by Charlotte M. B. Morrell. 21*s.*

Burritt (E.) The Black Country and its Green Border Land: or, Expeditions and Explorations round Birmingham, Wolverhampton, &c. By Elihu Burritt. Second and cheaper edition. Post 8vo. 6*s.*

—— **A Walk from London to Land's End.** With Illustrations. 8vo. 6*s.*

—— **The Lectures and Speeches of Elihu Burritt.** Fcp. 8vo. cloth, 6*s.*

Burroughs (John). *See* **Wake Robin.**

Bush (R. J.) Reindeer, Dogs, and Snow Shoes: a Journal of Siberian Travel. 8vo. 12*s.* 6*d.*

Bush Fighting. *See* **Alexander (Sir J. E.)**

Bushnell's (Dr.) The Vicarious Sacrifice. Post 8vo. 7*s.* 6*d.*

—— **Sermons on Living Subjects.** Crown 8vo. cloth. 7*s.* 6*d.*

—— **Nature and the Supernatural.** Post 8vo. 3*s.* 6*d.*

—— **Christian Nurture.** 3*s.* 6*d.*

—— **Character of Jesus.** 6*d.*

—— **The New Life.** Crown 8vo. 3*s.* 6*d.*

Butler (W. F.) The Great Lone Land; an Account of the Red River Expedition, 1869-1870, and Subsequent Travels and Adventures in the Manitoba Country, and a Winter Journey across the Saskatchewan Valley to the Rocky Mountains. With Illustrations and Map. Fifth and Cheaper Edition. Crown 8vo. cloth extra. 7*s*. 6*d*. (The first 3 Editions were in 8vo. cloth. 16*s*.)

The *Times* says:—"He describes easily and forcibly. He has a sympathy with the beautiful as well as a sense of the ridiculous. But his prejudices and his egotism are merely the weaknesses of a frank, hearty nature, and we have a personal liking for him when we take leave of him at the end of his wanderings."

"The tone of this book is altogether delightful and refreshing."—*Spectator*.

"The impression left on the mind by his narrative is one of profound interest."—*Morning Post*.

"This is one of the freshest and most interesting books of travel that we have had the pleasure of reading for some time past."—*Examiner*.

"There is a delightful breeziness and vigour about Captain Butler's style of writing."—*Leeds Mercury*.

"His fascinating volume . . . . not only exciting, but instructive reading."—*Pall Mall Gazette*.

"Captain Butler writes with rare spirit."—*Nonconformist*.

CALIFORNIA. *See* **Nordhoff.**

Carlisle (Thos.) The Unprofessional Vagabond. By Thomas Carlisle (Haroun Alraschid), with Sketches from the Life of John Carlisle. Fcap. 8vo. Fancy boards. 1*s*.

Changed Cross (The) and other Religious Poems. 2*s*. 6*d*.

Child's Play, with 16 coloured drawings by E. V. B. An entirely new edition, printed on thick paper, with tints, 7*s*. 6*d*.

Chefs-d'œuvre of Art and Master-pieces of Engraving, selected from the celebrated Collection of Prints and Drawings in the British Museum. Reproduced in Photography by Stephen Thompson. Imperial folio, Thirty-eight Photographs, cloth gilt. 4*l*. 14*s*. 6*d*.

China. *See* **Illustrations of.**

Choice Editions of Choice Books. New Editions. Illustrated by C. W. Cope, R.A., T. Creswick, R.A., Edward Duncan, Birket Foster, J. C. Horsley, A.R.A., George Hicks, R. Redgrave, R.A., C. Stonehouse, F. Taylor, George Thomas, H. J. Townshend, E. H. Wehnert, Harrison Weir, &c. Crown 8vo. cloth, 5*s*. each; mor. 10*s*. 6*d*

Bloomfield's Farmer's Boy.
Campbell's Pleasures of Hope.
Cundall's Elizabethan Poetry.
Coleridge's Ancient Mariner.
Goldsmith's Deserted Village.
Goldsmith's Vicar of Wakefield.
Gray's Elegy in a Churchyard.
Keat's Eve of St. Agnes.
Milton's l'Allegro.
Rogers' Pleasures of Memory.
Shakespeare's Songs and Sonnets.
Tennyson's May Queen.
Weir's Poetry of Nature.
Wordsworth's Pastoral Poems.

Christ in Song. Hymns of Immanuel, selected from all Ages, with Notes. By PHILIP SCHAFF, D.D. Crown 8vo. toned paper, beautifully printed at the Chiswick Press. With Initial Letters and Ornaments and handsomely bound. New Edition. 5*s*.

Christabel. *See* **Bayard Series.**

Christmas Presents. *See* **Illustrated Books.**

Chronicles of Castle of Amelroy. 4to. With Photographic Illustrations. 2*l*. 2*s*.

Clara Vaughan. *See* **Blackmore.**

Coffin (G. C.) Our New Way Round the World. 8vo. 12*s*.

Commons Preservation (Prize Essays on), written in competition for Prizes offered by HENRY W. PEEK, Esq. 8vo. 14*s*.

Compton Friars, by the Author of Mary Powell. Cr. 8vo. cloth. 10*s*. 6*d*.

Courtship and a Campaign; a Story of the Milanese Volunteers of 1866, under Garibaldi. By M. DALIN. 2 vols. cr. 8vo. 21*s*.

Cradock Nowell. *See* **Blackmore.**

Craik (Mrs.) The Adventures of a Brownie, by the Author of "John Halifax, Gentleman." With numerous Illustrations by Miss PATERSON. Square cloth, extra gilt edges. 5*s*.

A Capital Book for a School Prize for Children from Seven to Fourteen.

—— **Little Sunshine's Holiday** (forming Vol. 1. of the John Halifax Series of Girls' Books). Small post 8vo. 4*s*.

—— **John Halifax Series.** *See* **Girls' Books.**

—— **Poems.** Crown, cloth, 5*s*.

—— **(Georgiana M.) The Cousin from India,** forming Vol. 2. of John Halifax Series. Small post 8vo. 4*s*.

—— **Without Kith or Kin.** 3 vols. crown 8vo., 31*s*. 6*d*.

—— **Hero Trevelyan.** 2 Vols. Post 8vo. 21*s*.

Craik's American Millwright and Miller. With numerous Illustrations. 8vo. 1*l*. 1*s*.

Cruise of "The Rosario. *See* **Markham (A. H.).**

Cummins (Maria S.) Haunted Hearts (Low's Copyright Series). 16mo. boards. 1*s*. 6*d*.; cloth, 2*s*.

Curtis's History of the Constitution of the United States. 2 vols. 8vo. 24*s*.

DALTON (J. C.) A Treatise on Physiology and Hygiene for Schools, Families, and Colleges, with numerous Illustrations. 7*s.* 6*d.*

Dana (R. H.) Two Years before the Mast and Twenty-four years After. New Edition, with Notes and Revisions. 12mo. 6*s.*

Dana (Jas. D.) Corals and Coral Islands. Numerous Illustrations, charts, &c. Royal 8vo. cloth extra. 21*s.*

> "This handsome book is of a kind unfortunately too rare. An eminent traveller and naturalist has here endeavoured to present a popular account of a subject in which he has been one of the foremost investigators. . . . Professed geologists and zoologists, as well as general readers, will find Professor Dana's book in every way worthy of their attention."—*The Athenæum*, Oct. 12, 1872.

> "That his work is likely to be more popular than most accounts of the corals and coral polypes that we have seen, we have no doubt whatever." —*Saturday Review.*

Darley (Felix O. C.) Sketches Abroad with Pen and Pencil, with 84 Illustrations on Wood. Small 4to. 7*s.* 6*d.*

Daughter (A) of Heth, by WM. BLACK. Eleventh and Cheaper edition. 1 vol. crown 8vo. 6*s.*

Davies (Wm.) The Pilgrimage of the Tiber, from its Mouth to its Source; with some account of its Tributaries. 8vo., with many very fine Woodcuts and a Map, cloth extra. 18*s.*

> "Et terram Hesperiam venies, ubi Lydius arva
> Inter opima virûm leni fluit agmine Tibris."
> VIRGIL, Æn. II., 781.

Devonshire Hamlets; Hamlet 1603, Hamlet 1604. 1 Vol. 8vo. 7*s.* 6*d.*

De Witt (Madame Guizot). An Only Sister. Vol. V. of the "John Halifax" Series of Girls' Books. With Six Illustrations. Small post 8vo. cloth. 4*s.*

Dhow-Chasing. *See* **Sulivan.**

Draper (John W.) Human Physiology. Illustrated with more than 300 Woodcuts from Photographs, &c. Royal 8vo. cloth extra. 1*l.* 5*s.*

Dream Book (The) with 12 Drawings in facsimile by **E. V. B.** Med. 4to. 1*l.* 11*s.* 6*d.*

Duer's Marine Insurance. 2 vols. 3*l.* 3*s.*

Duplais and McKennie, Treatise on the Manufacture and Distillation of Alcoholic Liquors. With numerous Engravings. 8vo. 2*l.* 2*s.*

Duplessis (G.) Wonders of Engraving. With numerous Illustrations and Photographs. 8vo. 12*s.* 6*d.*

Dussauce (Professor H.) A New and Complete Treatise on the Art of Tanning. Royal 8vo. 2*l.* 2*s.*

—— **General Treatise on the Manufacture of Vinegar.** 8vo. 1*l.* 1*s.*

ENGLISH Catalogue of Books (The) Published during 1863 to 1871 inclusive, comprising also the Important American Publications.

This Volume, occupying over 450 Pages, shows the Titles of 32,000 New Books and New Editions issued during Nine Years, with the Size, Price, and Publisher's Name, the Lists of Learned Societies, Printing Clubs, and other Literary Associations, and the Books issued by them; as also the Publisher's Series and Collections—altogether forming an indispensable adjunct to the Bookseller's Establishment, as well as to every Learned and Literary Club and Association. 30*s.* half-bound.

*** The previous Volume, 1835 to 1862, of which a very few remain on sale, price 2*l.* 5*s.*; as also the Index Volume, 1837 to 1857, price 1*l.* 6*s.*

—— **Supplements,** 1863, 1864, 1865, 3*s.* 6*d.* each; 1866, 1867 to 1872, 5*s.* each.

—— **Writers,** Chapters for Self-improvement in English Literature; by the author of "The Gentle Life." 6*s.*

Erckmann-Chatrian, Forest House and Catherine's Lovers. Crown 8vo 3*s.* 6*d.*

—— **The Brothers Rantzau**: A Story of the Vosges. 2 vols. crown 8vo. cloth. 21*s.*

FAITH GARTNEY'S Girlhood, by the Author of "The Gayworthys." Fcap. with Coloured Frontispiece. 3*s.* 6*d.*

Favourite English Poems. New and Extended Edition, with 300 illustrations. Small 4to. 21*s.*

Favell (The) Children. Three Little Portraits. Crown 12mo. Four Illustrations. Cloth gilt. 4*s.*

"A very useful and clever story."—*John Bull.*

Few (A) Hints on Proving Wills. Enlarged Edition, sewed. 1*s.*

Fields (J. T.) Yesterdays with Authors. Crown 8vo. 10*s.* 6*d.*

Fleming's (Sandford) Expedition. *See* Ocean to Ocean.

Flammarion (C.) The Atmosphere. Translated from the French of CAMILLE FLAMMARION. Edited by JAMES GLAISHER, F.R.S., Superintendent of the Magnetical and Meteorological Department of the Royal Observatory at Greenwich. With 10 beautiful Chromo-Lithographs and 81 woodcuts. Royal 8vo. cloth extra, bevelled boards. 30*s.*

Franc (Maude Jeane) **Emily's Choice, au Australian Tale.** 1 vol. small post 8vo. With a Frontispiece by G. F. ANGAS. 5*s*.

—— **Marian, or the Light of Some One's Home.** Fcp. 3rd Edition, with Frontispiece. 5*s*.

—— **Silken Cords and Iron Fetters.** 5*s*.

—— **Vermont Vale.** Small post 4to., with Frontispiece. 5*s*.

—— **Minnie's Mission.** Small post 8vo., with Frontispiece. 4*s*.

Frey (H.) **The Microscope and Microscopical Technology.** 8vo. illustrated. 30*s*.

Friswell (J. H.) *See* Gentle Life Series.

—— **One of Two.** 3 vols. 1*l*. 11*s*. 6*d*.

GAYWORTHYS (The), a Story of New England Life. Small post 8vo. 3*s*. 6*d*.

Gems of Dutch Art. Twelve Photographs from finest Engravings in British Museum. Sup. royal 4to. cloth extra. 25*s*.

Gentle Life (Queen Edition). 2 vols. in 1. Small 4to. 10*s*. 6*d*.

THE GENTLE LIFE SERIES. Printed in Elzevir, on Toned Paper, handsomely bound, forming suitable Volumes for Presents. Price 6*s*. each; or in calf extra, price 10*s*. 6*d*.

I.

The Gentle Life. Essays in aid of the Formation of Character of Gentlemen and Gentlewomen. Tenth Edition.

"His notion of a gentleman is of the noblest and truest order. A little compendium of cheerful philosophy."—*Daily News.*

"Deserves to be printed in letters of gold, and circulated in every house."—*Chambers Journal.*

II.

About in the World. Essays by the Author of "The Gentle Life."

"It is not easy to open it at any page without finding some handy idea."—*Morning Post.*

III.

Like unto Christ. A New Translation of the "De Imitatione Christi" usually ascribed to Thomas à Kempis. With a Vignette from an Original Drawing by Sir Thomas Lawrence. Second Edition.

"Evinces independent scholarship, and a profound feeling for the original."—*Nonconformist.*

"Could not be presented in a more exquisite form, for a more sightly volume was never seen."—*Illustrated London News.*

IV.

Familiar Words. An Index Verborum, or Quotation Handbook. Affording an immediate Reference to Phrases and Sentences that have become embedded in the English language. Second and enlarged Edition.

"The most extensive dictionary of quotation we have met with."—*Notes and Queries.*

"Will add to the author's credit with all honest workers."—*Examiner.*

V.

Essays by Montaigne. Edited, Compared, Revised, and Annotated by the Author of "The Gentle Life." With Vignette Portrait. Second Edition.

"We should be glad if any words of ours could help to bespeak a large circulation for this handsome attractive book; and who can refuse his homage to the good-humoured industry of the editor."—*Illustrated Times.*

VI.

The Countess of Pembroke's Arcadia. Written by Sir Philip Sidney. Edited, with Notes, by the Author of "The Gentle Life." Dedicated, by permission, to the Earl of Derby. *7s. 6d.*

"All the best things in the Arcadia are retained intact in Mr. Friswell's edition.—*Examiner.*

VII.

The Gentle Life. Second Series. Third Edition.

"There is not a single thought in the volume that does not contribute in some measure to the formation of a true gentleman."—*Daily News.*

VIII.

Varia: Readings from Rare Books. Reprinted, by permission, from the *Saturday Review, Spectator,* &c.

"The books discussed in this volume are no less valuable than they are rare, and the compiler is entitled to the gratitude of the public for having rendered their treasures available to the general reader."—*Observer.*

IX.

The Silent Hour: Essays, Original and Selected. By the Author of "The Gentle Life." Second Edition.

"All who possess the 'Gentle Life' should own this volume."—*Standard.*

X.

Essays on English writers, for the Self-improvement of Students in English Literature.

"The author has a distinct purpose and a proper and noble ambition to win the young to the pure and noble study of our glorious English literature. To all (both men and women) who have neglected to read and study their native literature we would certainly suggest the volume before us as a fitting introduction."—*Examiner.*

XI.

Other People's Windows. By J. HAIN FRISWELL. Second Edition.

"The chapters are so lively in themselves, so mingled with shrewd views of human nature, so full of illustrative anecdotes, that the reader cannot fail to be amused."—*Morning Post.*

XII.

A Man's Thoughts. By J. HAIN FRISWELL.

German Primer; being an Introduction to First Steps in German. By M. T. PREU. 2*s.* 6*d.*

Getting On in the World; or, Hints on Success in Life. By WILLIAM MATHEWS, LL.D. Small post 8vo., cloth extra, bevelled edges. 6*s.*

Girdlestone (C.) Christendom. 12mo. 3*s.*

——— **Family Prayers.** 12mo. 1*s.* 6*d.*

Glover (Rev. R.) The Light of the Word. Third Edition. 18mo. 2*s.* 6*d.*

Goethe's Faust. With Illustrations by Konewka. Small 4to. Price 10*s.* 6*d.*

Gouffé: The Royal Cookery Book. By JULES GOUFFÉ, Chef-de-Cuisine of the Paris Jockey Club; translated and adapted for English use by ALPHONSE GOUFFÉ, head pastrycook to Her Majesty the Queen. Illustrated with large plates, beautifully printed in colours, together with 161 woodcuts. 8vo. Coth extra, gilt edges. 2*l.* 2*s.*

——— Domestic Edition, half-bound. 10*s.* 6*d.*

"By far the ablest and most complete work on cookery that has ever been submitted to the gastronomical world."—*Pall Mall Gazette.*

——— **The Book of Preserves; or,** Receipts for Preparing and Preserving Meat, Fish salt and smoked, Terrines, Gelatines, Vegetables, Fruits, Confitures, Syrups, Liqueurs de Famille, Petits Fours, Bonbons, &c. &c. By JULES GOUFFE, Head Cook of the Paris Jockey Club, and translated and adapted by his brother ALPHONSE GOUFFE, Head Pastrycook to her Majesty the Queen, translator and editor of "The Royal Cookery Book." 1 vol. royal 8vo., containing upwards of 500 Receipts and 34 Illustrations. 10*s.* 6*d.*

Girls' Books. A Series written, edited, or translated by the Author of "John Halifax." Small post 8vo., cloth extra, 4*s*. each.

1. **Little Sunshine's Holiday.**
2. **The Cousin from India.**
3. **Twenty Years Ago.**
4. **Is it True.**
5. **An Only Sister.** By Madame Guizot De Witt.

Gough (J. B.) The Autobiography and Reminiscences of John B. Gough. 8vo. Cloth, 10*s*. 6*d*.

Great Lone-Land. *See* **Butler.**

Grant (Rev. G. M.). *See* **Ocean to Ocean.**

Greenleaf's Law of Evidence. 3 vols. 84*s*.

Guizot's History of France. Translated by Robert Black. Royal 8vo. Numerous Illustrations. Vols. I. and II., cloth extra, each 24*s*.; in Parts, 2*s*. each (to be completed in about twenty parts).

Guyon (Mad.) Life. By Upham. Third Edition. Crown 8vo. 6*s*.

—— **Method of Prayer.** Foolscap. 1*s*.

HALL (E. H.) The Great West; Handbook for Emigrants and Settlers in America. With a large Map of routes, railways, and steam communication, complete to present time. Boards, 1*s*.

Harrington (J.) Pictures of Saint George's Chapel, Windsor. Photographs. 4to. 63*s*.

Harrington's Abbey and Palace of Westminster. Photographs. 5*l*. 5*s*.

Harrison (Agnes). *See* **Martin's Vineyard.**

Harper's Handbook for Travellers in Europe and the East. New Edition. Post 8vo. Morocco tuck, 1*l*. 1*s*.

Harz Mountains. *See* **Blackburn.**

Hawthorne (Mrs. N.) Notes in England and Italy. Crown 8vo. 10*s*. 6*d*.

Hayes (Dr.) Cast Away in the Cold; an Old Man's Story of a Young Man's Adventures. By Dr. I. Isaac Hayes, Author of "The Open Polar Sea." With numerous Illustrations. Gilt edges, 6*s*.

—— **The Land of Desolation;** Personal Narrative of Adventures in Greenland. Numerous Illustrations. Demy 8vo., cloth extra. 14*s*.

Hazard (S.) Santo Domingo, Past and Present; With a Glance at Hayti. With upwards of One Hundred and Fifty beautiful Woodcuts and Maps, chiefly from Designs and Sketches by the Author. Demy 8vo. cloth extra. 18*s*.

Extract from the notice in *Spectator*, March 22nd.—"This is a book that, in view of the St. Domingo Loan and the New Samana Bay Company, will prove peculiarly interesting to English readers."

—— **Cuba with Pen and Pencil.** Over 300 Fine Woodcut Engravings. New edition, 8vo. cloth extra. 15*s*.

"We recommend this book to the perusal of our readers."—*Spectator*.

"Mr. Hazard has completely exhausted his subject."—*Pall Mall Gazette*.

Hazlitt (William) The Round Table; the Best Essays of William Hazlitt, with Biographical Introduction (Bayard Series). 2*s*. 6*d*.

Healy (M.) Lakeville; or, Shadow and Substance. A Novel. 3 vols. 1*l*. 11*s*. 6*d*.

—— **A Summer's Romance.** Crown 8vo., cloth. 10*s*. 6*d*.

—— **The Home Theatre.** Small post 8vo. 3*s*. 6*d*.

Henderson (A.) Latin Proverbs and Quotations; with Translations and Parallel Passages, and a copious English Index. By Alfred Henderson. Fcap. 4to., 530 pp. 10*s*. 6*d*.

"A very handsome volume in its typographical externals, and a very useful companion to those who, when a quotation is aptly made, like to trace it to its source, to dwell on the minutiæ of its application, and to find it illustrated with choice parallel passages from English and Latin authors."—*Times*.

"A book well worth adding to one's library."—*Saturday Review*.

Hearth Ghosts. By the Author of 'Gilbert Rugge.' 3 Vols. 1*l*. 11*s*. 6*d*.

Heber's (Bishop) Illustrated Edition of Hymns. With upwards of 100 Designs engraved in the first style of art under the superintendence of J. D. Cooper. Small 4to. Handsomely bound, 7*s*. 6*d*

Higginson (T. W.) Atlantic Essays. Small post 8vo. cloth. 6*s*.

Hitherto. By the Author of "The Gayworthys." New Edition. cloth extra. 3*s*. 6*d*. Also in Low's American Series. Double Vol. 2*s*. 6*d*.

Hofmann (Carl) A Practical Treatise on the Manufacture of Paper in all its Branches. Illustrated by One Hundred and Ten Wood Engravings, and Five large Folding Plates. In One Volume, 4to, cloth; about 400 pages. 3*l*. 13*s*. 6*d*.

Hoge—Blind Bartimæus. Popular edition. 1*s*.

Holland (Dr.) Kathrina and Titcomb's Letters. *See* Low's American Series.

Holmes (Oliver W.) The Guardian Angel; a Romance. 2 vols. 16*s*.

——— (Low's Copyright Series.) Boards, 1*s*. 6*d*.; cloth, 2*s*.

——— **Autocrat of the Breakfast Table.** 12mo. 1*s*.; Illustrated edition, 3*s*. 6*d*.

——— **The Professor at the Breakfast Table.** 3*s*. 6*d*.

——— **Songs in Many Keys.** Post 8vo. 7*s*. 6*d*.

——— **Mechanism in Thought and Morals.** 12mo. 1*s*. 6*d*.

Home Theatre (The), by MARY HEALY. Small post 8vo. 3*s*. 6*d*.

Homespun, or Twenty Five Years Ago in America, by THOMAS LACKLAND. Fcap. 8vo. 7*s*. 6*d*.

Hoppin (Jas. M.) Old Country, its Scenery, Art, and People. Post 8vo. 7*s*. 6*d*.

Howell (W. D.) Italian Journeys. 12mo. cloth. 8*s*. 6*d*.

Hugo's Toilers of the Sea. Crown 8vo. 6*s*.; fancy boards, 2*s*.; cloth, 2*s*. 6*d*.; Illustrated Edition, 10*s*. 6*d*.

Hunt (Leigh) and S. A. Lee, Elegant Sonnets, with Essay on Sonneteers. 2 vols. 8vo. 18*s*.

——— **Day by the Fire.** Fcap. 6*s*. 6*d*.

Huntington (J.D., D.D.) Christian Believing. Crown 8vo. 3*s*. 6*d*.

Hymnal Companion to Book of Common Prayer. *See* Bickersteth.

ICE, a Midsummer Night's Dream. Small Post 8vo. 3*s*. 6*d*.

Illustrations of China and its People. By J. THOMSON, F.R.G.S. Being Photographs from the Author's Negatives, printed in permanent Pigments by the Autotype Process, and Notes from Personal Observation.

*** The complete work will embrace 200 Photographs, with Letter-press Descriptions of the Places and People represented. In Four Volumes, imperial 4to., price 3*l*. 3*s*. each Volume. The First Volume, containing Fifty Photographs, is now ready.

Subscribers ordering the Four Volumes at once will be supplied for 10*l*. 10*s*., half of which is to be paid on receipt of Vol. I., and balance on completion of the work. Non-subscribers' price is 3*l*. 3*s*. a Volume.

"In his succeeding volumes, he proposes to take us with him northward and westward; and if the high promise held out in the present instalment of his book be fulfilled in them, they will together form, from every point of view, a most valuable and interesting work. The photographs are excellent; . . . . artistically, they are all that can be desired. Accompanying each is a full, and what is somewhat unusual in books relating to China, an accurate description of the scene or objects represented."—*Athenæum*.

Illustrated Books, suitable for Christmas, Birthday, or Wedding Presents. (The full titles of which will be found in the Alphabet.)

Adventures of a Young Naturalist. *7s. 6d.*
Alexander's Bush Fighting. *16s.*
Anderson's Fairy Tales. *25s.*
Arctic Regions. Illustrated. 25 guineas.
Art, Pictorial and Industrial. Vol. I. *31s. 6d.*
Blackburn's Art in the Mountains. *12s.*
—— Artists and Arabs. *7s. 6d.*
—— Harz Mountains. *12s.*
—— Normandy Picturesque. *16s.*
—— Travelling in Spain. *16s.*
—— The Pyrenees. *18s.*
Bush's Reindeer, Dogs, &c. *12s. 6d.*
Butler's Great Lone Land. *7s. 6d.*
Chefs d'Œuvre of Art. *4l. 14s. 6d.*
China. Illustrated. 4 vols. *3l. 3s.* each vol.
Christian Lyrics.
Davies's Pilgrimage of the Tiber. *18s.*
Dream Book, by E. V. B. *21s. 6d.*
Duplessis' Wonders of Engraving. *12s. 6d.*
Favourite English Poems. *21s.*
Flammarion's The Atmosphere. *30s.*
Fletcher and Kidder's Brazil. *18s.*
Gœthe's Faust, illustrations by P. Konewka. *10s. 6d.*
Gouffe's Royal Cookery Book. Coloured plates. *42s.*
—— Ditto. Popular edition. *10s. 6d.*
—— Book of Preserves. *10s. 6d.*
Hazard's Santa Domingo. *18s.*
—— Cuba. *15s.*
Heber (Bishop) Hymns. Illustrated edition. *7s. 6d.*
Markham's Cruise of the Rosario. *16s.*
Milton's Paradise Lost. (Martin's plates). *3l. 13s. 6d.*
My Lady's Cabinet. *21s.*
Ocean to Ocean. *10s. 6d.*
Palliser (Mrs.) History of Lace. *21s.*
—— Historic Devices, &c. *21s.*
Peaks and Valleys of the Alps. *6l. 6s.*
Pike's Sub-Tropical Rambles. *18s.*
Red Cross Knight (The). *25s.*
Sauzay's Wonders of Glass Making. *12s. 6d.*
Schiller's Lay of the Bell. *14s.*
St. George's Chapel, Windsor.
Sulivan's Dhow Chasing. *16s.*
The Abbey and Palace of Westminster. *5l. 5s.*
Viardot, Wonders of Sculpture. *12s. 6d.*
—— Wonders of Italian Art. *12s. 6d.*
—— Wonders of European Art. *12s. 6d.*
Werner (Carl) Nile Sketches. 2 Series, each *3l. 10s.*

Index to the Subjects of Books published in the United Kingdom during the last 20 years. 8vo. Half-morocco. *1l. 6s.*

Innocent. By Mrs. Oliphant. 3 Vols. Crown 8vo. cloth. *31s. 6d.*

In the Tropics. Post 8vo. 6*s.*

In Silk Attire. *See* **Black, Wm.**

Is it True? Being Tales Curious and Wonderful. Small post 8vo., cloth extra. 4*s.*

(Forming vol. 4 of the "John Halifax" Series of Girls' Books.)

JACK HAZARD, a Story of Adventure by J. T. TROWBRIDGE. Numerous illustrations, small post. 3*s.* 6*d.*

John Halifax Series of Girls' Books. *See* **Girls' Books.**

Johnson (R. B.) Very Far West Indeed. A few rough Experiences on the North-West Pacific Coast. Cr. 8vo. cloth. 10*s.* 6*d.* New Edition—the Fourth, fancy boards. 2*s.*

"Variety and adventure abound in his book, which is written too with never-flagging spirit."—*Athenæum.*

KAVANAGH'S Origin of Language. 2 vols. crown 8vo. 1*l.* 1*s.*

Kedge Anchor, or Young Sailor's Assistant, by WM. BRADY. 8vo. 18*s.*

Kennan (G.) Tent Life in Siberia. 3rd edition. 6*s.*

"We strongly recommend the work as one of the most entertaining volumes of travel that has appeared of late years."—*Athenæum.*

"We hold our breath as he details some hair-breadth escape, and burst into fits of irresistible laughter over incidents full of humour.—*Spectator.*

Kent (Chancellor) Commentaries on American Law. 11th edition. 4 vols. 8vo. 4*l.* 10*s.*

Kilmeny. *See* **Black (Wm.)**

King (Clarence) Mountaineering in the Sierra Nevada. crown 8vo. Third and Cheaper Edition, cloth extra. 6*s.*

The *Times* of Oct. 20th says:—"If we judge his descriptions by the vivid impressions they leave, we feel inclined to give them very high praise."

"A fresh and vigorous record of varied kinds of adventure, combined with vivid pictures of mountain scenery, and with glimpses of wild life among Indians, Mexicans, and Californians, will commend itself to most readers."—*The Athenæum*

Kingston (W. H. G.) Ben Burton, or Born and Bred at Sea. Fcap. with Illustrations. 3*s.* 6*d.*

Koldeway (Captain) The Second North-German Polar Expedition in the year 1869-1870 of the ships "Germania" and "Hausa," under Command of Captain Koldeway. Edited and Condensed by H. W. Bates, Esq., of the Royal Geographical Society. 1 vol. demy 8vo., numerous Woodcuts, Maps, and Chromo-Lithographs —*In the Press.*

**AKEVILLE.** *See* Healy.

Land of the White Elephant. *See* Vincent.

Lang (J. D.) The Coming Event. 8vo. 12*s.*

Lascelles (Arthur) The Coffee Grower's Guide. Post 8vo. 2*s.* 6*d.*

Lee (G. R.) Memoirs of the American Revolutionary War. 8vo. 16*s.*

Like unto Christ. A new translation of the "De Imitatione Christi," usually ascribed to Thomas à Kempis. Second Edition. 6*s.*

Little Men. See Alcott.

Little Preacher. 32mo. 1*s.*

Little Women. See Alcott.

Little Sunshine's Holiday. *See* Craik (Mrs.)

Livingstone (Dr.), How I Found. *See* Stanley.

Log of my Leisure Hours. By an Old Sailor. Cheaper Edition. Fancy boards. 2*s.*

Longfellow (H. W.) The Poets and Poetry of Europe. New Edition. 8vo. cloth. 1*l.* 1*s.*

Loomis (Elias). Recent Progress of Astronomy. Post 8vo. 7*s.* 6*d.*

—— **Practical Astronomy.** 8vo. 10*s.*

Low's Copyright and Cheap Editions of American Authors, comprising Popular Works, reprinted by arrangement with their Authors:—

1. **Haunted Hearts.** By the Author of "The Lamplighter."
2. **The Guardian Angel.** By "The Autocrat of the Breakfast Table."
3. **The Minister's Wooing.** By the Author of "Uncle Tom's Cabin.
4. **Views Afoot.** By Bayard Taylor.
5. **Kathrina, Her Life and Mine.** By J. G. Holland.
6. **Hans Brinker: or, Life in Holland.** By Mrs. Dodge.

Low's Cheap Copyright Editions, *continued*—

7. **Men, Women, and Ghosts.** By Miss PHELPS.
8. **Society and Solitude.** By RALPH WALDO EMERSON.
9. **Hedged In.** By ELIZABETH PHELPS.
10. **An Old-Fashioned Girl.** By LOUISA M. ALCOTT.
11. **Faith Gartney.**
12. **Stowe's Old Town Folks.** 2*s.* 6*d.*; cloth, 3*s.*
13. **Lowell's Study Windows.**
14. **My Summer in a Garden.** By CHARLES DUDLEY WARNER.
15. **Pink and White Tyranny.** By Mrs. STOWE.
16. **We Girls.** By Mrs. WHITNEY.
17. **Little Men.** By Miss ALCOTT.
18. **Little Women.** By Miss ALCOTT.
19. **Little Women Wedded.** (Forming the Sequel to "Little Women.")
20. **Back-Log Studies.** By CHARLES DUDLEY WARNER, Author of "My Summer in a Garden."
    "This is a delightful book."—*Atlantic Monthly.*
21. **Timothy Titcomb's Letters to Young People, Single and Married.**

*** Of this famous little work upwards of 50,000 have been sold in America alone at four times the present price, viz. 1*s.* 6*d.* flexible fancy boards; 2*s.* cloth extra.

22. **Hitherto.** By Mrs. T. D. WHITNEY. Double Volume, 2*s.* 6*d.* fancy flexible boards.

*** This Copyright work was first published in this country in 3 vols. at 31*s.* 6*d.*; afterwards in 1 vol. at 6*s.* It is now issued in the above popular Series.

23. **Farm Ballads.** by Will. Carleton, price ONE SHILLING.

The *Guardian* says of "Little Women," that it is "a bright, cheerful, healthy story—with a tinge of thoughtful gravity about it which reminds one of John Bunyan. Meg going to Vanity Fair is a chapter written with great cleverness and a pleasant humour."

The *Athenæum* says of "Old-Fashioned Girl": "Let whoever wishes to read a bright, spirited, wholesome story get the 'Old-Fashioned Girl' at once."

*** "We may be allowed to add, that Messrs. Low's is the 'Author's edition.' We do not commonly make these announcements, but every one is bound to defeat, as far as he can, the efforts of those enterprising persons who proclaim with much unction the sacred duty of *not* letting an American author get his proper share of profits."—*Spectator,* Jan. 4, 1873.

Each volume complete in itself, price 1*s.* 6*d.* enamelled flexible cover, 2*s.* cloth.

Low's Monthly Bulletin of American and Foreign Publications, forwarded regularly. Subscription 2*s.* 6*d.* per annum.

Low's Minion Series of Popular Books. 1*s.* each:—

The Gates Ajar. (The original English Edition.)
Who is He?
The Little Preacher.
The Boy Missionary.

Low (Sampson, Jun.) The Charities of London. For the the year 1872. *1s.*

Ludlow (FitzHugh). The Heart of the Continent. 8vo. cloth. *14s.*

Lunn (J. C.) Only Eve. 3 vols. 31*s.* 6*d.*

Lyne (A. A.) The Midshipman's Trip to Jerusalem. With illustration. Third Edition. Crown 8vo., cloth. *10s. 6d.*

Lyra Sacra Americana. Gems of American Poetry, selected and arranged, with Notes and Biographical Sketches, by C. D. CLEVELAND, D. D., author of the "Milton Concordance." 18mo. *4s. 6d.*

ACALPINE; or, On Scottish Ground. A Novel. 3 vols. crown 8vo. *31s. 6d.*

Macgregor (John,) "Rob Roy" on the Baltic. Third Edition, small post 8vo. *2s. 6d.*

—— **A Thousand Miles in the "Rob Roy" Canoe.** Eleventh Edition. Small post, 8vo. *2s. 6d.*

—— **Description of the "Rob Roy" Canoe,** with plans, &c. *1s.*

—— **The Voyage Alone in the Yawl "Rob Roy."** Second Edition. Small post, 8vo. *5s.*

March (A.) Anglo-Saxon Reader. 8vo. *7s. 6d.*

—— **Comparative Grammar of the Anglo-Saxon Language.** 8vo. *12s.*

Marcy, (R. B.) Thirty Years of Army Life. Royal 8vo. *12s.*

—— **Prairie and Overland Traveller.** *2s. 6d.*

Marigold Manor. By Miss WARING. With Introduction by Rev. A. SEWELL. With Illustrations. Small Post 8vo. *4s.*

Markham (A. H.) The Cruise of the "Rosario" amongst the New Hebrides and Santa Cruz Islands, exposing the Recent Atrocities connected with the Kidnapping of Natives in the South Seas. By A. H. MARKHAM, Commander, R.N. 8vo. cloth extra, with Map and Illustrations. *16s.*

"The crew of the 'Rosario' were sent out from England in that wretched tub the 'Megæra.' Captain Markham's account of the cruise is pleasantly written."—*Standard.*

"We trust, therefore, that it may be generally read."—*Athenæum.*

Markham (C. R.) The Threshold of the Unknown Region. Demy 8vo. with Maps and Illustrations. [*In the press.*

*** The object of this Work is to give the public a correct knowledge of the whole line of frontier separating the known from the unknown region round the North Pole.

Marlitt (Miss) The Princess of the Moor. Tauchnitz Translations.

Marsh (George P.) Man and Nature. 8vo. 15*s.*

—— **Origin and History of the English Language.** 8vo. 16*s.*

—— **Lectures on the English Language.** 8vo. 15*s.*

Martin's Vineyard. By Agnes Harrison. Crown 8vo. cloth. 10*s.* 6*d.*

Matthews (Wm.) *See* **Getting on in the World.**

Maury (Commander) Physical Geography of the Sea and its Meteorology. Being a Reconstruction and Enlargement of his former Work; with illustrative Charts and Diagrams. New Edition. Crown 8vo. 6*s.*

Mayo (Dr.) *See* **Never Again.**

McMullen's History of Canada. 8vo. 16*s.*

Mercier (Rev. L.) Outlines of the Life of the Lord Jesus Christ. 2 vols. crown 8vo. 15*s.*

Meridiana *See* **Verne.**

Milton's Complete Poetical Works; with Concordance by W. D. CLEVELAND. New Edition. 8vo. 12*s.*; morocco 1*l.* 1*s.*

—— **Paradise Lost**, with the original Steel Engravings of JOHN MARTIN. Printed on large paper, royal 4to. handsomely bound. 3*l.* 13*s.* 6*d.*

Miss Dorothy's Charge. By FRANK LEE BENEDICT, Author of "My Cousin Elenor." 3 vols. crown 8vo. 31*s.* 6*d.*

Missionary Geography (The); a Manual of Missionary Operations in all parts of the World, with Map and Illustrations. Fcap. 3*s.* 6*d.*

Monk of Monk's Own. 3 vols. 31*s.* 6*d.*

Montaigne's Essays. *See* **Gentle Life Series.**

Morgan's Macaronic Poetry. 16mo. 12*s.*

Mother Goose's Melodies for Children. Square 8vo., cloth extra. 7*s.* 6*d.*

Mountain (Bishop) Life of. By his Son. 8vo. 10*s.* 6*d.*

My Summer in a Garden. See **Warner.**

My Cousin Maurice. A Novel. 3 vols. Cloth, 31*s.* 6*d.*

My Lady's Cabinet. Charmingly Decorated with Lovely Drawings and Exquisite Miniatures. Contains Seventy-five Pictures set in Frames, and arranged on Twenty-four Panels, thus representing the Walls of a richly adorned Boudoir. Each page or panel interleaved with Letterpress sufficient to explain the Subjects of the Drawings, and give the Names of the Artists. Printed on royal 4to., and very handsomely bound in cloth. 1*l.* 1*s.*

"The fittest ornament for a Lady's Cabinet which this season has produced."—*Athenæum.*

"Forms an excellent pretty book for the drawing-room table."—*Pall Mall Gazette.*

"A very pretty idea, carried out with much taste and elegance."—*Daily News.*

My Wife and I. *See* Mrs. **Stowe.**

**EVER Again**: a Novel. By Dr. MAYO, Author of "Kaloolah." New and Cheaper Edition, in One Vol., small post 8vo. 6*s.* Cheapest edition, fancy boards, 2*s.*

"Puts its author at once into the very first rank of novelists."—*The Athenæum.*

New Testament. The Authorized English Version; with the various Readings from the most celebrated Manuscripts, including the Sinaitic, the Vatican, and the Alexandrian MSS., in English. With Notes by the Editor, Dr. TISCHENDORF. The whole revised and carefully collected for the Thousandth Volume of Baron Tauchnitz's Collection. Cloth flexible, gilt edges, 2*s.* 6*d.*; cheaper style, 2*s.*; or sewed, 1*s.* 6*d.*

Nordhoff (C.) California: for Health, Pleasure, and Residence. A Book for Travellers and Settlers. Numerous Illustrations, 8vo., cloth extra. 12*s.* 6*d.*

Nothing to Wear, and Two Millions. By WILLIAM ALLEN BUTLER. 1*s.*

Nystrom's Mechanics Pocket Book. 10*s.* 6*d.*

OCEAN to Ocean. Sandford Fleming's Expedition through Canada in 1872. Being a Diary kept during a Journey from the Atlantic to the Pacific with the Expedition of the Engineer-in-Chief of the Canadian Pacific and Intercolonial Railways. By the Rev. GEORGE M. GRANT, of Halifax, N.S., Secretary to the Expedition. With Sixty Illustrations. Demy 8vo., cloth extra, pp. 372. 10*s.* 6*d.*

Old Fashioned Girl. See **Alcott.**

Oliphant (Mrs.) Innocent. 3 vols. Crown 8vo. cloth. 31*s.* 6*d.*

Only Eve. By Mrs. J. CALBRAITH LUNN. Three Vols. post 8vo. cloth. 31*s.* 6*d.*

Other Girls (The). *See* **Whitney (Mrs.)**

Our American Cousins at Home. By VERA, Author of "Under the Red Cross." Illustrated with Pen and Ink Sketches, by the Author, and several fine Photographs. Crown 8vo, cloth. 9*s.*

Our Little Ones in Heaven. Edited by Rev. H. ROBBINS. With Frontispiece after Sir JOSHUA REYNOLDS. Second Edition. Fcap. 3*s.* 6*d.*

PALLISER (Mrs.) A History of Lace, from the Earliest Period. A New and Revised Edition, with upwards of 100 Illustrations and coloured Designs. 1 vol. 8vo. 1*l.* 1*s.*

"One of the most readable books of the season; permanently valuable, always interesting, often amusing, and not inferior in all the essentials of a gift book."—*Times.*

—— **Historic Devices, Badges, and War Cries.** 8vo. 1*l.* 1*s.*

Paper Manufacture. *See* **Hofmann.**

Parsons (T.) A Treatise on the Law of Marine Insurance and General Average. By Hon. THEOPHILUS PARSONS. 2 vols. 8vo. 3*l.* 3*s.*

Parisian Family. From the French of Madame GUIZOT DE WITT; by Author of "John Halifax." Fcap. 5*s.*

"The feeling of the story is so good, the characters are so clearly marked, there is such freshness and truth to nature in the simple incidents recorded, that we have been allured on from page to page without the least wish to avail ourselves of a privilege permitted sometimes to the reviewer, and to skip a portion of the narrative."—*Pall Mall Gazette.*

Peaks and Valleys of the Alps. From Water-Colour Drawings by ELIJAH WALTON. Chromo-lithographed by J. H. LOWES, with Descriptive Text by the Rev. T. G. BONNEY, M.A., F.G.S. Folio, half-morocco, with 21 large Plates. Original subscription, 8 guineas. A very limited edition only now issued. Price 6 guineas.

Phelps (Miss) Gates Ajar. 32mo. 6*d.*; 4*d.*

—— **Men, Women, and Ghosts.** 12mo. Sewed, 1*s.* 6*d.* cloth, 2*s.*

—— **Hedged In.** 12mo. Sewed, 1*s.* 6*d.*; cloth, 2*s.*

—— **Silent Partner.** 5*s.*

Phillips (L.) Dictionary of Biographical Reference. 8vo. 1*l.* 11*s.* 6*d.*

Phillips' Law of Insurance. 2 vols. 3*l.* 3*s.*

Picture Gallery of British Art (The). Twenty beautiful and Permanent Photographs after the most celebrated English Painters. With Descriptive Letterpress. One Volume, demy 4to. cloth extra, gilt edges. 12*s.*

Picture Gallery of Sacred Art (The). Containing Twenty very fine Examples in Permanent Photography after the Old Masters. With Descriptive Letterpress. Demy 4to. cloth extra, gilt edges. 12*s*.

Pike (N.) Sub-Tropical Rambles in the Land of the Aphanapteryx. In 1 vol. demy 8vo. 18*s*. Profusely Illustrated from the Author's own Sketches, also with Maps and valuable Meteorological Charts.

"Rarely have we met with a book of travels more enjoyable, and few have been written by a sharper or closer observer. To recapitulate a tithe of the heads of the information he provides would exhaust the limits of the longest paragraph, and we must content ourselves with saying that he has left very little indeed to be gleaned by his successors in the task of bringing home to the English mind what a wealth of beauty and novelty there is to be found on the island."—*The Standard.*

Pilgrimage of the Tiber. *See* **Davies (Wm.).**

Plutarch's Lives. An Entirely New and Library Edition. Edited by A. H. CLOUGH, Esq. 5 vols. 8vo. 3*l*. 3*s*.

"'Plutarch's Lives' will yet be read by thousands, and in the version of Mr. Clough."—*Quarterly Review.*

"Mr. Clough's work is worthy of all praise, and we hope that it will tend to revive the study of Plutarch."—*Times.*

—— **Morals.** Uniform with Clough's Edition of "Lives of Plutarch." Edited by Professor GOODWIN. 5 vols. 8vo. 3*l*. 3*s*.

Poe (E. A.) The Works of. 4 vols. 2*l*. 2*s*.

Poems of the Inner Life. A New Edition, Revised, with many additional Poems, inserted by permission of the Authors. Small post 8vo., cloth. 5*s*.

"These books (Palgrave's and Trenche's) are quite beyond the range of the ordinary compiler, and praise similar in character, if not in degree, may be awarded to the careful Editor of the little volume before us."—*Spectator.*

Polar Expedition. *See* **Koldeway.**

Poor (H. V.) Manual of the Railroads of the United States for 1873-4; Showing their Mileage, Stocks, Bonds, Cost, Earnings, Expenses, and Organisations, with a Sketch of their Rise, &c. 1 vol. 8vo. 24*s*.

Portraits of Celebrated Women. By C. A. ST. BEUVE. 12mo. 6*s*. 6*d*.

Preces Veterum. Collegit et edidit Joannes F. France. Crown 8vo., cloth, red edges. 5*s*.

Preu (M. T.) German Primer. Square cloth. 2*s*. 6*d*.

Prime (I.) Fifteen Years of Prayer. Small post 8vo., cloth. 3*s*. 6*d*.

—— **(E. D. G.) Around the World.** Sketches of Travel through Many Lands and over Many Seas, 8vo., Illustrated. 14*s*.

Publishers' Circular (The), and General Record of British and Foreign Literature; giving a transcript of the title-page of every work published in Great Britain, and every work of interest published abroad, with lists of all the publishing houses.

Published regularly on the 1st and 15th of every Month, and forwarded post free to all parts of the world on payment of 8*s*. per annum.

Queer Things of the Service. Crown 8vo., fancy boards. 2*s*. 6*d*.

ASSELAS, Prince of Abyssinia. By Dr. JOHNSON. With Introduction by the Rev. WILLIAM WEST, Vicar of Nairn. (Bayard Series). 2*s*. 6*d*.

Ready, O Ready! or These Forty Years: A book for Young Fellows. By Captain ALLSTON, R.N. Small post 8vo., cloth extra. 3*s*. 6*d*.

Recamier (Madame) Memoirs and Correspondence of. Translated from the French, and Edited by J. M. LUYSTER. With Portrait. Crown 8vo. 7*s*. 6*d*.

Red Cross Knight (The). *See* **Spenser.**

Reid (W.) After the War. Crown 8vo. 10*s*. 6*d*.

Reindeer, Dogs, &c. *See* **Bush.**

Reminiscences of America in 1869, by Two Englishmen. Crown 8vo. 7*s*. 6d.

Reynard the Fox. The Prose Translation by the late THOMAS ROSCOE. With about 100 exquisite Illustrations on Wood, after designs by A. J. ELWES. Imperial 16mo. cloth extra, 7*s*. 6*d*.

"Will yield to none either in the interest of its text or excellence of its engravings."—*Standard.*

"A capital Christmas book."—*Globe.*

"The designs are an ornament of a delightful text."—*Times*, Dec. 24.

Rhyme of the Duchess May. *See* **Browning.**

Richardson (A. S.) Stories from Old English Poetry. Small post 8vo., cloth. 5*s*.

Rochefoucauld's Reflections. Flexible cloth extra. 2*s*. 6*d*. (Bayard Series.)

Rogers (S.) Pleasures of Memory. *See* **"Choice Editions of Choice Books."** 5*s*.

Romance (The) of American History. By Prof. De Vere. Crown 8vo. cloth. 6*s*.

ANDEAU (J.) *See* **Sea-Gull Rock.**

SANTO DOMINGO, Past and Present. *See* **Hazard.**

Sauzay (A.) Marvels of Glass Making. Numerous Illustrations. Demy 8vo. 12*s*. 6*d*.

Schiller's Lay of the Bell, translated by Lord Lytton. With 42 illustrations after Retsch. Oblong 4to. 14*s.*

School Books. *See* **Classified.**

School Prizes. *See* **Books.**

Sea-Gull Rock. By Jules Sandeau, of the French Academy. Translated by ROBERT BLACK, M.A. With Seventy-nine very beautiful Woodcuts. Royal 16mo., cloth extra, gilt edges. 7*s.* 6*d.*

"A story more fascinating, more replete with the most rollicking fun, the most harrowing scenes of suspense, distress, and hair-breadth escapes from danger, was seldom before written, published, or read."—*Athenæum.*

"It deserves to please the new nation of boys to whom it is presented."—*Times.*

"The very best French story for children we have ever seen."—*Standard.*

"A delightful treat."—*Illustrated London News.*

"Admirable, full of life, pathos, and fun. . It is a striking and attractive book."—*Guardian.*

"This story deserves to be a great favourite with English boys as well as with French."—*Saturday Review.*

"Can be recommended alike for the graphic illustrations and admirable subject-matter."—*John Bull.*

"Is quite a gem of its kind. It is beautifully and profusely illustrated."—*Graphic.*

"A finely illustrated and beautifully adorned volume."—*Daily News.*

Seaman (Ezra C.) Essays on the Progress of Nations in civilization, productive history, wealth, and population ; illustrated by statistics. Post 8vo. 10*s.* 6*d.*

Sedgwick, (J.) Treatise on the Measure of Damages. 8vo. 1*l.* 18*s.*

Shadow of the Rock. *See* **Bickersteth.**

Shakespeare's Songs and Sonnets, selected by J. HOWARD STAUNTON ; with 36 exquisite drawings by JOHN GILBERT. See "Choice Series." 5*s.*

Shawl Straps. *See* **Alcott.**

Sheridan's Troopers on the Borders. Post 8vo. 7*s.* 6*d.*

Sidney (Sir Philip) The Countess of Pembroke's Arcadia, edited, with notes, by the author of "Gentle Life," 7*s.* 6*d.* Large paper edition. 12*s.*

Silent Hour (The), Essays original and selected, by the author of "The Gentle Life." Second edition. 6*s.*

Silent Partner. *See* **Phelps.**

Silliman (Benjamin) Life of, by G. P. FISHER. 2 vols. crown 8vo. 1*l.* 4*s.*

Simson (W.) A History of the Gipsies, with specimens of the Gipsy Language. 10*s.* 6*d.*

Smiley (S. F.) Who is He? 32mo. 1*s.*

Smith and Hamilton's French Dictionary. 2 vols. Cloth, 21*s.* : half roan, 22*s.*

Snow Flakes, and what they told the Children, beautifully printed in colours. Cloth extra, bevelled boards. 5*s.*

Socrates. Memoirs, from Xenophon's Memorabilia. By E. LEVIEN. Flexible cloth. 2*s.* 6*d.* Bayard Series.

Spayth (Henry) The American Draught-Player. 2nd edition. 12mo. 12*s.* 6*d.*

Spenser's Red Cross Knight, illustrated with 12 original drawings in facsimile. 4to. 1*l.* 5*s.*

Spofford (Harriet P.) The Thief in the Night. Crown 8vo., cloth. 5*s.*

Spray from the Water of Elisenbrunnen. By GODFREY MAYNARD. Small Post 8vo. Fancy Boards. 2*s.* 6*d.*

St. Cecilia, a modern tale of Real Life. 3 vols. post 8vo. 31*s.* 6*d.*

St. George's Chapel, Windsor, or 18 Photographs with descriptive Letterpress, by JOHN HARRINGTON. Imp. 4to. 63*s.*

Stanley (H. M.) How I Found Livingstone. Including Travels, Adventures, and Discoveries in Central Africa. Illustrations, Maps, &c. 8vo. cloth. 21*s.*

Steele (Thos.) Under the Palms. A Volume of Verse. By THOMAS STEELE, translator of "An Eastern Love Story." Fcap. 8vo. Cloth, 5*s.*

Stewart (D.) Outlines of Moral Philosophy, by Dr. McCosh. New edition. 12mo. 3*s.* 6*d.*

Stone (J. B.) A Tour with Cook Through Spain; being a Series of Descriptive Letters of Ancient Cities and Scenery of Spain, and of Life, Manners, and Customs of Spaniards. As Seen and Enjoyed in a Summer Holiday. Illustrated by Photographs produced by the Autotype Process. Crown 8vo. cloth. 6*s.*

Stories of the Great Prairies, from the Novels of J. F. COOPER. With numerous illustrations. 5*s.*

Stories of the Woods, from J. F. COOPER. 5*s.*

——— **Sea,** from J. F. COOPER. 5*s.*

Story without an End, from the German of Carové, by the late Mrs. SARAH T. AUSTIN, crown 4to. with 15 exquisite drawings by E. V. B., printed in colours in facsimile of the original water colours, and numerous other illustrations. New edition. 7*s.* 6*d.*

——— square, with illustrations by HARVEY. 2*s.* 6*d.*

——— **of the Great March,** a Diary of General Sherman's Campaign through Georgia and the Carolinas. Numerous illustrations. 12mo. cloth, 7*s.* 6*d.*

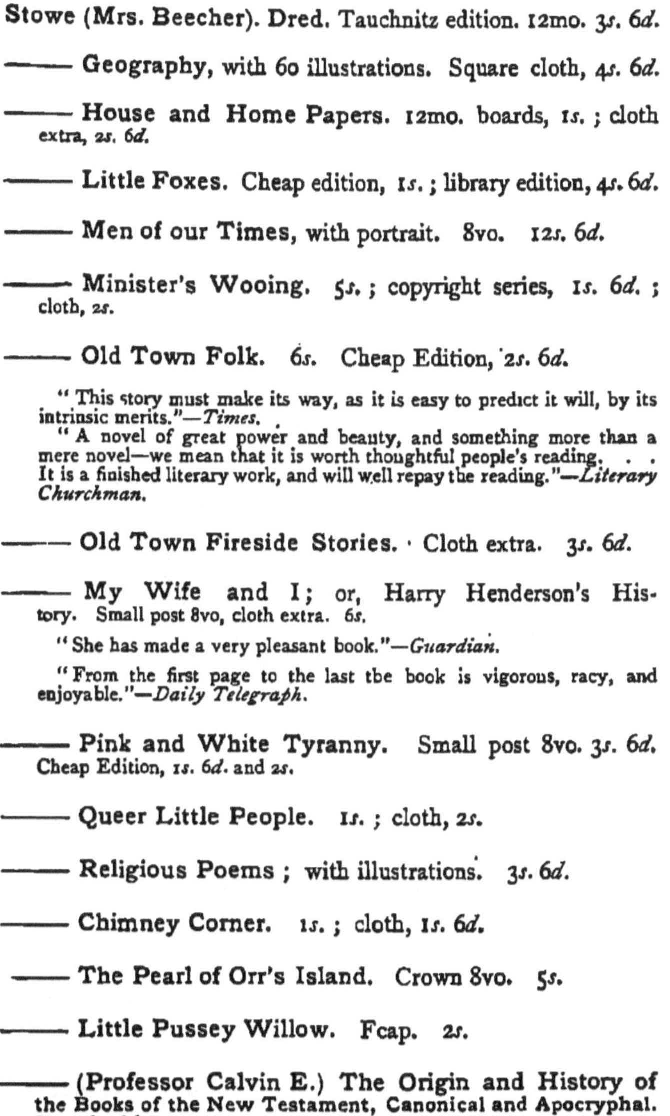

Stowe (Mrs. Beecher). Dred. Tauchnitz edition. 12mo. 3*s*. 6*d*.

—— **Geography,** with 60 illustrations. Square cloth, 4*s*. 6*d*.

—— **House and Home Papers.** 12mo. boards, 1*s*.; cloth extra, 2*s*. 6*d*.

—— **Little Foxes.** Cheap edition, 1*s*.; library edition, 4*s*. 6*d*.

—— **Men of our Times,** with portrait. 8vo. 12*s*. 6*d*.

—— **Minister's Wooing.** 5*s*.; copyright series, 1*s*. 6*d*.; cloth, 2*s*.

—— **Old Town Folk.** 6*s*. Cheap Edition, 2*s*. 6*d*.

"This story must make its way, as it is easy to predict it will, by its intrinsic merits."—*Times.*

"A novel of great power and beauty, and something more than a mere novel—we mean that it is worth thoughtful people's reading. . . It is a finished literary work, and will well repay the reading."—*Literary Churchman.*

—— **Old Town Fireside Stories.** Cloth extra. 3*s*. 6*d*.

—— **My Wife and I;** or, Harry Henderson's History. Small post 8vo, cloth extra. 6*s*.

"She has made a very pleasant book."—*Guardian.*

"From the first page to the last the book is vigorous, racy, and enjoyable."—*Daily Telegraph.*

—— **Pink and White Tyranny.** Small post 8vo. 3*s*. 6*d*. Cheap Edition, 1*s*. 6*d*. and 2*s*.

—— **Queer Little People.** 1*s*.; cloth, 2*s*.

—— **Religious Poems;** with illustrations. 3*s*. 6*d*.

—— **Chimney Corner.** 1*s*.; cloth, 1*s*. 6*d*.

—— **The Pearl of Orr's Island.** Crown 8vo. 5*s*.

—— **Little Pussey Willow.** Fcap. 2*s*.

—— **(Professor Calvin E.) The Origin and History of the Books of the New Testament, Canonical and Apocryphal.** 8vo. 8*s*. 6*d*.

STORY'S (JUSTICE) WORKS:

Commentaries on the Law of Agency, as a Branch of Commercial and Maritime Jurisprudence. 6th Edition. 8vo. 1*l.* 11*s.* 6*d.*

Commentaries on the Law of Bailments. 7th Edition. 8vo. 1*l.* 11*s.* 6*d.*

Commentaries on the Law of Bills of Exchange, Foreign and Inland, as administered in England and America. 4th Edition. 8vo. 1*l.* 11*s.* 6*d.*

Commentaries on the Conflict of Laws, Foreign and Domestic, in regard to Contracts, Rights, and Remedies, and especially in regard to Marriages, Divorces, Wills, Successions, and Judgments. 6th Edition. 8vo. 1*l.* 15*s.*

Commentaries on the Constitution of the United States; with a Preliminary Review of the Constitutional History of the Colonies and States before the adoption of the Constitution. 3rd Edition. 2 vols. 8vo. 3*l.* 3*s.*

Commentaries on the Law of Partnership as a branch of Commercial and Maritime Jurisprudence. 6th Edition, by E. H. BENNETT. 8vo. 1*l.* 11*s.* 6*d.*

Commentaries on the Law of Promissory Notes, and Guarantees of Notes and Cheques on Banks and Bankers. 6th Edition; by E. H. BENNETT. 8vo. 1*l.* 11*s.* 6*d.*

Commentaries on Equity Pleadings and the Incidents relating thereto, according to the Practice of the Courts of Equity of England and America. 7th Edition. 8vo. 1*l.* 11*s.* 6*d.*

Commentaries on Equity Jurisprudence as administered in England and America. 9th Edition. 3*l.* 3*s.*

Treatise on the Law of Contracts. By WILLIAM W. STORY. 4th Edition, 2 vols. 8vo. 3*l.* 3*s.*

Treatise on the Law of Sales of Personal Property. 3rd Edition, edited by Hon. J. C. PERKINS. 8vo. 1*l.* 11*s.* 6*d.*

Sub-Tropical Rambles. *See* Pike (N.)

Suburban Sketches, by the Author of "Venetian Life." Post 8vo. 6*s.*

Sullivan (G. C.) Dhow Chasing in Zanzibar Waters and on the Eastern Coast of Africa; a Narrative of Five Years' Experiences in the suppression of the Slave Trade. With Illustrations from Photographs and Sketches taken on the spot by the Author. Demy 8vo, cloth extra. 16*s.* Second Edition.

Summer in Leslie Goldthwaite's Life, by the Author of "The Gayworthys," Illustrations. Fcap. 8vo. 3*s.* 6*d.*

Swiss Family Robinson, 12mo. 3*s.* 6*d.*

AUCHNITZ'S English Editions of German Authors. Each volume cloth flexible, 2*s.*; or sewed, 1*s.* 6*d.* The following are now ready:—

On the Heights. By B. AUERBACH. 3 vols.

In the Year '13. By FRITZ REUTER. 1 vol.

Faust. By GOETHE. 1 vol.

Undine, and other Tales. By Fouqué. 1 vol.

L'Arrabiata. By PAUL HEYSE. 1 vol.

The Princess, and other Tales. By HEINRICH ZSCHOKKE. 1 vol.

Lessing's Nathan the Wise.

Hacklander's Behind the Counter, translated by MARY HOWITT.

Three Tales. By W. HAUFF.

Joachim v. Kamern; Diary of a Poor Young Lady. By M. NATHUSIUS.

Poems by Ferdinand Freiligrath. Edited by his daughter.

Gabriel. From the German of PAUL HEYSE. By ARTHUR MILMAN.

The Dead Lake, and other Tales. By P. HEYSE.

Through Night to Light. By GUTZKOW.

Flower, Fruit, and Thorn Pieces. By JEAN PAUL RICHTER.

The Princess of the Moor. By Miss MARLITT.

An Egyptian Princess. By G. EBERS. 2 vols.

Ekkehard. By J. V. SCHEFFEL.

Tauchnitz (B.) German and English Dictionary, Paper, 1*s.*; cloth, 1*s.* 6*d.*; roan, 2*s.*

——— French and English. Paper 1*s.* 6*d.*; cloth, 2*s.*; roan, 2*s.* 6*d.*

——— Italian and English. Paper, 1*s.* 6*d.*; cloth, 2*s.*; roan, 2*s.* 6*d.*

——— Spanish and English. Paper, 1*s.* 6*d.*; cloth, 2*s.*; roan, 2*s.* 6*d.*

—— New Testament. Cloth, 2*s.*; gilt, 2*s.* 6*d.* *See* New Testament.

Tayler (C. B.) Sacred Records, &c., in Verse. Fcap. 8vo, cloth extra, 2*s.* 6*d.*

"Devotional feeling and sentiment are the pleasing characteristics of the Rector of Otley's charming and elegant little volume of poems. . . . Fluency, fervour, and ready command of rhyme—criticism must willingly accord to the Rev. C. B. Tayler . . attractive and lovable little volume of verse."—*Morning Post.*

cellent boys' book. We devoutly wish we were a boy to enjoy it."—*Times*, Dec. 24.

"Full of the most astounding submarine adventures ever printed."—*Morning Post.*

"Illustrated with more than a hundred engravings that make the hair stand on end, and published at a low price. If this book, which is translated from the French, does not 'go,' boys are no longer boys. . . . Grave men will be equally borne along in the grasp of the accomplished author."—*Standard.*

Very Far West Indeed. *See* **Johnson.**

Viardot (L.) Wonders of Italian Art, numerous photographic and other illustrations. Demy 8vo. 12*s*. 6*d*.

—— **Wonders of Painting,** numerous photographs, and other illustrations. Demy 8vo. 12*s*. 6*d*.

—— **Wonders of Sculpture.** Numerous Illustrations. Demy 8vo. 12*s*. 6*d*.

Vincent (F.) The Land of the White Elephant: Sights and Scenes in South-Eastern Asia. A Personal Narrative of Travel and Adventure in Farther India, embracing the countries of Burmah, Siam, Cambodia, and Cochin China, 1871-2. With Maps, Plans, and numerous Illustrations. 8vo. cloth extra. [*In the press.*

AKE ROBIN; a Book about Birds, by JOHN BURROUGHS. Crown 8vo. 5*s*.

Warner (C. D.) My Summer in a Garden. Boards, 1*s*. 6*d*.; cloth, 2*s*. (Low's Copyright Series.)

—— **Back-log Studies.** Boards 1*s*. 6*d*.; cloth 2*s*. (Low's Copyright Series.)

We Girls. *See* **Whitney.**

Webster (Daniel) Life of, by GEO. T. CURTIS. 2 vols. 8vo. Cloth. 36*s*.

Werner (Carl), Nile Sketches, Painted from Nature during his travels through Egypt. Facsimiles of Water-colour Paintings executed by GUSTAV W. SEITZ; with Descriptive Text by Dr. E. A. BREHM and Dr. DUMICHEN. Imperial folio, in Cardboard Wrapper. 3*l*. 10*s*.

CONTENTS OF THE SECOND SERIES:—Banks of the Nile near Achmins—Coffee-house at Cairo—Money broker in Esneh—Tombs of Kalifs of Cairo—Assuan—The Temples of Luxor.

*** PART I., published last year, may still be had, price £3 10*s*.

Westminster Abbey and Palace. 40 Photographic Views with Letterpress, dedicated to Dean Stanley. 4to. Morocco extra, £5 5*s*.

Wheaton (Henry) Elements of International Law. New edition. [*In the press.*

When George the Third was King. 2 vols., post 8vo. 21*s*.

Where is the City? 12mo. cloth. 6*s*.

White (J.) Sketches from America. 8vo. 12*s*.

White (R. G.) Memoirs of the Life of William Shakespeare. Post 8vo. Cloth. 10*s*. 6*d*.

Whitney (Mrs. A. D. T.), The Gayworthys. Small post 8vo. 3*s*. 6*d*.

—— **Faith Gartney.** Small post 8vo. 3*s*. 6*d*. And in Low's Cheap Series, 1*s*. 6*d*. and 2*s*.

—— **Hitherto.** Small post 8vo. 3*s*. 6*d*. and 2*s*. 6*d*.

—— **Summer in Leslie Goldthwaite's Life.** Small post 8vo. 3*s*. 6*d*.

—— **The Other Girls.** Small post 8vo., cloth extra. 3*s*. 6*d*.

—— **We Girls.** Small post 8vo. 3*s*. 6*d*. Cheap Edition, 1*s*. 6*d*. and 2*s*.

Whyte (J. W. H.) A Land Journey from Asia to Europe. Crown 8vo. 12*s*.

Wills, A Few Hints on Proving, without Professional Assistance. By a PROBATE COURT OFFICIAL. Fourth Edition, revised and considerably enlarged, with Forms of Wills, Residuary Accounts, &c. Fcap. 8vo, cloth limp. 1*s*.

Woman's (A) Faith. A Novel. By the Author of "Ethel." 3 vols. Post 8vo. 31*s*. 6*d*.

Wonders of Sculpture. *See* Viardot.

Worcester's (Dr.), New and Greatly Enlarged Dictionary of the English Language. Adapted for Library or College Reference, comprising 40,000 Words more than Johnson's Dictionary. 4to. cloth, 1,834 pp. Price 31*s*. 6*d*. well bound; ditto, half mor. 2*l*. 2*s*.

"The volumes before us show a vast amount of diligence; but with Webster it is diligence in combination with fancifulness,—with Worcester in combination with good sense and judgment. Worcester's is the soberer and safer book, and may be pronounced the best existing English Lexicon."—*Athenæum*.

Words of Wellington, Maxims and Opinions, Sentences and Reflections of the Great Duke, gathered from his Despatches, Letters, and Speeches (Bayard Series). 2*s*. 6*d*.

Work: a Story of Experience. By LOUISA M. ALCOTT. In 2 vols. Crown 8vo. 21*s*. cloth.

Young (L.) Acts of Gallantry; giving a detail of every act for which the Silver Medal of the Royal Humane Society has been granted during the last Forty-one years. Crown 8vo., cloth. 7*s*. 6*d*.

CHISWICK PRESS:—PRINTED BY WHITTINGHAM AND WILKINS, TOOKS COURT, CHANCERY LANE.

www.ingramcontent.com/pod-product-compliance
Lightning Source LLC
Chambersburg PA
CBHW022116300426
44117CB00007B/728

* 9 7 8 3 7 4 4 7 6 0 7 2 0 *